MIKE BREARLEY

The Art of
CAPTAINCY

CORONET BOOKS
HODDER AND STOUGHTON

Copyright © 1985 by Mike Brearley Limited
First published in Great Britain in 1985 by
Hodder and Stoughton Limited

Coronet edition 1987

Second impression 1988

British Library C.I.P.

Brearley, Mike
    The art of captaincy.
    1. Cricket – Team captains
    I. Title
    796.358   GV927.5.T4

    ISBN 0-340-41029-9

Printed and bound in Great Britain for Hodder and
Stoughton Paperbacks, a division of Hodder and
Stoughton Limited, Mill Road, Dunton Green,
Sevenoaks, Kent (Editorial Office: 47 Bedford
Square, London WC1B 3DP) by St Edmundsbury
Press Limited, Bury St Edmunds, Suffolk. Photoset
by Rowland Phototypesetting Limited, Bury St
Edmunds, Suffolk.

The Art of
CAPTAINCY

To MISCHA and LARA

Contents

Introduction

'Why do so many players *want* to be captain?' Derek Underwood wondered, perplexed. It is a good question. A French general was once tactlessly asked, after a famous victory, if it hadn't really been won by his second-in-command. He thought for some time before answering. 'Maybe so,' he replied. 'But one thing is certain: if the battle had been lost *I* would have lost it.'

In 1981, shortly after being recalled as England's captain, I had a letter which read curtly:

> Dear Brearley,
> There is an old Italian proverb: if you want to know
> that a fish is bad look at its head,
>   Yours sincerely . . .

A captain is held responsible when things go wrong; and any rottenness in him rapidly spreads through the whole organism. Moreover, he tends to *feel* responsible when the side does badly. He may of course be right. But there may also have been nothing more that he could have done.

Captaincy can be a hassle. At the level of county cricket, the captain is responsible (in most cases) for how long everyone practises in the nets, for insisting on or making optional physical exercises during rain-affected days, for arranging cars and passengers for away trips; and so on. He may delegate some of these jobs, but disputes or problems will be referred back to him. In club cricket, the captain has to deal with last-minute withdrawals from the team (as when the long-distance lorry-driver phones from Turin on a Saturday morning warning that he might be late – an example I was recently told). He has to ensure that everyone gets to the ground; and after smiling at the opposition during the match is supposed to entertain them after it.

What is more, cricket captains do not have the luxury of being elevated above the activity of those they lead. It is easier for a football manager

Introduction

to 'play God', to read the riot act to the players, because he does not have to perform himself. Sales managers don't sell, foremen don't hump bricks. All cricket captains bat and field, and some bowl. We receive repeated intimations of our own fallibility.

Despite all this, there are, as Underwood implies, many who aspire to the job. Why, incidentally, do so many more regard themselves as potential captains now than, say, thirty years ago? It is an interesting sociological question which I look at in Chapter Two. The fact is that there are plenty of us who feel that we know best and like the idea of putting that 'knowledge' into practice. It is more agreeable to tell others what to do than to be told what to do. We like being bossy.

We also prefer stimulation to mental inactivity. There are those who, as Ranjitsinhji wrote in *The Jubilee Book of Cricket*, 'grow grey in the service of the game and are astonishingly ignorant about it'. These cricketers are content to leave tactics, man-management and the rest to others. Between innings they play poker or flick through magazines. They prefer being punted in a gondola through Venice to organising the trip and planning the route. But we actual and potential captains are a very different breed. We are struck by the length of time that may elapse between one knock and the next. Above all, we are fascinated by the complexity and variety of the game. We see that, tactically and psychologically, there is infinite scope for sense, sensitivity and flair. There are also, necessarily, almost unlimited ways in which we can go wrong.

For various reasons, the role of leadership is more significant in cricket than in any other sport. In the first place even in its shortest form each game lasts too long, and its pace is too slow, for excitement and intuition to achieve all or most of a team's aims.

Then, changes in conditions and climate make an enormous difference to what is tactically required or possible. Just as the batting and bowling skills needed for playing on a dead strip of baked earth at Karachi are a world apart from those called for on a bouncy 'flier' at Perth or on an old-style 'sticky-dog' at Brisbane or on a damp, green pitch in murky light at Manchester, so the tactics will have to be equally diverse. Even on one day, in one place, the ball may suddenly start to swing when the atmosphere changes, and the new ball offers totally different opportunities for attack from one fifty overs old. Hand in hand with this versatility in tactics goes the requirement of flexibility in approach by the players and, above all, by the captain. Like the conductor of an orchestra, he determines the attitude of the players and of the team as a whole to each situation.

I have mentioned two factors that help to differentiate cricket from other sports and make the leader's contribution more crucial, one to do with time-span and tempo, the other to do with variation in conditions. The whole book will, in part, constitute an extension, in detail, of this claim. At this point, I will merely add one other feature: the variety of roles within a team.

K. S. Ranjitsinhji and W. G. Grace at Jamnagar, India, in Grace's last years. Grace
did not captain England until he was forty, in 1888. He was still captaining the side at
the time of Ranji's first Test appearance in 1896, and at a public dinner in
Cambridge in 1908, the Doctor told his audience, 'I assure you you will never see a
batsman to beat the Jam Saheb if you live for a hundred years.'

Ranji wrote about captaincy: 'To treat a man as an automaton is the best way to
make him one, and an automaton is precisely what is not required as a cricketer.'
No one, to be sure, ever accused either Ranji or W. G. of playing cricket in a
stereotyped way.

It takes all sorts: Alvin Kallicharran (5 feet 4 inches) batting with Joel Garner (6 feet 9 inches).

Unlike a rowing eight, a cricket eleven works only by dint of differentiation. The skills, like the shapes and sizes of their owners, are diverse. I have always felt it to be one of the charms of the game that it accommodates the vast Colin Milburn and the svelte Michael Holding, the towering Joel Garner and the tiny Gundappa Viswanath. Amongst the fielders, we need skilful specialists in the slips; and agile, deft movers halfway out. We need courageous close fielders; and good runners and throwers in the deep. There is the wicket-keeper, whose job is unique and calls for at least a book to do justice to its subtleties and range. A well-balanced side will have steady batsmen as well as brilliant ones; Desmond Haynes as well as Viv Richards. Indeed, Peter Roebuck, who for many years went in at Number Four for Somerset, described his job as staying in long enough to prevent Richards (the Number Three) and Ian Botham (at Number Five) from being at the crease together: for when they were, Botham would try to hit the ball further, and higher, than Richards, and their partnerships, though dynamic and unnerving to opposition bowlers and captains, were unproductive. Roebuck's role was as vital to the team as it was unspectacular. The range in bowling skills is equally diverse, from fast to slow, with all the variations of swing, cut, bounce and spin.

The captain must know how to deploy whatever skills his players have at their disposal. He must enable them to widen their own range, to have the confidence to experiment. (My last remark, like many generalisations, is a partial truth, and the partial truth expressed by its opposite also needs saying: he must sometimes discourage experimentation in a batsman or a bowler, and insist upon a dogged orthodoxy.) In short, a captain must get the best out of his team by helping them to play together without suppressing flair and uniqueness.

Cricket's range separates it from a sport such as rowing. Apart from the cox, eight men (or women) have much the same job as each other, and that job does not vary greatly over the period of the race. Each oarsman submerges himself in the whole, and much of his pleasure derives from being part of an efficient machine. The cox takes over each person's decision-making; he becomes the mind for a single body. But even he has few parameters within which to exercise his thought.

Or take a sport that is much closer to cricket: baseball. Both have individual duels within the setting of a team game. Both have 'throwers' and 'strikers', speed of delivery and swing or curve. Yet the scoring arc of baseball is $90°$, a quarter of cricket's; in cricket the ball bounces, which produces a whole new world of deviation and trajectory; and the pitcher's assistants, his fielders, are deployed in relatively unchanging positions, while the bowler's arc scattered about in all sorts of patterns, sometimes clustered together and nearly all behind the batsman, sometimes higgledy-piggledy and nearly all in front of him, in as many different arrangements as there are shapes of the cricket grounds themselves, which may be round, oval, rectangular or, more likely, any old shape. Canterbury even has a large tree inside the playing area, while Lord's drops eight feet from one side to the other. It is no accident that cricket's literature is richer than that of rowing or baseball.

What is surprising is that so little has been written about the art of captaincy. There are excellent chapters by Ranjitsinhji, Sir Donald Bradman and others. The only study I know of that deals specifically, and in an informed and perceptive way, with cricket captaincy is Ray Illingworth's little book, but even that is slight; of its 118 pages thirty-three deal in a chatty way with the qualities of a few individuals.

The discovery of this curious gap in the literature was one motive for the present attempt. But however prolific the bibliography had been I think I would still have been tempted to add to it. For one thing, it was a great privilege to captain Middlesex for twelve years, and England on four tours and in thirty-one Tests, and I should like to be able to convey something of the fascination of the job at this level. But my own fascination with tactics began decades before. I have loved the game for as long as I can remember, and would, like many youngsters, persuade anyone to come and bowl to me, even, as a last resort, my great-aunt. From a very early age, my father was instilling in me not only a straight bat and a pointed left elbow (which had a suspiciously Yorkshire quality) but also a sense of who was bowling and why someone else should have been; of where certain fielders stood and why they ought to have been elsewhere (though no doubt these 'oughts' would have been misplaced during the three years that my father was himself captain of Brentham Cricket Club, in Ealing, while I grew from eight years old to eleven).

My earliest memory of *being* a captain goes back to the football field, and a match between City of London School Under-12s against Forest School. We considered Forest pretty hot stuff, so we were surprised and pleased to be holding them at 0-0 shortly before half-time. Then came the excruciatingly exciting moment; we were awarded a penalty, by the Forest ref. Penalties were almost unheard of in those days and at that level, but were glamorous and dramatic so we had practised them for hours. Just as school cricket captains open both batting and bowling, football captains take penalties; this I knew, in the safely hypothetical time before the Actual Penalty, and I had even gone so far as to develop my own style, wrong-footing the goalkeeper by using the outside of my right foot. So far so good. But when the whistle blew, and Mr Lodge – a delightful man, I discovered, whom years later I occasionally met at first-class cricket grounds – pointed at the spot, I panicked. I dashed around asking everyone who should take the penalty ('Please say me. Please don't say me'). I tried to persuade the other 'star' – Warren Pantzer, the centre-half – to face the fearful responsibility. In the end, it had to be me. Needless to say, all subtlety about placing the ball or using the outside of the foot had completely disappeared from my mind. I just ran at the ball and kicked it as hard as I could in the general direction of the goal. What happened next shows the curious state I was in. The ball hit the bar and bounced back. I knew well the rule that states that after the penalty kick some other player must be the next to touch the ball. At that instant, I remember both realising that fact with perfect clarity *and* quite cold-bloodedly gambling on Mr Lodge's not knowing it; so I kicked the ball into the net. I was wrong about Mr Lodge, and the final score was: Forest 5 – City of London 0.

Even as I write this, I tremble and sweat from reliving the anxiety of the awful moment as well as from embarrassment at my absolute lack of coolness. Captaincy material, was I? It is hard to believe.

Thirty years on, I am nervous, though less so, at the challenge of trying to put into words something of the possibilities of the art of

Horace Brearley coaching at City of London School in 1959.

captaincy. This book also makes a bridge between one career and another. It is an effort at capturing part of the essence of what played a big part in my life for a long time.

This book is not, though, an autobiography. If I have taken examples from my own experience, that is because these are the examples whose detail I know best. Nor is it a history of captaincy, which I am not qualified to write. Nor again is it a handbook on captaincy, though I hope that captains young and old may find in it practical hints that will help them, whatever their level, despite the fact that the book deals mainly with the first-class game.

So much for what the book is not: what *is* it? If the word did not call to mind ancient, dusty and probably unreadable tomes, I would call it a 'treatise on captaincy'. I hope, too, that it will turn out to contribute to broader discussions about the interactions of individuals and groups and, in particular, about the relations between leaders and led. Some of the contents will be familiar to the managers who have listened to – and contributed to – my seminars on leadership and motivation.

I should like to end this introduction with an appeal to any would-be captains among my readers: please don't be put off by my going on about how many ways one can go wrong! Much of what I say will be a reminder of what you all know already, but perhaps have not put into words. Parts of the book may consist of ideas, ploys, aspects of the job which have not occurred to you before. It is often easier to describe sickness than health, defects rather than perfection. An occupational hazard for a coach, for example, is to harp on about the faults in a youngster's batting or bowling instead of stressing his strengths. Nevertheless, an account of good batting will include much about batsmen's shortcomings, and an account of health will talk about diseases. The danger is that just as one who embarks on the latter may end up a hypochondriac, so someone who reads my book may give up any idea of becoming a captain.

Please don't! Learning about indigestion need not stop us eating, though it may change our habits of eating. We should never give up what we enjoy because we discover that it is more complex and difficult than we realised. Most things are. Think of batting; or having children! Two of the great pleasures of life have innumerable snares.

Captaincy is difficult. But we must also do justice to a quite opposite criticism of the book, that I make complex something essentially straight-forward. A man said to me recently, 'Motivation is basically simple; it's a matter of bringing the best out of people.' Batsmen may be overcoached; it is said of Ian Botham that he is a wonderfully *natural* cricketer. As Kapil Dev remarked recently, 'There is no room for *copying* anyone else's play at Test level.' Without doubt we have to be natural to be captains, too; we must be ourselves. Every good captain leads his side in his own way, as suits his own personality. He must be willing to follow his hunches. The captain, like the batsman or the mother, is impeded and stilted in his performance if his head is constantly cluttered up with theories.

The trouble is that not every spontaneous response is appropriate or valid. How can a mother 'behave naturally' if what she longs to do is strangle her brat? Or a batsman if, whenever a slow bowler tosses one up, he is irresistibly tempted to slog it over mid-wicket? It is true that captaincy is at best often a matter of intuition; but only if the intuition has been honed and trained and developed along the right lines. The heart must be in the right place, but so must the mind and its attention to detail.

The kindest, or perhaps most flattering remark made about me as a captain was in an article by Mihir Bose. He wrote that my Brahminical attention to detail managed to avoid fussiness because the spirit of my captaincy was sound. The principle is right, though the Middlesex players who played under me would by no means all, or always, have agreed with its application. It also leads me to my next question: how *does* a captain think?

CHAPTER ONE

Captaincy in action

What sorts of things *do* go on in the captain's head? And what makes thinking difficult for him?

As captain, you sometimes feel the whole operation is on the verge of collapse. You are swayed by conflicting demands: both short-term and long-term, tactical and psychological: amongst your own players one is fuming, another sulking: your opponents are rampant, or perhaps eking out their resources better than you feel they should be. Even the umpires may add to your confusion.

At Perth, in 1978, during the second Test, there was a brief period on the third day, in which I felt under siege from all directions. We had scored 309 in our first innings, on a pitch that had helped seam bowlers. Our own bowlers had made excellent use of the conditions to reduce Australia to 128 for eight. At this point, Peter Toohey, who was playing well and had reached 50, was joined by Geoff Dymock – a tail-ender with no great pretensions to batting but with a competent defence, especially when able to push forward in safety.

Our problems started when we tried to give Dymock the strike, by allowing Toohey a single at the start of the over. This was reasonable enough in theory, but in practice the policy can have drawbacks. Toohey turned Hendrick to long-leg, for instance: the ball went between two deep fielders, and the batsmen scuttled back for two. Next ball he took the offered single. Then a leg-bye enabled the batsmen to change ends again. We were playing eight-ball overs in that series so less than half the over had gone by, Toohey had strike again, and four runs had already been scored, none of which might have accrued with orthodox fields.

However, we did succeed in keeping Toohey from most of the strike; I discovered later that he received only twenty-two balls while Dymock faced fifty-three. Our problem was getting rid of Dymock. The ball was by now softer, and the sun had eased the pitch. The irrational furore that had erupted six months earlier, when Bob Willis had hit Iqbal

Qasim, the Pakistan night-watchman, in the face, had led to an undue namby-pambiness about bouncers being bowled at tail-enders. In the current series Graham Yallop, the Australian captain, and I, had to agree before each match which tail-enders were exempt from bouncers and which were to be allowed a certain leeway. (The situation was absurd; it was like requiring Don Bradman to bat with one arm behind his back against second-string bowlers.) Anyway, in this Test, Dymock had been designated a borderline case in this respect: he was to have impunity from bouncers to begin with, but if he hung around for a while we were to be allowed to bowl him some.

As Dymock's assurance increased I said to umpire Robin Bailhache

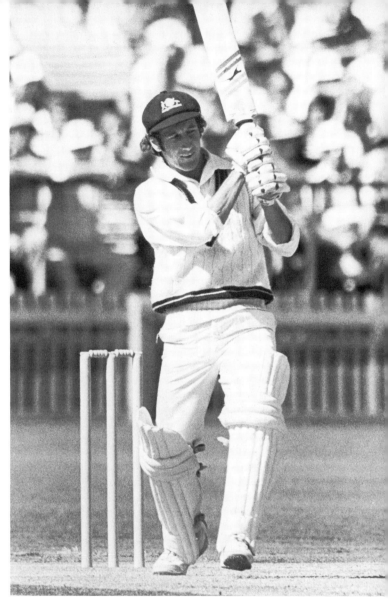

LEFT Ian Botham bowling at Perth, second Test, 1978. His match figures were an uncharacteristic 0–100, and at one stage he lost his temper while trying to prove that Peter Toohey could not hook. This was one of the few occasions on which Botham's impetuosity as a bowler overrode his cricketing sense. RIGHT Peter Toohey batting during the Perth Test. His duel with Ian Botham – decidedly won by Toohey – led to an awkward situation for the captain.

that I thought he warranted a bouncer or two. Bailhache agreed, but told me to make sure they were occasional. (I'm surprised that he didn't insist on the bowler waving a red flag to let the batsman know when it was coming.) I also reverted to orthodox field-placing for Toohey. I felt that some of our momentum had left us – the necessary tension and urgency can be hard to sustain in bowler and fielders alike when several fielders are thrown back to allow a single. This change was costly, however, as the batsmen took ten runs off an over from John Lever, and fourteen – all pulls by Toohey – off the next, intemperately bowled by Ian Botham. He was annoyed at being told to pitch the ball up to Dymock, and then only being allowed one bouncer in eight balls at him; but as this over

Viv Richards and Collis King during their crucial stand of 139 in 15 overs. Bob Taylor is the wicket-keeper. Richards is the hardest batsman to contain in modern cricket, while King tore our 'fill-in' bowlers to shreds.

was the sixty-fifth and the second new ball was due at the end of it Botham's attempt to prove a point with Toohey was particularly inappropriate.

We took the new ball. As he handed it to me, the other umpire, Tom Brooks, said, 'We don't think you should bowl bouncers at Dymock with the new ball.' I refused to accept this, arguing that it was *my* decision, not theirs. Brooks replied that it was the umpires' responsibility to ensure that tail-enders did not get hurt. I disagreed again: in my view, anyone who walks to the crease accepts a risk. The umpires should prevent sheer intimidation, and should be prepared to step in to protect a tail-ender who clearly cannot defend either himself or his wicket. The mere threat of a bouncer often makes a man play differently, and less well. My conversation with the umpires was amiable: but the outcome was a blunt confrontation. I refused to instruct our bowlers not to bowl bouncers at Dymock, and they threatened to report me if we did.

Meanwhile Willis, who was to bowl the next over, was indignant with Botham. His main concern was that I shouldn't let *him* bowl any more. 'Don't give the new ball to Guy; he could go for twenty an over.' When I arrived at slip, Botham was fuming too. He wanted revenge on Toohey. Meanwhile Lever was disgruntled at being taken off – after only two overs – for Willis, and the umpires were threatening to report me. *And* we were in a winning position! To restore some sanity to the proceedings, I told Hendrick to get loose to bowl the next over.

As it happened, Hendrick bowled Dymock with his second ball, so the matter went no further, and we could all calm down; but how far my decision was the outcome of reason I don't know. Hendrick was certainly the most economical of our seam bowlers; he was also the most phlegmatic and the least likely to bowl bouncers at anyone.

Certainly it is a requirement of captaincy not to panic in such situations. Another failing is to be reduced to helplessness. However bad things are there are always options that would be less catastrophic than others. I remember feeling close to impotence in the World Cup Final in 1979, when Collis King and Viv Richards cut loose. Admittedly we had to bowl Geoff Boycott, Graham Gooch or Wayne Larkins for twelve overs, which was, in those conditions, like attacking tanks with pea-shooters. But it was a mistake to ask Larkins, of the three, to bowl at all. He was out of both practice and confidence. His two overs cost 26 runs.

A captain can be saved from tactical or other mistakes by sound advice, given at the right moment. Or the timely word may crucially restore a bowler's confidence. On the last day of the Headingley Test in 1981 Dennis Lillee and Ray Bright were, at the last gasp, clawing back the game for Australia by their robust and shrewd batting. Willis, who had rampaged his way through the main Australian batsmen, was suddenly and momentarily uncertain. Lillee had flicked him over the slips for four, and cut him for two more boundaries. When Bob over-adjusted his line Lillee helped him off his legs for a three. The pair had taken Australia from 75–8 to 110–8 in a mere four overs. I knew, too, that Bob rarely bowled at his best against the great fast bowler: a failing that stemmed, he thought, not only from the latter's ability to improvise with the bat, but also from the unnerving realisation that he himself could become a helpless target when the roles were reversed. During a single over in 1974 two of Lillee's deliveries had narrowly missed his nose as he played robotically forward; his plight looked so desperate that Greg Chappell came up from slip to implore Bob not to keep lunging suicidally down the pitch.

Now, at this tense moment, with Australia only 21 runs short of victory, Bob needed some clear word from me: something more definite than mere encouragement. As I walked towards him before the start of his next over, Mike Gatting ran up to me. 'Tell him to bowl *straight* at Dennis,' he said. 'It doesn't matter much what length.' I realised he was right, and said just that to Bob. Four balls later, Lillee scooped the ball – a straight, well-pitched-up delivery – towards mid-on, and Gatting himself raced in, dived and caught the ball inches above the ground.

Advice may, of course, be misguided; and it is then the captain's fault if he follows it. World Cup Final again. At tea, we were 79–0 off twenty-five overs. The target was another 208 runs from thirty-five overs, five of them to be bowled by the potentially weak link in the West Indies' attack, Richards or King. Batting: Boycott and Brearley. To come: Randall, Gooch, Gower, Botham, Larkins and Edmonds (not to mention Old, Taylor and Hendrick). The tactics? Plain as a pikestaff, one would have thought: to go all out for a rate of six an over from the first over after tea, aiming at seven or more against Richards/King.

What happened? In the next thirteen overs we scored 50 runs, Richards conceding only 23 off six overs; then Garner – whose hand when he delivers the ball comes from above the sightboards at the Nursery End – took five wickets in eleven balls. We collapsed from 129–0 to 192 all out.

Why? When we walked off for the tea interval on that lovely midsummer afternoon we felt that we had done pretty well: 79–0 was preferable to 90–3. Our score was, I felt, a launching-pad for an onslaught. The rest of the team were buoyant and enthusiastic. After downing several glasses of iced lemon squash, I started to discuss our tactics as I changed clothes and tried to rub myself dry with a towel. I had two cups of tea and a rock cake. I rolled a couple of cheese sandwiches up in a paper napkin in anticipation of my dismissal and as a bulwark against champagne, ours or the West Indies'. And I was talked out of my plan.

My idea was that we should have a hit. I would tell Boycott to look to score faster, while I myself would take any number of risks. But one of the lessons of one-day cricket that has been learned by us professionals with difficulty is the value of having wickets in hand. All too often teams have thrown games away by outright slogging.

With this in mind, Botham pressed me not to take too many chances:

Geoff Boycott and I on an occasion that had a happier outcome – against Australia at Trent Bridge in 1977, when our opening partnership was worth 154 in the second innings, and England won by seven wickets. In the World Cup final we felt we had done reasonably well at tea, when the score was 79–0 after 25 overs; but we got our tactics wrong thereafter.

we still had a long way to go. And Randall, similarly, with his 'Carry on, skip, it's magic', urged moderation. I doubt if I asked Boycott, because I knew how reluctant he was to throw caution to the wind; but the advice that was uttered echoed his unvoiced approach, and I was swayed. Not that it would ever have been easy to score 287 in sixty overs against Holding and Roberts, Garner and Croft, however flat the pitch. Pakistan had made a brave effort to chase a big score – 294 – in the semi-final at the Oval, but despite brilliant innings of 81 by Majid Khan and 93 by Zaheer Abbas they too had fallen increasingly behind the rate required, and ended 43 runs short.

There is no guarantee that if I had stuck to my original plan the outcome would have been different; but our chances would have been a little better as Gooch, Gower, Botham and the others would have had some space in which to play themselves in.

In fact, the decision-making process is often a matter of ideas being thrown in, played with, criticised, until it is hard to say *whose* idea it is that the captain eventually acts on – and is judged by. In retrospect, it

Denis Compton about to be caught by Arthur Morris off the bowling of Ray Lindwall, fifth Test, at the Oval, 1948, for only 4 runs. The Australian captain, Bradman, apparently recalled Compton being dismissed in exactly the same manner early in an innings before the War. A nice example of the importance of memory for captains and bowlers alike, and it contributed to the outcome of the match.

is easier to recall the spectacular successes and defeats rather than the buzz of reflection, intuition, bluff and memory that actually makes up the job.

John Lever once maintained that one of a bowler's main weapons is a good memory. I should like to bask in a couple of dismissals that depended on that, together with freakish good fortune. In 1982 we played a weakened Nottinghamshire side at Trent Bridge. The pitch helped bowlers, and once we had scored 383 in our first innings we were in a strong position. The main danger-man would be Clive Rice, the fine South African all-rounder. In their first innings Norman Cowans, our young fast bowler, was making the ball lift from a little short of a length around Rice's off-stump. I noticed that Rice was looking to force the ball away off the back foot. Two years before we had caught him in the slips from this shot; but I could also remember the ball sailing over the slips from a thicker edge. So I moved Radley from orthodox gully to a rarely-used position, behind fourth or fifth slip, perhaps twenty-five yards from the bat. Next time the batsman tried the shot the ball flew precisely to Radley.

When Notts followed on Rice's dismissal was even more fortuitous. We tried the same ploy as in the first innings, but by now the pitch was less bouncy, and Cowans not quite so fast, so I switched Radley to a deepish backward short-leg. Rice favours a flick off his legs which can go in the air in this direction. Roland Butcher had caught him in that position in 1977. With much display, I adjusted Radley's location, and he, entering into the joke, exaggeratedly marked it with his boot. Lo and behold, in the same over, Rice clipped the ball straight to him.

I need hardly stress that one is rarely so fortunate as this; but we may as well enjoy such manoeuvres when they work.

I also still squirm to think of opportunities missed, of hunches *not* acted on. In 1967, on the Under-25 tour of Pakistan, our first representative match was on a fine batting pitch at Lahore. Pat Pocock, the Surrey off-spinner, took a wicket, and Mushtaq Mohammad came in. He was the best batsman in the opposing side; but I knew that he tended to stab at the ball early in his innings. I wanted Pocock to have a short square-leg, in case he did this and the ball turned, but Pocock preferred not to risk a man there: I let him have his way. Sure enough, a few deliveries later, Mushtaq hastily pushed forward, and the ball lobbed up in a gentle arc from bat and pad to where the short-leg would, and should, have been. Mushtaq gave us no second chance, and scored 132.

By contrast with this, it is arguable that I sometimes put too much pressure on the bowlers by wanting over-attacking fields. Mike Kirkman, a leg-spinner who played only a few first-class matches, remembers me doing this to him at Cambridge, way back in 1963. I apparently insisted on a silly-point, and refused him a deep extra-cover – and this against Rohan Kanhai on an easy Fenner's pitch! Dermott Monteith, the Irish slow left-arm bowler who played occasionally for Middlesex, felt that I made him nervous by moving his one-saving man at short fine-leg to a catching position before he had relaxed and found a rhythm. John Emburey, Phil Edmonds and Geoff Miller all felt similarly early in their careers; though for the most part they would agree that they had to learn to bowl with attacking fields sooner or later. Such matters of timing, confidence and degree of attack are delicate issues on which there may well be no clear-cut answers.

Similar problems arise with regard to the dilemma between orthodoxy and experiment. In 1981, in a Sunday League match, Lancashire needed over 100 runs in the last twelve overs, and I told our bowlers to adopt what was then the orthodox policy in such situations – to keep bowling straight and pitch the ball fairly well up.

The rationale is, in part, that if the batsman misses the ball he is out. The old Middlesex and England leg-spinner Jim Sims used to drum this into my head when I went to Lord's for coaching as a schoolboy of sixteen. 'Michael,' he would say, in his surreptitious, confidential manner, 'a straight ball has a certain lethal quality about it.' Here Jim would pause, before delivering the dramatic summing-up from the corner of his mouth: 'If you miss it you've 'ad it.' He also told me that he had once taken eight wickets against Sussex at Lord's, which the *Evening Standard* had described as 'Sims takes eight wickets with long-hops'. 'What they failed to say,' he said, 'was that six of them long-'ops were *straight* long-'ops.'

A second reason for bowling straight and well-up against batsmen who are hitting out is that one can control the direction in which the batsman hits the ball; it is hard to hit such deliveries square with or behind the wicket, whereas short-of-a-length bowling can be pulled or cut, hoiked or deflected, in any direction.

On this occasion, however, Clive Lloyd was batting; we were able to control the direction of his shots, but not their distance. Lloyd kept hitting the ball for six, or so hard along the ground that it would beat defensive fields, and Lancashire eventually won off the last ball. I felt that we should not have allowed them to win, despite Lloyd's immense power and skill, and I think my policy was too rigid. We ought to have varied our bowling more, experimenting, perhaps, with an occasional bouncer or slower ball; or to have switched to bowling outside his off-stump when the shorter boundary was on the leg-side. Simon Hughes, our young quick bowler, asked me if he could try a slower ball or a bouncer in the last over, from which nine were needed, but I told him not to take the chance.

I shall have much more to say about tactics in a later chapter. The examples that I have given show clearly enough that the captain must be alive to different possibilities of attack and defence, of experiment and conventionality. They have also shown how there is, or should be, a constant interaction between the captain and other players. It is his responsibility to sort out good from bad advice, and to know when to, and when not to, seek it. It is also an important facet of captaincy to be able to deal with many conflicting demands at the same time.

The captain may also have to pay attention to the role that a certain player has in a team. Roles may be restrictive or enabling. For instance, Willis had, in 1981, been the spearhead of England's attack for a decade. But during the previous two years there were periods when his ability to bowl fast appeared to be waning. At the same time, Graham Dilley had been emerging as a genuinely fast bowler, but he was still raw and had, in Willis's words, to be mothered and used mainly in short spells. Moreover, in 1980 and 1981 Ian Botham could be depended on less to bowl reliably and aggressively for long periods.

All these factors meant that, in the early part of the 1981 season, Bob was called upon to bowl more overs in a day than before. It was impossible for him to keep going flat out throughout. He had therefore begun to aim more for accuracy than for speed. His role in the attack had gradually, and without explicit recognition, changed from that of the front-line strike bowler to being – partially at least – a stock bowler.

In the first innings of the Headingley Test Bob had bowled pretty well, but without taking a wicket. He had not reached maximum pace, partly for the reasons already mentioned, partly too because he was anxious about even more no-balls if he aimed for that final edge of speed. On the evening before the last day, when Botham's prodigious innings had given us an outside chance, we talked in the bar. Willis himself made the crucial suggestion that in the first innings we had been too concerned to bowl a good length and let the pitch 'do' the rest. Shouldn't we, and he in particular, bowl faster and straighter? I agreed. Graham Gooch underlined the point. 'Even Gatt is harder to bat against when he really runs in,' he said. I told Bob to forget about no-balls, the thought of which had made him hold back. On a pitch with such uneven bounce the harder the ball hits it the more devastating its variations will be. Moreover, bowling on the next day would be an all-or-nothing affair, a huge effort without thought of conservation of energy.

We were, in effect, restoring Bob's old role to him. The effect was spectacular – eight wickets for 43 runs, and a nailbiting win by 19 runs.

I should like to end this chapter by looking at this final, dramatic innings from my own point of view, as captain, to indicate the sorts of consideration that entered into my decisions.

The first question was, who should open the bowling? We had four seamers for the match, and in the first innings I had started with Willis and Old. Willis and Dilley had both preferred to come up the hill from the Football Stand End, with the wind slightly behind them, while Old and Botham wanted the other end. Such an amiable division is rare; as the match went on, and the wind veered, there was a time when all four were keen to bowl from the Kirkstall Lane End. At times a captain has to point out to his bowlers that someone has to bowl the other end, and that batsmen cannot choose theirs: but hills and winds do make a considerable difference. Running downhill, a bowler is liable to bowl no-balls, over-pitch and generally lose control. Running up the hill, on the other hand, a bowler may find himself under-pitching, straining to get to the crease and, especially if the wind too is against him, he may lose his fire.

By the last day of the match the wind and the bowlers' preferences were again as they had been on the first, but I chose to open with Dilley and Botham. I felt Dilley's batting (he had scored a brave 56) had lent him confidence. He had a high wicket-taking rate with the new ball. I also thought that if the match became tense it would be impossible to expect him to bowl his first spell when we had few runs to play with. I would give him two or three overs in which to click; if he didn't, I would bring Willis on early. The other choice was also influenced by what had happened so far. Botham's bowling, like his batting, had been transformed. If anyone could create a miracle it was he. As he took off his pads, undefeated on 149, I reminded him of our conversation before the match in which I had commiserated with him for the way in which he had been harassed and pursued by the media. I had added, half-joking, that he would probably score a century and take twelve wickets in the match! Now, almost a week later, I mentioned that he still owed us six wickets.

Well before we went on to the field, I told all four fast bowlers who would be starting. I made a brief exhortatory speech to the team before we went out. 'More aggression, more liveliness, more encouragement for the bowlers,' I said. '*They're* the ones who are nervous now.' I think I also said then what I had said at the end of the first day's play, when Australia were 210–3: 'On this pitch, a side could be bowled out for 90.'

Botham's first ball was a long-hop, his second a half-volley, and Graeme Wood hit both for four. In the third over, we had a stroke of luck; Wood misjudged a half-volley from Botham and edged to Taylor. Despite these three bad balls, Botham was bowling well, but without sharp movement or real pace. I was more worried about Dilley. His first two overs went for 11 runs. I decided to take him off. Moreover, he told me he was feeling a thigh strain. I sent him off to have Bernard Thomas, the team's physiotherapist, look at it. He was soon back on the field, strapped up, with the message that he could bowl through the injury if needed.

LEFT Headingley, 1981. Botham on the way to his remarkable 149 not out. On this unpredictable pitch, where any batting approach was liable to be undone by an unplayable delivery, he had licence to bat with total freedom.

RIGHT Graham Dilley about to bowl at John Dyson, Headingley, 1981. Despite his pace and promise, Dilley was still relatively inexperienced. In a tight situation such a bowler can pose problems for his captain: 'Can I risk bowling him, and if so, when, and for how long?'

For the sixth over I gave the ball to Willis. He said, 'Faster and straighter, right?' I nodded. At once he bowled well, coming up the hill as he wished.

The wind should have helped Botham's outswing; in fact, the ball was swinging little in the bright sunshine. Trevor Chappell and John Dyson struggled on, beaten from time to time, but nudging runs here and there. As we had decided before the innings began, we kept a third man and a fine-leg to stop the edges and deflections from going for too many runs over the fast outfield.

After he had bowled five overs, Willis said to me, 'Give me a go at the other end.' I had just replaced Botham with Old at that other end, hoping, probably vainly, that he might be able to swing the ball out. My reaction, playing for time, was, 'You mean you've had enough of coming uphill into the wind?' This acknowledged Bob's problem (the wind had again veered slightly) without committing myself. The response probably also expressed irritation that he should suddenly prefer the other end and thereby make my plans less clear-cut. Willis replied, grumpily, 'Okay, I'll carry on here then.'

During the next over, Old's second, I put Bob's question to Bob Taylor and Botham. They favoured giving Willis the choice of ends. Ian said, 'He's looked our most dangerous bowler.' I agreed. We must give Willis his head. I indicated as much by signalling to him down at fine-leg.

Someone had to bowl the next over from the Grandstand End. I was not keen to try Dilley again, as I feared that he might be expensive.

Captaincy in action

Botham was a possibility, but he had not looked penetrative. Old was the more likely bet to bowl with Willis, but he could not bowl two consecutive overs. I decided to put Peter Willey on. Not only for want of anyone better: he had turned his off-breaks even on the first day, so he was bound to find some assistance from the pitch on the fifth. I felt, too, that neither Dyson nor Chappell would go on to the attack against him. Anxious about taking undue risks, they might give a catch to a close fielder, and even if not, two or three overs should not prove costly. This was almost certainly the last chance to see if Willey's spin looked capable of making a decisive contribution. (I still felt that we might miss John Emburey after all, whose omission from the twelve had been a difficult decision: but selection is not the issue at this stage in the book, nor was it a factor at this point in the match, so I will leave it until later.)

Willey bowled three overs. They did not look particularly dangerous, though the ball did turn. At least they cost only four runs. After them I reverted, with conviction, to Old.

Meanwhile, Bob was steaming in downhill. We reminded him not to worry about no-balls and encouraged him to keep harrying the batsmen as he was doing. At last his – and our – luck changed. First Willis bowled a perfect bouncer at Chappell who, hurriedly protecting his face, could only lob the ball up for Taylor to catch. Next over, Old twice hit Dyson painful blows on the hand as he pushed tentatively forward. There was nothing tentative about the bowling or the fielding now. Old, too, was bowling with more aggression than earlier in the match, and his contribution as the accurate, mean foil to Willis proved invaluable. Until Bright took 10 off his last over with a couple of slogs to leg he was hit for only 11 runs in the eight overs he bowled.

Willis summoned up all his energy for his last over before lunch. In four balls he took two wickets – those of Kim Hughes and Yallop. Once Hughes had gone, with the score 58–3, we knew we had a real chance. We roused Bob still further: he must surely fancy getting Yallop out this time. Yallop lasted just three balls, beautifully caught by Gatting at short-leg off a nasty, kicking delivery.

The score was 58–4. We lunched – in the dressing-room, at such a crucial stage – knowing that the odds must have come down from 500–1 to about 6–4.

We spent some time trying to predict how the remaining batsmen would play. Rod Marsh might well 'have a go'. In the first innings of the first Test, at Nottingham, on a similar pitch, he had slogged a quick 19 before being caught off a skier at long-leg. Geoff Lawson and Lillee too might have a swing (if we got down to them) especially if we pitched the ball up. Dyson, Allan Border, and Bright would probably 'graft' – that is, fight it out by orthodox batting. One thing was clear: we must keep running at them, and attacking.

It was also clear that, unless there was an unpredictable change, I should rely on Willis to bowl until the death from the top – Kirkstall

Lane – end. There was also no difficulty in deciding to continue with Old, especially as Border was the next batsman; Old has always fancied left-handers.

In the event he soon bowled Border, for a duck, and Willis dismissed Dyson and Marsh in quick succession, the latter falling to another fine catch, this time by Dilley, a few feet in from the boundary at fine-leg: 74–7. Between overs Bob came up to tell me that umpire David Evans had told him not to bowl bouncers at Lawson. I was surprised. Lawson is a more than competent batsman – except against the bouncer. 'Forget it,' I retorted to Bob. 'But don't bother with an out-and-out bouncer at first; just short of length, rib-height.' Next over, with his very first ball at Lawson, Bob had him caught behind: 75–8.

Willis had taken six wickets in six overs, after bowling thirty-seven overs in the match without a single wicket. In fifty-eight minutes seven wickets had fallen for 19 runs, on a pitch playing little worse than in the first innings, when the same batsmen had amassed 401–9.

This extraordinary match still had an unnerving twist or two in its tail, and some awkward captaincy problems calling for quick decisions. Australia may have been 75–8; but they still needed only 55 to win. In four overs Lillee and Bright added 35. I have already mentioned Willis's

Bob Willis bowling to Kim Hughes, first innings, Headingley Test. At this stage nothing was going right for Willis or for England; indeed, his Test career seemed over, and England's chances of winning the series minimal. Willis's 8–43 in the second innings changed everything. This was the second match in 104 years of Test cricket in which a side won after following on, the first being at Sydney in 1894 when England won by 10 runs after rain turned the pitch into a quagmire. The 1896 Test at Manchester came close. Oddly enough, in that game Australia needed an almost identical score – 125 – to win, and there was a heroic spell of bowling from another fast bowler, Tom Richardson; he sent down 42.3 five-ball overs and took six wickets for 76 runs. But on that occasion Australia scraped home by three wickets.

block against bowling at his best to Lillee. Lillee is no mug with the bat, capable of shrewd improvisations as well as a resolute correctness. We soon saw that he had settled for unorthodoxy – a policy that was entirely justified by the conditions.

As soon as Willis dropped short Lillee stepped back and poked the ball high over me at first slip for four. I decided that we had to guard against that shot, so I took Gooch from third slip and put him at deep fly slip, behind second slip. Again Lillee made room to cut, this time beating Dilley at wide third-man: another four. Immediately Willis was forced to switch either his length or his line, or both. So Lillee deftly moved the other way, towards off-stump, and clipped the ball away to backward square-leg for three more runs. When he cut another four, and Bright connected with two solid, though risky blows to leg off Old we were suddenly back on the defensive, on the brink of defeat. This was the point at which Gatting helped us to dismiss Lillee. At this stage we could afford only two close catchers, both at slip. We had been forced to have two third-men, as well as a backward point and an extra-cover. And short-leg had gone back to backward square-leg, saving one. Now Lillee tried to play more conventionally – again a reasonable approach, as we had so few close fielders. He may have changed his mind when he saw the ball well pitched up, and decided too late to drive it.

Terry Alderman, the last man in, really is a moderate batsman. I was not in favour of wasting bouncers on him. But Bright had the strike, at the end of Willis's over. I took Old off and brought Botham back. This too seemed a straightforward decision. However well Old had bowled Bright had obviously got used to his action and had picked him up all too easily: a change was essential. Australia still needed 20 runs, so I decided to allow Bright a single at the beginning of the over, if he chose to take it. We could then bowl at Alderman. Bright accepted the single. I discussed fields with Ian. We agreed that we needed a mid-off, as Alderman's lunge forward might give him runs in this direction. We also needed a square-leg, rather than a short-leg, to cut off thick edges or nudges on the leg-side. We were left with only three close fielders. Two should be at slip. I was not sure if we could afford a third slip, as there would then be a wide open space backward of cover. I asked Botham which he preferred, third slip or gully. He wanted the extra slip; he was right. Agonisingly, two sharp chances went to Old in exactly that position, and he missed both. Perhaps it was as well that it was a Yorkshireman standing at third slip at that moment.

But a few moments later it was all over. Appropriately, Willis finished the match in a perfect, most emphatic way, clean bowling Bright middle-stump with a yorker. Australia were all out for 'Nelson' – 111. It was only the second time in Test history, and the first this century, that a side had won after following on.

CHAPTER TWO

On class and charisma:
choosing a captain

Imagine that a company whose business is to make recommendations to the boards of other companies on the appointment of senior personnel has been employed by the committee of an ailing county side to seek a captain for them. And then imagine that they are perceptive and knowledgeable not only about management but also about cricket.

What qualities would they most hope to find in the captain? Is there in any sense a blueprint for their man?

I suppose there are entirely general requirements. The man must have some ability as a player. He must have common sense. He needs to know the game, and have 'leadership qualities', whatever they are. He must be willing from time to time to take an unpopular line.

These remarks seem hardly worth making. Yet as soon as we probe, the water rapidly becomes muddy.

To take the first point first: how *much* ability as a player is called for? The Maharaja of Porbandar captained the first All-Indian team to tour England in 1932; he played in only six matches, invariably batted late in the order, and did not bowl. His tally for the tour was 6 runs in six innings. I doubt if our 'headhunting' company would recommend Porbandar for India's World Cup Squad, or for reviving the fortunes of, say, Leicestershire in the late '60s or Derbyshire in the mid '70s. Even the *Wisden* of the day commented that, 'no injustice is being done to him by saying that, admirably fitted as he was in many respects for the job, his abilities as a cricketer were not commensurate to the task.' Porbandar is a joke, a relic of a bygone age and culture. But what of Brearley, as captain of England? *Private Eye* suggested that my favourite piece of music was Haydn's Duck Quartet, as that was what I usually scored. I was certainly no Len Hutton or M.J.K.Smith, or even Douglas Jardine with the bat, but no Porbandar either.

Nevertheless, the job becomes that much harder when, as captain, you are struggling to find your own form. In 1978–9, in Australia, I knew

On class and charisma: choosing a captain

A perennial problem for selectors, especially in England where there has been a long tradition of picking captains who have not been worth their place as players alone.

what it was like to be regarded as a liability to the team one week and as the Duke of Wellington a week later.

This was the tour which took place in direct competition with World Series Cricket. While England had lost six leading players of whom four or five would have been in our touring party, Australia had lost seventeen, of whom probably seven or eight would have been in their Test side if available. We won the first two Tests against Yallop's team; but in the third, at Melbourne, we were resoundingly beaten. In that match I scored 0 and 1, after dropping two catches at slip on the first day. My tally from six Test innings was then 37. There were the inevitable comparisons with Mike Denness's situation at the same stage of the 1974–5 tour; he had scored 65 runs from his six innings, but England were 0–2 down in the series. Denness decided to leave himself out of the side for the fourth Test.

I, too, considered this move. But Willis, the vice-captain, and Doug Insole, the tour manager, told me briskly not to give it another thought, and we decided at once that I should play. Others enjoyed keeping the thought alive: Tony Greig, for example, who came to have tea in my hotel room in Sydney the day before the fourth Test, remarked on the irony of my having the same room that Denness had had four years before. It was not until a year later that I learned that Denness's team had stayed in another hotel.

To cut a long story short, we won this fourth Test match as a result of a quite amazing come-back from a hopeless position. I batted better, scoring 17 and 53; but it was the victory that reinstated, indeed elevated my reputation. In fact, while the whole team did show an admirable grit in fighting back, my contribution was, from a tactical point of view, minimal. Our position after two days was such that almost anyone could have said what *had* to be done: the problem was doing it.

That series also illustrated in a clear-cut way the different approaches adopted by England and Australia to choosing a captain. Traditionally, England have appointed the captain first, and then co-opted him to pick the team, while Australia have selected their best eleven and made one of them captain. In 1978, neither Yallop nor I would have been captain had the methods been reversed.

Historically, the English attitude has been connected with class distinctions. Until well after the Second World War, the view was that a bunch of professionals needed an amateur as captain. (A similar view applied in the West Indies, until 1960.) The Australians valued 'leadership qualities' less; at least on the surface, for I presume that they were not entirely unconcerned whether they had in their eleven a man capable of leading the side. Similarly, for England it was not an entirely irrelevant consideration that the captain should be a decent player.

In an ideal world each system would produce the same result. But it can happen that the best tactician is nowhere near being the best player; and then the relative values of personal performance as against leadership ability have to be weighed up. Such balancing may, naturally, be called for at any level in the game, but the most notorious examples occur in the selection of Test captains.

The difference in Australia's and England's approach to captaincy is well-known. What is not so well-known is that Australia moved closer to our method after their 5–1 defeat under Yallop in 1978–9, when Hughes was named captain for the tour of India in advance of the rest of the party. (There was a variation on our method which I will discuss in Chapter Four.)

In England, too, we oscillate in the emphasis we place on a person's experience or reputation as a captain alone. This oscillation depends on recent successes or failures. For example, in the Australian season following our win there, we were decisively beaten, 3–0, in the three-match series. At the end of that tour, I announced that I would not be available for future tours. The man chosen to replace me for the home series against West Indies had had no previous experience as a captain; there was, further, no question about his being good enough for the side, since he was at that time the best all-rounder in the world. I refer of course to Ian Terence Botham who, incidentally, I too felt should succeed me.

A little more than a year later the selectors were debating another change. England had, not surprisingly, struggled against West Indies

On class and charisma: choosing a captain

and then Australia; Botham himself had had a rough time with bat and ball. Now the cry in the press and elsewhere was for someone at the helm who was without doubt qualified as a captain, whether or not he would be included on playing ability alone. My name and Keith Fletcher's were most widely bandied about as possible choices; but the press mentioned also others even less likely to be selected except as captain, like Roger Knight of Surrey or John Barclay of Sussex. At that time, no one talked of Bob Willis or David Gower or Graham Gooch, though they were firmly established in the team.

Part of this shift in the stress on captaincy *per se* lies in the image of potential captains, and how that image fits in with the mood of the cricketing public of which the selectors form a part. In 1982, for example, when Peter May took over from Alec Bedser as chairman of the selectors, Willis replaced Fletcher for the home series against India and Pakistan. I believe that this choice had much to do with the respective images of these two in May's mind; one extrovert, dominant, prepared to castigate players for lack of will, personally courageous; the other retiring, less intense, more reflective. Two years before, Botham had seemed a perfect antidote to me, as he was charismatic and of heroic stature.

Partly, too, such a shift reflects a genuine conflict. We *do* value tactical shrewdness and the ability to bring the best out of the players: we are also rightly reluctant to 'carry' a Porbandar in any side.

Certainly the *best* player is not necessarily an adequate captain, any more than the best salesman makes a sales manager. Indeed, the outstandingly gifted may well find it difficult to understand the problems of the average performer in their field. The Peter Principle is that people are inevitably promoted beyond their sphere of excellence. Nevertheless, at any level of the game, the captain, as with the sales manager, needs to be at least an adequate performer in the practical, first-order skills, otherwise it will be extremely difficult for him to gain the respect of the team, and to keep his own self-respect. I would go so far as to say that he *should* be worth his place in the side as a player alone, unless he has unequivocally proved his value as a captain. In 1977, just to remind the reader, when I was appointed captain of England in place of Greig, I had been picked as a batsman for the previous six Tests.

So, we have established the not very novel point that our headhunters must take into account both playing skills and leadership ability. But how are they to spot leadership qualities in those who have never had experience of the job? Clearly we constantly do form an impression of someone's potential on the basis of what we know of them (though I recall Tacitus's cautionary *mot* about the Emperor Galba, that he was *capax imperii nisi imperasset* – capable of ruling, if he had not ruled). Each appointment is to some extent a guess, every step in life has an element of uncertainty. But everyone who has ever captained a side once captained for the first time. Someone must have made a favourable judgement about his potential.

TOP A. G. Steel, captain of England in 1886 and 1888, wrote that 'amateurs
always have made, and always will make, the best captains; and this is only natural.'
This Gentlemen side of 1899 contained four notable England captains – W. G. Grace,
C. B. Fry, A. C. MacLaren, and Hon F. S. Jackson. The caption for the original
photograph described the players with initials; the umpires, being professionals,
were plain Sherwin and West.

BOTTOM First All-India team to tour England, 1933, with H. H. Maharaja Porbandar
as captain. Porbandar was said to have owned more Rolls-Royces than he scored
runs on the tour. He was a composer, the author of at least seventy-one tunes, best
known of which was 'Oriental Moon' – which was what *he* usually scored.

On class and charisma: choosing a captain

I keep flourishing this phrase 'leadership qualities'; what would our headhunters take this to mean? Again, this is a large question, to which much of the book is an attempted answer. Here I should like to discuss one approach to leadership that is sometimes suggested – that the great captains, like others who command respect, have some indefinable quality called 'charisma'.

Charisma originally had a religious meaning. It was a God-given grace of the personality capable of inspiring others by means of love, admiration, affection or a touch of fear. 'I'd follow him anywhere,' someone says. Or, 'They'd do anything for him.' Charisma is an effulgence of personal qualities, innate, or at any rate not capable of being acquired by study. In England, charisma and leadership have traditionally been associated with the upper class; with that social stratum that gives its members what Kingsley Amis called, 'the voice accustomed to command'.

Until 1954, every captain of England was an amateur; that is, he was not paid to play cricket. (The Latin root implies that amateurs played because of love of the game, rather than for anything so base as money.) Before the War, and for some time afterwards, the distinction was secure. Amateurs had different changing-rooms, stayed in better hotels, and emerged on to the playing area through separate gates. They stated when they were able to play, which explains why a cricketer of G. O. Allen's stature played only 146 matches for Middlesex in a career spanning

England's first professional captain appointed, May 1952. Len Hutton never relished the job. He once said that he wished he played golf, since then he would not have to travel with eleven others who couldn't stand the sight of him.

twenty-six seasons. Their names were represented differently on score-cards, either as 'Mr' or with 'Esq', or with the initials before rather than after their surnames. In 1950 Fred Titmus played his first game at Lord's. It was a fine Saturday, with a good crowd. An announcement came over the loudspeaker: 'Ladies and gentlemen, a correction to your scorecards: for "F. J. Titmus" read "Titmus, F. J." '

As late as 1960 I played for the Middlesex 2nd XI at Hove. I was still at school; this was only my second game with a mainly professional side. I was told to change in a large room, plush with carpets and sofas, along with our captain R. V. C. Robins (Esq). The other ten – all professionals – were changing in a tiny makeshift room virtually under the showers. Perhaps it was not entirely a coincidence that I was run out twice in the match.

By no means all the amateurs in cricket were High Tories in background or style. They had simply gone on from school to Oxbridge, been good at cricket, and followed a natural route into the first-class game. (Indeed, until 1981 the *Wisden* 'Births and Deaths' list marked out those of us who played for Oxford or Cambridge as 'Mr'.) Trevor Bailey and M. J. K. Smith were among those who took up secretarial jobs with their county sides in order to enable them to afford to play. The post-war amateurs became more like the members of Margaret Thatcher's cabinet than of Harold Macmillan's; more, too, like the latter than like the MCC Committee of the 1950s, when Lord Monckton was alleged to have said that in comparison to it Macmillan's cabinet was a group of 'pinkos'. Being an amateur not only kept one's status honourable amongst one's friends; it also opened up, for the better players, the chance of the ultimate honour – the England captaincy. Wally Hammond, after all, had changed from being a professional with this aim in mind.

Ted Dexter was undoubtedly one with the personality, style, and looks to fit his Radley background. Imperious as a player and, at times, as a man, it was not for nothing that he was widely known as 'Lord Ted'. Dexter scorned run-accumulation as much as he might money-grubbing, and it was typical that he would often get out to fourth-change bowlers who, he thought, ought not to be allowed to bowl.

I have already mentioned the West Indies' attitude to captaincy. For many decades the leader had to be white. It was axiomatic that no black man could be considered. Thus when in 1960 Frank Worrell was appointed captain for the tour of Australia it was a turning-point in West Indian cricket. (His leadership also marked a telling transformation in the performance of the team, whose success has continued almost unbroken until the time of writing.)

In England the abolition of the amateur/professional distinction did not formally arrive until 1962. Now that there is no restriction according to colour or social origin, far more players have become candidates for the captaincy of county or country, and more still see themselves as candidates. Captaincy is no longer a job reserved for members of a

Frank Worrell in 1957. Three years later he became captain of West Indies, the first black man to hold the job. Richie Benaud writes of him that 'when things threatened to get out of hand, Frank was there with his calm air of authority, his smile and the husky laugh which was instantly recognisable.' In the famous tied Test at Brisbane in 1960, Wes Hall dropped a crucial catch in the last over, knocking Rohan Kanhai – who was poised under the ball – out of his way in his enthusiasm. At this moment, Worrell simply walked over to Hall – who was bowling the over – put his arm round his shoulders, and told him to relax. Wes reckoned that it was Worrell's calming influence which got him back on the rails.

Worrell was a fine captain. He was sound tactically, though perhaps he failed to realise in the tense climax to the Lord's Test of 1963, when Cowdrey came to the crease in the last over with his arm in plaster with six runs needed and one wicket to fall, that West Indies had by far the better chance of winning. He was chivalrous; though in the same Test he allowed the over-rate to decline to a very low level by the standards of the day. Above all, the team would do anything for him. C. L. R. James tells how Roy Gilchrist was driven for five fours in an over by Cowdrey in a festival game in 1957; Worrell was captain and he had told Gilchrist that in festival games you don't bowl bouncers. Gilchrist preferred to bowl half-volleys and be driven for four after four rather than run the risk of appearing to disobey Frank Worrell.

certain caste, and one result is that there is more rivalry, envy, and even jostling for position. In common with other members of society cricketers are not as humble as they once were; they no longer compare their own lot only with that of their nearest rivals. They say 'why not me?' about a wider range of possibilities. This fact itself implies alterations in the task of the captain.

However, my main point is that it has long been recognised that the charisma of a leader is not a matter of social origin. I have already used the word to describe Botham, for his power, combativeness, and his ability to transcend the limitations of the ordinary cricketer. He also has a rare generosity to those of less ability; he values the stodgy but resolute contribution of a hardworking batsman, even if his score might only be 15 or 20, and a word of acknowledgement from him means more than fulsome praise from others.

In a quite different way Brian Close had charisma. He of all the captains I have known led from the front. His courage was notorious. Fielding incredibly close in at short square-leg, the great dome of his head thrust belligerently forward, he was regularly struck by the ball. The story goes that it once rebounded from his forehead to second slip. 'Catch it!' Close shouted. After the catch the Yorkshire players hurried up to him. He assured them he was all right. 'But what if it had hit you an inch lower?' one asked. 'He'd have been caught in t' gully,' Close replied.

Less apocryphal is the episode of his catch to dismiss Gary Sobers for 0 in the match between England and the Rest of the World at the Oval in 1970. The pitch was easy-paced, and Sobers was one of the most powerful hookers the game has known. Few players apart from Close would have stood at short square-leg to Sobers on such a pitch, even before he had scored. The bowler, John Snow, produced a token bouncer, and Sobers, seeing it early, was quickly in position to smash it to the square-leg boundary. I am convinced that any other cricketer with an ounce of sense would, in Close's position, have thrown himself to the ground, protected his head and closed his eyes. But the indomitable Close did not even flinch. As luck would have it, Sobers was too early with his shot, and too high; the ball touched the bottom edge of his bat, was deflected on to his hip, and bounced up for what turned out to be a simple catch. Close, still in position, and still looking, caught him.

In the Lord's Test against West Indies in 1976 we had gained a first-innings lead. West Indies were batting cautiously against Underwood and Pocock in their second innings; but were beginning to fret. Close, in his usual suicidal position, turned to David Steele at backward short-leg and whispered, 'They're getting fed up; they'll have a lap (i.e. a sweep) in a minute. I'll get in t' road, and you catch t' rebound.' This was, of course, in pre-helmet days; I cannot imagine Brian wearing one anyway. He is also alleged to have maintained that a cricket ball can't hurt you as it's only on you a second. Such neglect of personal safety is, if not admirable, certainly awesome.

On class and charisma: choosing a captain

My last example of a charismatic captain is the reverse of the caricature with which I began. Ian Chappell was an anti-hero, firmly anti-Establishment. In many ways he was an inspiring, tough and shrewd captain; but he also nudged cricket in the direction of gang warfare. I never played against Australia in a Test when he was captain, but in 1979 I did play against South Australia when he was in charge. In that match, which admittedly occurred in the turbulent aftermath of the Packer division, I was struck by the lounging hostility of their fielders and the way remarks would be directed out of the corner of the mouth, half out of earshot of the batsman but not, I felt, particularly complimentary to him.

I had always admired Ian's attitude to umpiring decisions until that match. It was quintessentially Australian – never walk, but never show dissent either. In one Test against England in Australia, the sixth, at Melbourne, in 1974–5, he was given out twice in the match caught at the wicket when the ball had merely touched his pads. He marched off in his usual trenchant way, allowing none of the spectators to know that the umpire had made a mistake. In the 1979 match I was referring to, however, I squeezed a ball into the slips: I thought I played it off the toe of the bat into the ground. On appeal the umpire gave me not out. The fielders made their disappointment very clear; in response to which I said with some heat, 'I played it into the ground.' At the end of the over Ian muttered to me as he crossed, 'You do the batting, we'll do the appealing, and leave the umpiring to the umpire, Mike.' However, he was, in this match, unable to live up to this admirable sentiment. For when it came to his turn to bat, on his first ball (a bouncer which he tried to evade) the umpire (wrongly, in my opinion) refused to allow him to run for a leg-bye; whereupon Chappell threw down his bat and gloves in disgust, remonstrated with the umpire, and caused play to be held up. When the next ball was eventually bowled, Botham had him caught at the wicket for a duck.

Charisma seems to me a most limited asset to a captain. It helps in the early stages: any cricketer would be inclined to give Botham, or Close, or Dexter or Ian Chappell the benefit of any doubt about his decisions. Their mistakes would be tolerated for longer, and with less resentment, than would, say, the Maharaja of Porbandar's (unless the members of the latter's team depended on him for their livelihood. A story of cricket historian David Frith's hints at Porbandar's not being unaware of pecuniary influences – he is said to have been in the habit of presenting diamond-encrusted tie-pins to umpires – *before* the match!).

But honeymoons come to an end, and charisma does not imply steadiness, patience, concentration, or considerateness, all invaluable in a captain. Above all, placing too much emphasis on charisma might well involve ignoring the central requirement of a captain, namely, that he knows his task. Charisma is not the same thing as leadership.

The case of Dexter proves the point. His main failing was that he

Colin Cowdrey and Brian Close opening for England against Pakistan, third Test, the Oval, 1967. Boycott had gone sick, so Close moved up to Number One. On the day before the match, Close had had to attend a disciplinary hearing at Lord's to explain his alleged time-wasting and, worse, striking a spectator during a county match at Birmingham a few days before. On the day after the Test it was announced that Cowdrey, not Close, would captain the MCC touring team to West Indies in the following winter. Cricket and the England captaincy has thrown up several juxtapositions such as this photo illustrates – north v. south, professional v. amateur: Close v. Cowdrey, Illingworth v. Cowdrey, Illingworth v. Denness, Boycott v. Brearley.

easily became bored. In all three matches that I played under him in South Africa in 1964–5 there were periods in which he had lost interest and was more concerned with getting his golf-swing right at square-leg than with who should be bowling or with what field. He was an excellent theorist on the game; but when his theories failed to work, or he had no particular bright ideas, he would drift; and the whole team drifted with him. I would guess that Dexter was, in those days, more interested in ideas than in people.

Or take Close. Of course his personal qualities were inseparable from his captaincy, and they unquestionably enhanced it. Physically, he was immensely hard, and no one would risk provoking him. His players also felt affection for him. On top of this, he was a fine attacking captain. He was much happier when his team was 'on the go' in the field, trying anything to get a wicket (when, too, he could caper about at the batsman's feet as happy as a hippo in wet mud), than when they had to fall back on defence or containment. But his strengths as a captain had less to do with his courage than with his shrewdness and competitiveness. Towards the end of his career, his wish to 'make things happen' had an unsettling

On class and charisma: choosing a captain

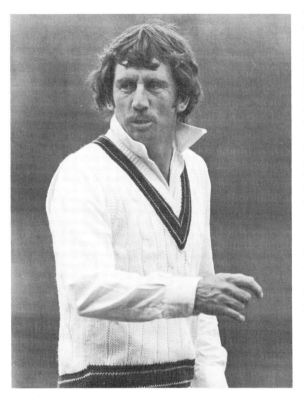

Ian Chappell. Benaud's words about Keith Miller, that 'he would be horrified if anyone thought that under the brash man's exterior there lurked a generous heart', apply to Chappell. He was a players' captain, not only in his ability to bind the group together and argue their case, but also in his using every opportunity for confrontation with outsiders towards that end. Nevertheless there were cliques within his teams, and those who were unwilling to put on the rebellious front that was almost a uniform for his side could feel out of things.

Ian Botham's anxiety about criticism while captain of England seems to be reflected in this defensive look and pose.

effect on the team, especially on the bowlers; for Brian found it hard to let things happen of their own accord, or to allow the bowlers to find a rhythm and to force a batsman into error by tying him down first.

Botham too has sufficient tactical sense; his main problem, apart from the loss of his own form, was that he has been too sensitive to criticism. He allowed people to niggle and upset him. Even the England players became cautious about offering advice if they suspected that Ian would not agree with it.

So: birth, breeding, superficial attractiveness are dangerous grounds on which to select a leader. Yet for almost a century England and the counties restricted their choice of captains to a small percentage of those who played first-class cricket. The reverse attitude is equally inappropriate. As Jim Swanton once remarked, 'There is such a thing as *inverted* snobbery.' Either way, to search for the charismatic leader implies ignoring the needs of the task, and (to continue with the helpful categories of John Adair's *Action-Centred Leadership*) is an inadequate substitute for the complicated personal qualities required to motivate individuals and the group.

So far we have established that our captain-seeking company would not ignore first-order skills (batting, bowling, etc); that they would not restrict themselves to any particular social sub-group (McKinsey's, the management consultants, recently showed that none of ten outstandingly well-managed companies showed any indications of nepotism, class distinction or elitism in their selection or promotion practices) and that charisma, the possession of readily discernible charm or magnetism, is an inadequate basis for choice of leader. Instead, they would want to make their assessment on two grounds: how well does a candidate know the game (and how ready is he to learn)? And, secondly, will he be able to motivate the others?

A few words about the task. The type of knowledge required will be practical, not theoretical. We have all known those who are brilliant at theorising, but who cannot make decisions and have no common sense. This syndrome is not unknown among university graduates. A captain's decisions are practical, and share with others of this type the feature that they often have to be made on imperfect evidence. You move a man from backward short-leg to third slip: you can never know for certain that the next ball will not lob up exactly where your fielder had been. This 'glorious uncertainty' of cricket is one factor in a tendency amongst down-to-earth players to denigrate thought; so often they have heard theories based on assumption rather than on fact. They know from experience the role luck plays in the short-term.

In my first year as captain of Middlesex we played a ten-over game against Glamorgan at Ebbw Vale. As we fetched our bags from the cars (the rain had unexpectedly stopped at about tea-time) I said excitedly, 'We'll have to think about this!' The senior players found this hilarious: *think* about a ten-over match! About a sheer slog! I can see their point;

in those days I did have too much confidence in the power of thought in predicting or controlling events.

I can remember in that first season in 1971 referring to *Wisden* to discover which types of bowlers had been most successful the year before against each of the counties we played. I now think this was a pretty fatuous exercise: current conditions are far more relevant than the patterns of a year before. However, I also believe that there are no activities on which thought, properly and appropriately carried out, cannot be a help. A captain and a team *do* need to think about their approach to a ten-over match, and about how it might differ from a forty-over encounter.

Sir Donald Bradman goes so far as to say that any good captain should be an avid reader of the game and know not only its laws but also a fair degree of its history. I find this far-fetched: every captain I have known would have been found lacking in this respect. Awareness of cricket's history would not harm a captain; but I find it hard to see how it could be of much practical help.

So our potential captain should be able to talk sense about tactics; he should value thought, provided that it is down-to-earth: he will be interested in, perhaps even passionate about, this side of the game. He will also be aware that there is no *one* task of captaincy; there are many different tasks, with varying degrees of immediacy. I shall be discussing this point in the next chapter.

Let us return to the question of motivation. Can we make any remarks that are not entirely predictable about the sorts of qualities that enable a man to bring the best out of others? What will the headhunters look for?

Clearly they will not be satisfied if they find someone who, like a contemporary of G. O. Allen's, was (in Allen's words) 'excellent on tactics, but his word didn't count for sixpence as no one would listen to him.'

I have said that a captain has from time to time to be prepared to take an unpopular line. He must have a measure of independence. He cannot always be 'one of the boys'. He will have to criticise individuals or even the whole group, and say things, or insist on activities, that they do not like. He will have to be able to drop senior players from the team, and give them the news. He must be prepared to recommend that some members of a staff be sacked.

Nevertheless, he must be able to engage with his players, to communicate with them. He cannot keep a glacial distance. I often envied captains who never lost their tempers; but I noticed, too, that this coolness was sometimes bought at the expense of involvement. Nor is it likely that any captain will be able to keep his team enthusiastic if he is positively and widely disliked by them. There was, in the 1960s, a county captain in the West Country whose bowlers tried to hit him with the ball whenever he had a net.

A captain should not crave affection from his players; but nor should he court, or make a virtue of, their disaffection. He should always, too, be available to players, whether to listen to their ideas or to their complaints. In choosing a captain, some such assessment of a man's personality is essential.

What about more humdrum biographical facts about the candidates? Does his age matter? (I presume that it is not sexist to assume, in our present context, that the candidates will be male.) Should he come from the current staff of a side, or from outside? Is he likely to be a batsman or a bowler?

With regard to age, I myself found that dealing with players significantly older than myself was, on the whole, harder than dealing with the rest. Not everyone feels the same, though there must be at least a trace of unease in most people when, in a situation as intimate and domestic as a cricket dressing-room, they are installed in authority over men almost old enough to be their fathers. The 'fathers', too, often resent this reversal. However, other captains find that it is the arrogance or insolence of youth that they find hardest to stomach; and for some it is the rivalry and envy of their peers. The main problem in appointing a very young man as captain of, say, a county side is of course lack of experience. I think our headhunters would be unwilling to lay down any hard-and-fast criteria on this issue.

They would take a similar line on the question of whether to find an insider to take over the ailing team, or an outsider. The more feeble the side has become, and the longer its decline has lasted, the more reason there is to import. For by then some at least of the likely candidates from within will already have been tried. Moreover, the pattern of apathy and expectation of defeat will have become entrenched. For an insider both to see it clearly and to manage to change it will be difficult though not of course impossible. In his unobtrusive and unselfish way Jim Watts gradually steered Northamptonshire from the doldrums in the early '70s to being a team that held their heads high and a force to be reckoned with ten years later. No doubt there are many other such cases.

Nevertheless the more dramatic uplifts have often been caused by the arrival of a captain from outside. I will mention two such examples. First, Tony Lock at Leicester. Lock's achievement was remarkable in that he captained Leicestershire for only two years yet his impact was immediate. Moreover, Leicestershire's brief rise in the county championship did not outlast his presence as captain. The figures are striking. In 1963 and 1964, the county finished sixteenth; in the following year they were fourteenth. In 1966, Lock's first season at Leicester, they rose six places to eighth in the table, and in his second year he lifted them a further five places to third, equal in points with Kent, who finished second. After Lock's departure the side declined again; ninth in 1968 (again under the leadership of Maurice Hallam, who had preceded Lock). And in Illingworth's first two seasons as captain, in 1969 and 1970, the county finished fourteenth and fifteenth. Not that statistics tell the whole story. *Wisden* states in 1967 that:

'The former Surrey and England player was clearly resolved to make a success of his captaincy and infected his team with his own exuberance, which was an important factor in recording eight wins, the most since 1961. Lock's urgent approach to his duties delighted supporters and brought a lively response from the players, evidence for which was often to be seen in the field . . . The season should prove to have been most useful in rebuilding Leicestershire's morale, and the effects of this ought soon to be seen in 1967.'

Indeed they were. Next year *Wisden* commented on his 'drive and brilliance on the field', and remarked that he 'sustained a belief in the capacity to win'. I never played against a side that Lock captained, but I can imagine his energy, optimism and enthusiasm combined with a shrewd cricketing brain. And if confirmation of these remarks were needed, his achievement in leading Western Australia to their first-ever

Imran Khan as captain of Pakistan, Leeds, 1982. At this time, shortly before a stress fracture of his left shin forced him to give up bowling, possibly permanently, Imran had become a wonderful all-rounder. As a captain, he struggled. The main task was interesting: to choose the moments to attack with Abdul Qadir, the leg-spinner, and himself, and to defend with his other, pedestrian bowlers. I felt that he left Qadir and himself on far too long at a time, and failed to give singles to ensure that vulnerable batsmen ended up at the right end. In that series Ian Greig and Derek Pringle, for example, had no clue against Qadir, yet Imran allowed them to hang around at the non-striker's end while a much more competent batsman, like Gatting, kept the strike.

outright win in the Sheffield Shield in his first season as captain underlines his immense contribution. In the previous four seasons – 1962–3 until 1966–7 – Western Australia had been fourth (out of five), fifth, second and fourth.

My second example is Eddie Barlow's brief period as captain of Derbyshire. The county had been propping up the table during most of the '70s when halfway through 1976 Barlow became their fourth captain in five seasons. In the six seasons between 1971 and 1976 they had finished fifteenth twice, sixteenth once and seventeenth (last) three times. Under Barlow they were seventh in 1977 and, though they dropped to fourteenth in 1978, they reached the final of the Benson and Hedges Cup in that season. These figures may not sound so impressive as Lock's, but I have a vivid impression of the transformation he brought to his team. At last Derbyshire looked and played like a side that believed they could win. Barlow was a fitness fanatic himself and one of the first county captains to insist on intensive training for a county squad. Their improved physical shape no doubt helped them; but far more important was the tremendous improvement in morale which he inspired.

Finally, will the search for a new leader be concentrated mainly on batsmen or bowlers? On openers or middle-order batsmen? And what of wicket-keepers? We might compare this issue with a parallel one in business: is the best managing director most likely to have been an economist or an accountant, a sales manager or a marketing man?

By far the largest proportion of captains, at least at the level of first-class cricket, has been provided by those who are predominantly batsmen. This pattern arises partly from the class distinctions I have spoken of: gentlemen batted, players bowled, a pattern repeated in services cricket. I remember while at school playing a Combined Services team composed mainly of officers; the bowling was opened, however, by Stoker Healey and Private Stead. Since captains came from the ranks of the gentlemen, it is not surprising that few captains were bowlers.

But are there any intrinsic reasons for the bias? Would the headhunters of the 1980s find any reason for preferring a batsman? Bradman for one, in *The Art of Cricket*, maintained that the captain should, ideally, be a batsman; for it is extremely hard for bowlers to be objective about their own craft. They tend either to over-bowl themselves or not to bowl enough, from conceit, modesty or indeed self-protection. The captain has decisions to make and a job to do while his team is batting, to be sure. But by far the greater part of his work is to be done in the field, changing the bowlers and fielders, keeping everyone alert. There is a strong case, therefore, against giving the job to someone whose primary task is to bowl.

On the other hand, two of the best post-war international captains were Richie Benaud and Illingworth. Indeed, Illingworth argues in his book *Captaincy* (Pelham, 1980) that the all-rounder, and especially the slow-bowling all-rounder, are, all else being equal, in the best position for the job. Unlike fast bowlers, they do not have to inject so much adrenalin and aggression into their bowling; nor is it quite so physically exhausting. Being bowlers and batsmen, they should be able to understand the mentality of both. It is therefore easier for them to criticise both. One of Illingworth's refrains as captain and as manager was that he could not understand seam bowlers who were unable to bowl on one side of the wicket. ('I could do it better blindfold,' he used to say.) Expecting high standards of himself both as batsman and bowler, it was easier to demand them of others. Moreover, a bowling captain is in a position to convince the rest of the team that a declaration is well-timed if he will be relying on himself, among others, to prove it right.

I would agree there is a strong case for having an all-rounder, if he is a slow or medium-paced bowler, as captain. The one argument against is, however, a strong one: is he in the best position for deciding when

Mike Procter, bowling for Gloucestershire against Hampshire, 1977. An exception to the rule about fast bowlers not making good captains. Vintcent van der Bijl, who played under Procter for Natal, speaks of his ability to develop each player's natural game and of the enthusiasm that he brought to every match. The umpire is Barry Meyer.

to bowl himself? In my view, Illingworth's main flaw as a captain was in not bowling himself enough.

I have already implied my opinion about fast bowlers as captains; it takes an exceptional character to know when to bowl, to keep bowling with all his energy screwed up into a ball of aggression, *and* to be sensitive to the needs of the team, both tactically and psychologically. Willis in particular has always shut himself up into a cocoon of concentration and fury for his bowling. Our headhunters should recommend a fast bowler only as a last resort; unless, perhaps, they have a man of Mike Procter's qualities available.

The captain who is a batsman is also liable to display his own short-comings. First, I think, there is a greater risk that he will not understand his bowlers. Richard Hutton once complained to me that I expected the

David Bairstow
captaining Yorkshire in
1984. The job is never
easy for a 'keeper; but
Bairstow had a more than
usually difficult task in
taking over after the bitter
dissension over the
sacking and reinstatement
of Boycott, and the
removal of Illingworth
from the position of
manager. Bairstow coped
manfully, and his
extrovert energy helped
the county to start the
season well, though the
momentum could not be
maintained.

bowlers to perform like automata, and his criticism was probably just. I had never had to charge in twenty-five or thirty yards and hurl the ball as fast as I could at the stumps. More empathy is called for in the batsman-captain. I do not mean that he needs to know a great deal about the mechanics of bowling, though doubtless this would at times be a help. Rather, he needs to enter imaginatively into the mind of his bowlers, young and old, quick and slow, and learn how to get the best out of them.

There is also a minor drawback in being an opening batsman. Any opener starts to feel signs of nerves when the opposition have lost eight or nine wickets, or are likely to declare. For the captain who also opens the batting the transition from concentrating on taking these last wickets (which may require him to spur on tired bowlers and deal with his own and the side's frustration) to the kind of calmness that he needs for his next job is stark. Close used to urge me to give myself more chance as a batsman by going in lower in the order, at least in Tests.

On class and charisma: choosing a captain

From a purely tactical viewpoint, the man who is in the best position to see what the bowlers are doing, and to judge the nature of the pitch, is the wicket-keeper. He is often the first to know that a bowler is tiring from the way the ball comes into his gloves. What is more, he can often advise the bowler if there is something slightly wrong; for example, if he is running in too fast or not fast enough, if he seems to be straining. It is often the 'keeper who knows whether a slow bowler is bowling a little too fast or too slow, too short or too far up, for a particular pitch or batsman. Titmus, the great Middlesex off-spinner, would constantly check with John Murray behind the stumps on all these aspects of his craft.

Yet remarkably few 'keepers have become captains; and many of those who have have quickly given up the job. One problem is simply logistic. The captain needs to talk to his bowlers. The wicket-keeper may be seventy yards away from his opening bowler when he starts his run-up. And though a similar problem confronts a captain who fields at slip, at least he is not encumbered by pads for his repeated sprints from bowler to fielding position.

The main problem, however, seems to be the degree of concentration that 'keeping entails. Not only do they have to expect to take each delivery, but whenever the ball is struck they have to prepare for a throw-in, which often means dashing up to the stumps. Taylor was one who found, in a few months of captaining his county side, that one role adversely affected the other; he was no longer 'keeping at his best. Wicket-keepers make invaluable advisers to the captain; rarely captains themselves. I would rate Rodney Marsh the exception to this rule. For behind the abrasive front was a thoughtful, astute and humorous man, whose players, when he led Western Australia, were totally committed to him. The Australian Board, however, were not. But their prejudice was not based on technical considerations, such as having a wicket-keeper as captain. For them he was tarred with the same brush as Ian Chappell, the brush of revolution and extremism. Greg Chappell, with his more dignified air, they could stomach as captain; but they refused to swallow Marsh. This was a major mistake; he might well have proved a more imaginative Test captain than Greg.

CHAPTER THREE

Taking stock: the nursery end

One part of the captain's job is visible to all. He is the one who leads the rest out of the pavilion, and who then, by nodding his head or pointing his arm, manipulates them on the field. His task is tactical, his decisions immediate and short-term. On his performance in this sphere he is judged.

But there is also another side to the captain's role, hidden from the general view like the dark side of the moon, where he assesses, plans and prepares. Here, some of the work is directed to longer-term aims. It starts as soon as he is appointed, if not before. At any level of cricket, being invited to captain a side rarely comes as a complete surprise, so most new captains will already have thought about the team that they might inherit, its strengths and weaknesses, its co-operative and its recalcitrant members. Even where the offer does emerge from 'the blue', a man should have grounds for confidence about the set-up that he is to join before accepting. He should feel that *he* has a fair chance of carrying the job off, for a start. He will want to be convinced, especially if the club is not his own, that it treats its players adequately. He may well hesitate unless he is sure that the side has some unrealised potential, though he may consider that he is duty-bound to make the attempt, even if he is not sanguine about the prospects.

At school level some of these issues will not arise for the captain designate; but even here captaincy has its hinterland. It is unfortunate for many youngsters today that their schools no longer play cricket (if they ever did). Neither Gatting nor Ian Gould, both England players, had any chance to play the game at their schools in the 1970s. Don Bennett, the Middlesex coach, runs the county's indoor cricket coaching during the winter; he not infrequently finds that a group of schoolboys who have attended enthusiastically and shown promise throughout the previous winter tell him when they come again in September that they have not played cricket at all since March. Fortunately, the gap is being partially closed by the selfless efforts of those who run junior teams and youth-coaching at established clubs.

However, let us imagine a twelve-year-old boy whose teacher tells him he will be captain of the under-13s next season. At this age, the staff will presumably be in charge of the organisation of sport in the school. But is there any scope for an enterprising youngster to plan for the season?

I suppose that even Bennett's disappointed winters-only cricketers might have done something about their plight. In India, I was told of a school which, in the heady atmosphere of Independence, regarded cricket as an imperialist game and refused to have anything to do with it. The school had not reckoned, however, with the enthusiasm of the majority of the boys. A group of frustrated thirteen-year-olds had the nerve to ask for a meeting with a noted industrialist of the city, who happened to be the headmistress's father. They told him their sad story. He said that yes, it must be distressing; but what did they wish him to do about it? 'Well,' they replied, taking deep breaths, 'we reckon it would cost 2,100 rupees to get a pitch made and buy some equipment. We wondered if . . .' Next day, a cheque for 2,100 rupees arrived with a message asking to whom it should be made out. Thus the school cricket team was founded, and their benefactor turned up at the first match with an enormous thermos flask containing enough cold lemon squash for the team; and with some stern words about their careless batting.

Not every enterprise is so rewarded, but nor does it require such temerity. The under-13 XI captain-elect could, indeed should, start thinking about his opportunity well in advance of the first match. His school might, for example, have no organised winter practice, and yet be within easy reach of a cricket school or sports centre. Perhaps he himself could find this out, and propose to the cricket teacher that a group of those who wished to do so might go there. Such opportunities are more widely available than they were; my own first experience of an indoor net occurred when I was fifteen, and was rarely repeated until I was invited to the county's winter nets at seventeen.

If the school has a gym, or a playground, the children can, at minimal expense, be helped to learn the skills of the game and at the same time have a lot of fun. The school may be persuaded to put up a net in the yard; or to organise some coaching in the gym during lunch hours or after school. For the latter, a few old bats, tennis balls and lacrosse balls are all that is needed. Or, again, they could write off to the MCC for a set of rules for six-a-side indoor cricket, which has caught on well in recent years.

None of these ideas is, of course, the prerogative of the young captain. It will be particularly up to him, however, to begin to consider the likely make-up of his team. Who will be his best batsmen and bowlers? Did they as under-12s have a good wicket-keeper? Who will help him make his decisions on the field? He may go to the library and read whatever he can find on the subject of captaincy, trying to understand the basic field settings, and so on. Whenever he reads cricket articles in the papers or listens in to commentary on radio or television, he will be especially attentive for what is said about the efforts and tasks of captains. Perhaps he will even suggest to his teacher that he write to the county club in their area to see if one of the players would come and talk to them about captaincy or other aspects of the game.

Clearly, these basic remarks need not apply only to schoolboys. There are so many types and levels of club cricket that it is hard to generalise. However, I can imagine a new captain reflecting on whether he wishes to alter the club's cricketing priorities. He may, for example, want a more serious approach, with success on the field counting for more than sheer bonhomie. He may be in favour of the team playing all-out to win on Saturdays, while on Sundays their more relaxed attitude could continue, in which the aim is to ensure that everyone who plays is given a chance with bat or ball, and that no one hogs the show. Both approaches have their adherents: the new captain may be able to steer the club in either direction.

He may also concern himself with practice and coaching within the club. How much attention has been given to the state of the nets? Is there a structure of youth cricket within the club, through which the senior sides may expect to receive a flow of promising players?

For a new county captain, there is no question of there being doubt about his aims for the club: players, committee and supporters alike want success on the field. The captain may – almost certainly will – have scope for making everyone more acutely aware of this aim, for toughening the players and for convincing the committee about the need for decisive action to make it possible. But there will be agreement about the aim itself, and his own tenure will depend on its being achieved – at least in part.

Let us presume that the captain has been appointed in the autumn for the following season, and that he has automatically become a member of the cricket sub-committee, if not also of the general committee of the club. (The latter makes all the decisions, basing them on recommendations from its various sub-committees, such as finance, youth cricket and so on.) The presumption of ex-officio membership of the cricket sub-committee is now universal; it was not so in all counties even as recently as the late 1960s. Yorkshire, for example, whose record in personnel relations has been authoritarian, did not have Close on any committee when he was captain of the club. He was not even a member of the selection committee; from whom he would receive a list of twelve names for the next match. In such a set-up, the notion of responsibility as applied to the captain becomes a mockery.

However, those days are over. The issues on which the new captain's opinion will first be sought are likely to be mundane, but important. Is he happy with the arrangements for winter nets? And what programme does he advocate for the players' pre-season training and practice?

The relevance of winter nets has declined as the number of professionals spending the winter abroad has increased. If the captain himself stays at home, these weekly practices, indoors of course, give him an opportunity of getting to know those who are also in England – often, but not always, the less experienced members of the staff. He will also be able to see teenagers who have played for the county's Young Cricketers XI in the previous season, and anyone else who is recommended for a trial. This is primarily the domain of the county coach; but liaison between him and the captain is essential.

Pre-season practice is more important. Fitness has only recently been considered a matter that needs special attention by cricketers. In 1965, my first full year on the Middlesex staff, possession of a tracksuit would have been considered irrelevant and even pretentious. Not many years before, Denis Compton used to turn up at Lord's for the first time half an hour before the first match of the season, borrow a bat and score a hundred. Compton was a genius, and thus a law to himself. But the general belief was then and continued to be that fitness for cricket was achieved simply by playing the game. Alec Bedser, for instance, would regularly bowl 1,200 overs per season without push-ups or sprints.

To some extent it is true that fitness for cricket can best be achieved by cricket activities. Only by spending six hours in the field regularly can one be fresh to open the batting at 6 p.m. However, all cricketers can enhance their performance by better all-round fitness. They are also aided in avoiding injuries. Thomas's most significant contribution to the England team as physiotherapist was in the field of prevention. Bowlers who had constantly suffered from muscle injuries – to their hamstrings, say, or groins – became less prone to such breakdowns. Regular exercising also prolonged people's careers and mitigated or delayed the effects of arthritis in over-used joints. Geoff Arnold was one who gained by a routine of training. But the two men whose careers have been most miraculously revived and extended by dedication to hard work are Lillee and Willis.

I was present at a conversation between Tony Greig and Willis at Sydney shortly after the Centenary Test in 1977. Greig was hinting at an imminent development in cricket which would mean new opportunities (an allusion to World Series Cricket, a meaning I totally failed to grasp). He told Bob that he needed to be able to bowl in a day an opening spell of seven overs, six of them flat out; a second spell of, say, six overs, five of them fast; and then a third spell of six overs, again with five at top speed – nineteen overs a day, of which sixteen would be really hostile, rather than fourteen, of which eight were. Willis had already adopted Thomas's approach. Now he used hypnosis to push his body further than before. Since that time he regularly ran five miles a day, on top of stretching and exercises appropriate to speed and mobility. Lillee, even before Willis, had devised a vigorous programme for himself that enabled

Grim stretching exercises on the practice area, Sydney Cricket Ground, 1982–3 tour. This was where John Maclean was injured in the nets on the day before a Test. The slim tower on the left of the picture supports one of the Packer floodlights. Foreground: Bob Willis with Bernard Thomas. Background: Allan Lamb and Liam Botham.

him to recover from a serious back injury and to become again the greatest bowler in the game.

Even for batsmen and fielders much, though not all, of this applies. Injuries can be avoided, and an extra foot of speed, an extra inch of suppleness that avoids a narrow run-out or turns a half-chance into a chance can be achieved.

The impetus for the change in attitude arose partly from the sporting scene at large, partly from the arrival of one-day cricket. In one-day matches, outfielding and speed between the wickets count for more than in longer games; and the improved standards are maintained in three- and five-day cricket. No longer is it conceivable that a fast bowler should have to chase the ball back to the long-on boundary, as Alan Moss had to do at the end of a long day at Lord's in the early '50s; finishing his follow-through, he turned round to see an ageing Sims edging towards square-leg from mid-on, saying out of the corner of his mouth, 'I'm sorry, Al old boy, but you'll have to go.'

All counties now arrange for some physical training in April. At Middlesex we have been fortunate in having a Loughborough graduate, Graham Barlow, on our playing staff; he was sensitive to the different capacities of, say, eighteen-year-olds and forty-year-olds, and aware of the different requirements of batsmen and bowlers.

The new captain will have to decide how prominent a role this aspect of preparation will play, and how long the whole period should be. My view was that a week of this – to me, boring – activity was enough; after which Bedser's old-fashioned attitude was mainly right, and the important thing was to practise *and* train via cricketing skills. I do believe, though, that, especially in the cold of an average English spring, warm-up exercises are valuable.

Just as sheer physical exercise, however imaginatively organised, becomes a bore, so I find can unmitigated net practice. My view is that a week of full-time net practice is sufficient. Beyond that, standards become sloppy and efforts flag. So the rest of the time – perhaps one more week – should be devoted to practice matches and middle practice. At Lord's we had a particular problem. Because Middlesex do not own the ground, and because the square at Lord's is over-used, we found an understandable reluctance within the MCC to allow us on to the square in April. In fact, I can remember this happening only once in my time there. After a while I accepted the position, and therefore asked the secretary to arrange several one-day friendly matches instead.

Here the captain will have to make decisions with his opposite number about how these are to be taken: we used to have an agreement with Surrey that each pair of batsmen would stay at the crease for forty minutes or so, regardless of whether they got out. (Norman Featherstone was actually out to each of the first three balls of such a match.) I came to think that such laxity is a mistake, and encourages looseness. The players' attitudes are improved by realistic practice matches.

I used to find this whole pre-season period hard work. As captain, I was responsible for deciding the overall programme. Although the coach would share it, I came to feel that, at least for the first-team squad, nets worked better if I was definitely in charge, and if I insisted on the practice being serious and energetic, while also taking care that it did not drag on too long. Moreover, the captain and coach have to decide how to occupy the players during rain. We would often trust to the good sense of individuals, and simply say that we expected them all to take some exercise that they found helpful, whether that was a several-mile run through London's parks or an indoor net, a game of squash or exercises under the arbours on the Nursery ground.

One other perennial decision concerned reporting back. Barbados would regularly ring to ask if Wayne Daniel could play for them in a crucial match ten days after we were due back. On the one hand, it seemed ridiculous to stop a man playing high-class cricket rather than watching the rain fall in London; on the other, if Daniel were to be allowed leeway others would expect it, and some degree of acclimatisation *is* necessary. Roland Butcher found this out to his – and our – cost, when he pulled a muscle in a snow-storm a couple of days after a late return from the Caribbean. Our best season, 1980, coincided with our taking a tough line with all players, requiring them to come back on time.

Most of these problems sound petty; many need only be dealt with as they occur. But the job does include them, and some forethought about how to tackle them may help.

During this period, from, say, November to April, and throughout the first season, the new captain will be assessing the playing strengths of the county and establishing his links with the players. If his predecessor was deposed, and is still on the staff, it may be worth making a special effort to get his co-operation. He will, apart from all else, have much valuable knowledge about the whole set-up.

The new captain will also quickly come to recognise any others who may be disgruntled, possibly because their claims to the captaincy have been overlooked. He should be alive to schisms. I have known county teams divided into those who had played Test cricket and the rest: the Middlesex team of the late '60s had this tendency. Younger players were not expected to voice opinions; there was a lack of mutual respect. It is the captain's job to try to unify the team, and the first step in such integration will be his awareness that it is lacking.

He will also make an assessment of strengths and weaknesses. As he pencils in his team for the first match, he may be uncomfortably aware of the weakness of the middle-order batting, or the lack of a fast bowler or a class spinner. He may find a team too many of whom are in their late thirties or it may lack experience. The more successful the side becomes, the greater will be the need for quality and depth among the reserves, for two reasons: one is that there may well be extra Test calls, and secondly whenever a team is challenging in several competitions at the same time there are certain to be injuries; the players are bound to push themselves hard in each match, and one is tempted to play key players even when they are not fully fit.

During these first months of contact with his players, the captain will form, and modify, all sorts of views about them individually and as a group. Is there, perhaps, a tendency to complacency? Is the side as a whole resolute when the going is hard? Is the dressing-room atmosphere conducive to a sharing of problems or insights, or does each jealously guard his ideas from the rest?

The committee, ultimately, has responsibility for the management of the club, and for its long-term viability. But no captain worth his salt will think only in terms of a single season, despite the fact that this is likely to be the limit of his appointment. He will accept that it is part of his job to help build a side – or, rather, a staff – for the future as well as for the present.

But the building may first require demolition. Space may be needed for new acquisitions or for the development of those already there. Sometimes one or two players can affect the whole so adversely that they need to be removed, like rotten apples from a barrel. At the end of Illingworth's second season with Leicestershire, he ensured the departure of the county's two most successful batsmen, Clive Inman and Peter

Marner, on the grounds that the team would never function as such while they were around. (I make no comment on the correctness of Illingworth's judgement in this case; I offer it as an example of what *may* have to be done.)

Such drastic action may not be needed. Talent needs to be respected and nurtured. It is up to the captain, with the help of others, to integrate and accommodate such players if at all possible. I shall return to the problem of difficult individuals and those who warrant special treatment in a later chapter, but I should like to mention here that in my opinion the England selectors were wrong to leave Edmonds out of the tour parties to Australia in 1982–3 and to New Zealand and Pakistan in 1984. He can indeed be hard to handle; but it is the job of captain and managers to do just that, and not to select four spinners all inferior in ability to Edmonds to avoid such problems, particularly when he had had successful seasons at home in 1982 and 1983.

Indeed, the most reliable way of improving a team is to improve its talent. To borrow a story from the cricket writer, Michael Melford: as the jockey, allegedly Fred Archer, said to the noble owner who asked why he had not come on the scene earlier in the race, 'I couldn't come without the horse, your Grace.'

In the short run, horses must also be picked for courses, as we will see in the chapter on selection. But it is equally essential to form a longer-term view of a side's shortcomings and to set out to fill the gaps.

There are two methods of doing this. One is to transplant specimens that have already grown to maturity in someone else's garden; the other to grow from seed. The drawbacks of transplants are that they might not enjoy the new soil, they might elbow out half-grown native stock, and they might prove expensive. Seeds, however, may not survive, or may take years to become established.

When I started as Middlesex captain in 1971, I was struck by the speed with which clubs like Leicestershire and Northamptonshire snaffled up players who had become disgruntled or simply lacked opportunity at other clubs. Mike Turner and Illingworth, for example, seemed free of the red tape that hampers counties which go through every relevant committee before approaching a player with a firm offer (or indeed before responding with conviction to the approach of a player). Moreover, they knew what they wanted.

During my first few seasons we tried to sign Bob Cottam, Norman McVicker and Mushtaq Mohammad, and failed with all three. One reason was that with living costs so high in London our offers were not sufficiently attractive financially. I regarded it as a priority for Middlesex to improve its level of pay in real and comparative terms, and I think that the club did, at least to a modest degree, manage to make this possible. It was also important that the attractions of a potential player should not blind one to the values of the current staff; new recruits should never be paid more than our own top players. Alan Connolly, the Australian Test bowler, had a brief and disappointing time with Middlesex. But it started, in 1969, on the wrong footing when the committee, in their justifiable eagerness to sign him, offered more than they had to Titmus and Murray who, as all-rounders, were in effect doing two jobs to Connolly's one. Some of the home side naturally resented this; they took it out on the enthusiastic but naive Australian, and he never, I think, felt wholeheartedly welcomed or completely at home.

Not that money alone is sufficient to lure a playing staff of the necessary quality. We could offer the attraction of regular cricket at a fine ground; but we also had to promise positive and enjoyable cricket and a reasonably happy environment. Many of our key players, particularly the bowlers, have come from other counties. Mike Selvey and Emburey were from Surrey, the latter being prepared to serve several years as Titmus's understudy rather than walk into the first team of any one of about twelve or fourteen counties. Edmonds chose Middlesex ahead of Kent, Leicestershire and others. Allan Jones was on the point of emigrating to New Zealand when we heard that he was free and signed him for the 1976 season.

The club also evolved a clearer, more realistic policy towards overseas players; so that as well as the admirable Daniel, we also had the benefit of the tremendous skills of Vintcent van der Bijl and Jeff Thomson.

Our signing of Thomson for a single year in 1981 evoked some criticism, a few club members even going so far as to resign in protest. At first glance one may well wonder why there was an issue at all. We could not persuade van der Bijl to come back; the rules allowed, for one more year, a second overseas player. If we could find one who would unquestionably strengthen our side, were we not duty-bound to offer him terms?

There are, however, arguments against this point of view, the main one being that we thereby retarded the development of our own players. But I also sensed some envy or disapproval of our determination to maintain our success. Ought we, the critics implied, to want to win so much?

As to the main argument: one problem for 2nd XI players is indeed insufficient match play. All 2nd XIs play too little cricket. The reserve team at Manchester United play almost as many games as their seniors, but cricket clubs cannot afford the expenses of such a programme, let alone the salaries of the extra players who would be required to make 2nd XI cricket as intensive as that of the first team. Net practice is no substitute for playing in matches; and there are limits to how far one can progress when playing against inferior opposition. On the other hand, our reserve bowling strength was still thin, and raw. In previous seasons there had been occasions when young bowlers had to play for the County XI despite having lost confidence. Inexperienced players are sometimes relieved to be left out. One factor in their development is indeed opportunity; but another is a degree of protection.

I felt that Thomson's presence was a blessing in disguise for some of our younger bowlers, who learned a lot by playing and practising with a man of his stature, as they had the previous season with van der Bijl. Signing on class players like these two is rarely resented by the rest of the staff.

Some committee members were tempted to allow us to rest on the laurels of 1980. But as Titmus used to say, it is harder to stay at the top than to get there. We were right to sign Thomson!

Being clear about one's needs for ready-made players who have already performed well elsewhere, and keeping one's ear close to the ground for them, is one thing. Even more important is to produce a reliable crop of home-grown players, and this too has been done in Middlesex. Thanks to the efforts of Ted Jackson, Jack Robertson and others, Middlesex colts cricket is now well established. At club level, there was a rapid growth of colts cricket in the late '60s. By 1971 over ninety clubs in the county ran colts teams as compared with only three in the mid '60s. This development was particularly crucial at a time when opportunities for playing cricket at school were declining.

I also believe that the formation of the Middlesex League (and other local leagues) was a good thing for our county cricket. The existence of a highly competitive senior league has improved standards generally, and also provided a sharper testing ground for youngsters near 2nd XI standard. The portents began to look good when our 2nd XI and under-25 XI became, in the mid 1970s, arguably the best in the country. Our coach, Don Bennett, had shown sound judgement in the young players we took on, and they arrived in the 1st XI looking the part.

By the late '70s and early '80s we had the best attack in England. Those who captained Middlesex in the 1960s – and perhaps throughout the post-war period – must have envied their successor the marvellous bowlers we have had in the last few years: Daniel, Selvey, Edmonds and Emburey as the resident quartet, with the occasional visiting maestros, van der Bijl and Thomson. And now, bursting forth from the chorus, Cowans, Hughes and Neil Williams. There have been guest appearances by the mellow master Titmus, and an important early contribution from euphonious Jones the Grunt. And if Daniel, say, broke a (ham) string, waiting in the wings there were, by 1982, some admirable reserves. Indeed by 1983 three of those vying for places as fast bowlers were in their early twenties and had learned their cricket locally. In the '60s, by contrast, too much had depended on Titmus, who frequently had to come on after fifty minutes to restore some semblance of order, even on a pitch helpful to the seamers. After Alan Moss retired in 1963, only Titmus and John Price were regularly capable of match-winning per-formances with the ball, and there was never the necessary depth of effective bowling.

Taking stock: the nursery end

In the long-term, the only solution was to develop, discover and attract the requisite quantity and quality of bowlers. In the meantime, what might a captain have made of such material? His first prerequisite – and this can be vital in the short-run – is to be lucky: with the weather and pitches; with the toss in some conditions (often it is irrelevant, sometimes crucial); in winning the close matches which could go either way; and indeed in his timing. Illingworth wrote about me that I was 'the luckiest of England captains, enjoying lucrative success against sub-standard Test teams'. (Perhaps Botham was the unluckiest; as I wrote to him in March 1981, when he was about to embark, at Kingston, Jamaica, on his tenth Test as captain, nine of them against the West Indies, 'My advice is to find someone else to captain England against.')

It will be clear now that the captain must not only make the most of current resources, he must also assume part of the responsibility for building a successful side. Given time, he cannot for ever excuse the side's failure on grounds of insufficient talent. It will be equally clear that the captain is not *solely* responsible for a team's persistent mediocrity, or indeed for its repeated successes. In the first place, he will need to establish a good working relationship with the committee. In the remainder of this chapter I will discuss this further, and also the interactions with other key figures behind the scenes – coach, physiotherapist, groundsman and, in some cases, manager.

Twenty years ago, committees were considerably more Victorian than they are now. I remember feeling that the visit to the dressing-room of a senior committee-man, watch-chain dangling, smacked of a Dickensian mill-owner's visit to a shop-floor. The players would stiffen into attitudes of modest respect. And if the committee-man's mien had a benevolent aspect, that was probably because he stood to lose nothing by the workmen's inefficiency. It was easy then to be struck by the fact that a professional game was being run entirely by amateurs who had no personal stake in the business. For them, it was a hobby. We players were amused by stories such as the one told by Peter Richardson; how, when he was captain of Worcestershire in 1953, the county had an exceptionally good morning against the Australians, taking several of their wickets for 80 or so runs. In the lunch interval Richardson was congratulated by the chairman of the cricket sub-committee, who added that he had but one small criticism to make: he and his fellow committee members had noticed, he said, that all the runs Australia had scored had come from shots that went through gaps in the captain's field.

Committees were also liable to have assumptions about class that were unwarranted. In 1972, my second year as captain of Middlesex, I made my own position uncomfortable by disclosing, naively, to the rest of the players the fact that I had been awarded a rise in salary that made me a hundred pounds better off than anyone else. Nowadays, I would advocate a much larger differential in pay between captain and the rest, on the grounds of the additional responsibilities of the job. But the aspect of this modest award that most irked the players was the fact that the previous professional captains – Titmus and Peter Parfitt – had not received any such financial recognition. It was only with the arrival of a Cambridge graduate that the committee saw fit to acknowledge the importance of the role financially. I was, nevertheless, surprised to be asked by one member of the committee, 'Of course, you do have a private income, don't you?' – as if it were inconceivable that a man of a certain background could possibly live off the wages – when did cricket clubs start calling the players' pay 'salaries'? – of a professional cricketer.

There still are, inevitably, many committee-men who contribute little more than hot air and expensive aromas. Committees still tend to be in practice self-perpetuating; but I have increasingly come to respect their contribution. Many committee members work hard and unostentatiously for the club. They run junior teams. They travel the country as chairmen of selectors, or phone from far-flung places at 7.30 a.m. to discuss the balance of the side. They run the bar in the supporters' box. The chairman of Essex CCC regularly helps out in the car park on busy Sundays.

And the attitude towards the players, at least at Middlesex, has radically changed. There is far more communication, in which players, too, are more open and forthright. There is more representation of players on the sub-committees of the club. Both formally and informally, there is a sense of common purpose between the two groups. The captain's role in this exchange is crucial. In the General Committee, where final decisions are taken, he is the one representative of the players, and is responsible for ensuring that those who run the club at least understand the players' point of view. He can facilitate a more open interaction; it may require his initiative to persuade the committee to take more trouble to explain its problems, for example its financial difficulties, to the players.

The captain should also take seriously his formal obligations, to attend all committee meetings where a topic that materially affects the players is on the agenda. He should certainly concern himself closely in the discussions about levels of pay and comparisons between players' pay; about the timing of the award of a county cap (which is a mark of a cricketer's emergence from apprenticeship); and of benefits. He should also keep an eye on the pay and conditions of work for the junior members of the staff. In the mid-1970s we arranged, for the first time, for those who were on duty at Lord's but not playing in a county match to be remunerated for their lunches; and for 2nd XI players to have their membership fees for a local club paid for by the county.

Earlier in this chapter I described how archaic the 1960s' attitude to fitness now seems. Twenty years from now cricketers will, I think, regard the present approach to coaching as equally antiquated. Most professional cricketers, myself included, have been unwilling to learn. When in 1964 no less a batsman than Wally Hammond commented quietly to me after he saw me batting in a net in Durban that he thought my hands and arms were too tense, I listened, but with inward reservations. Not until ten years later was I ready to take in that lesson, and it needed further, periodical reinforcements. We distrust theory, and are apprehensive lest change bring catastrophe in its train. (With some cause: for example, correcting a failure to get across behind a ball just outside the off-stump may lead to increased vulnerability to LBWs.) In so far as we do listen, we learn haphazardly, with the odd tip from coach, opponent, or ex-player. Our steadiest help comes, probably, from our team-mates.

And, just as players are reluctant to be coached, many coaches, I find, are reluctant to coach. In county clubs the coach is often a man who has not quite made it to the top as a player. He may lack the confidence to intervene with the better players, though they may benefit as much as anyone from the right advice, given at the right time and in the right spirit. County coaches thus often restrict their domain to the 2nd XI, leaving the responsibility for helping first-team players squarely on the captain.

While official coaches, from modesty or lack of confidence, refrain from coaching, unofficial ones are free with their criticisms and advice. My Cambridge tutor once remarked that too many people believe that others should be doing just what they themselves find interesting -- that because they accelerate particles, say, so should we all. No doubt the physicists whose speciality this is are no less partisan to their own style than are the cricketing particle-accelerators, the fast bowlers. Fred Trueman, for one, conveys the impression that no one can be a high-class fast bowler unless their action closely resembles his own. When he offered to take Graham Dilley to the nets in Perth in 1979, I politely discouraged him: for Dilley's method and approach have always been quite different from Trueman's, and I was not confident that his peculiar skills would be left intact. I think I was right to shield Dilley from the squalls of advice that he was liable to receive at that time, much of it short-lived and contradictory. By the 1980-1 tour of West Indies, he had completely changed his action and lost his speed. As Michael Holding said, he was no longer being natural.

The amateurish approach to coaching could be verified by a brief inspection of the standard of net pitches on first-class grounds. They are, on average, a scandal to the profession. Players used to make a point of arriving early for matches at Leicester simply in order to enjoy the luxury of a safe net pitch. In 1979 John Maclean's Test career for Australia was shattered when a ball rose from a length and gashed his eyebrow. This occurred on the day before a Test, in the nets at the Sydney cricket ground. Further evidence of lack of professionalism is provided by the reluctance that players and counties alike have shown in making use of mechanical aids to coaching, in particular of videos and bowling machines. The video, like the tape for a musician, is the most

Coaching styles, 1952. In that year MCC initiated a crusade for Group Coaching to coach cricket to the millions. It cost £15,000. Included in this picture, taken at Lilleshall, are Bill Voce and 'Tiger' Smith. The only trouble with this method is boredom. Today we would be more likely to see a hectic game of six-a-side cricket.

instructive device imaginable. Not only does it produce evidence about technical deficiencies (the cricketer is often as surprised to see the positions he gets into as is a child on first hearing his own voice on a tape-recorder); but also it can boost one's confidence. It was by means of a video of myself batting in the indoor nets at Lord's in 1981 that I noticed that my right foot was going not back and across to fast bowling but straight back. More important, when I was not confident, I thought, watching myself bat: 'That bloke *can* bat!'

It ought to be a basic provision of the coaching system of any professional club to make an extended tape of each player when in good form. He should be filmed both in the middle and in the nets. Such a tape would be a touchstone for the individual; in lean days it would remind him of his strengths. And it could be used by coach and player together to pinpoint the ways in which his method had deteriorated or improved.

Yet many counties have not even access to camera and video. In 1971, when I asked Middlesex to buy one, the county decided that it would be too expensive. And I myself, though I made regular use of the equipment

Don Wilson, MCC head coach, demonstrates the camera and video equipment at the Indoor School at Lord's.

MCC installed at Lord's in 1979, never had the energy or drive to put into practice my scheme for a video dossier on each player.

The first bowling machine to be seen at Lord's became known as the 'Chris Old', since it kept on breaking down. (Especially, the joke was, when hit for four.) But now MCC have a machine originally used in baseball. It is safe and reliable; and it imparts spin as well as speed, so that the ball can be made to swing sharply. A skilled 'feeder' can even introduce an element of uncertainty by dropping the ball into the machine in different ways. Such a contraption serves many functions. Not least, it removes the inherent unsatisfactoriness of net practice, namely that batsmen need more practice, and of a different type, than bowlers can profitably give. A bowling machine frees bowlers to practise according to *their* needs, not according to the batsmen's. Moreover, its mechanical regularity enables a batsman to practise a particular shot repeatedly. He can remind himself of his assets and remedy weaknesses. He can also gradually quicken his reflexes for facing sheer pace; this machine can 'bowl' at 120 mph!

Most top cricketers are, as I have said, complacent or cynical about their chances of being helped to improve. In this respect, they are unlike top musicians or other artistic performers who will keep aside some periods of each year to visit their personal guru, who knows their work through and through.

There are cricketing exceptions, the most striking of whom is Boycott. Boycott is a perfectionist who believes in practising for hours at a stretch. On tour, he would frequently return to the nets after the official practice was over – if he could find anyone to bowl at him. And he has confidence in the advice of Johnny Lawrence, the ex-Somerset leg-spinner, who runs what in Yorkshire they call 'sheds'; an indoor cricket school near Barnsley, which Boycott visits frequently.

Most players can, no doubt, point to moments in their careers when some profitable advice was given, and received, as a result of which their performances moved into a higher gear. One such watershed for me came in 1974, and can be dated precisely. On 8 May, on the first day of Middlesex's three-day match at Edgbaston, I scored a stodgy 78 in three and a half hours. I hit only three boundaries. 'Tiger' Smith, formerly the county wicket-keeper and later their coach, at that time eighty-nine years old, had watched me play. He showed me how tense I was in face, hands and arms. Using his walking stick as a bat, I came to see how much easier it is to swing it if the body relaxes. He offered me only one piece of technical advice: that I should stand up more, to enable the bat to swing straight down close to my body like a pendulum. 'Let the hands go to the line of the ball,' he said. In my anxiety in the middle earlier that day (and earlier in my career) I had poked my head too far to the off-side; my balance was poor, my eyes did not remain level, and the bat tended to go 'round' rather than 'through' the ball.

Until 1974 I had been a moderate county batsman, averaging in the late 20s or early 30s. From 1974 on – apart from one disastrous season in 1978 – I regularly averaged 40 or above in county cricket. Smith's advice – of which the technical part was probably the least important – was integral to my progress. When, four years later, I found myself in a bad patch (after breaking my left arm at the beginning of that year) many critics who had little knowledge or memory of the contribution this upright stance with high back-lift had made to my improvement as a batsman now pinned the responsibility for my decline on to it. And I, equally obstinate in being wedded to a method that had perhaps become rigid, was unable to notice that at times my head went up and down like an oil-well pumphead as the bowler bowled. I was nodding like a mechanical donkey.

I did, at last, emerge from the doldrums. I retained the peculiar stance for a year or two longer, deciding that I didn't really need it only in 1980. It had on the whole served me well; it had been *my* route to a better and more productive style.

This hiccup in my development that occurred in 1978 was not, of course, attributable only to errors of technique. A more serious error was spotted by Ian Botham, and goes back to tension; to what Hammond and Smith had in their different ways also pointed out. At that time I was gripping too hard with my right hand. Ian showed me how loosely his hand held the bat, caressing it lightly with only the tips of middle finger and thumb. And *he* hit the ball hard enough!

Soon after my talk with Tiger Smith I read *A Life of One's Own* by Joanna Field. The author was writing about table tennis: 'What surprised me was that my arm seemed to know what to do by itself, it was able to make the right judgements of strength and direction quite without my help. Here the internal gesture required seemed to be to stand aside.'

Standing aside feels, to the Puritan mind, shockingly like irresponsibility. But it can, often, be the only way to let potentialities flower, to allow one's body to do what it is capable of.

If we define a good coach as 'One who enables the potentialities of others to flower', Tiger Smith certainly qualifies: his advice helped me to my best season yet. It came from the right man (I already knew, respected and liked him) and at the right time (I had just played an innings which was, though full of endeavour, never without strain). It is no use having all the knowledge of technique in the world if you don't know, as a coach, how and when to impart it. The horse may not want to drink – or he may be unable to.

Cricket is so much a matter of confidence; no one can learn unless he believes that he can learn, and that he's worth teaching. For a batsman very much out of form, Tiger's instructions would often be that he should arrive early and have a long net, on a good wicket, with bowlers who bowled to his strengths. We need constantly to be reminded of our good qualities in order to get into a frame of mind which is suitable for amending our faults.

There are no pat answers to the fundamental questions that arise about the balance between control and spontaneity, between discipline and freedom. Advice that is appropriate in one situation may be inappropriate in another. Sheer technique is something else, which simply has to be learned. Which all goes to show that coaching is an infinitely difficult, fascinating and perfectible art. The difficulty of doing it well is part of what explains (and sometimes justifies) cricketers' instinctive caution about coaching. Like other such skills, including captaincy, it is often done by rote. Too often the spirit of the teaching is critical and negative. And even appropriate advice may come at the wrong time, or not be properly followed up.

I have already hinted at the captain's responsibility with regard to coaching. He must, I think, be prepared to intervene directly with a player. He cannot divorce his expectations of a bowler on the field from the bowler's capacity to carry them out. And even where he is not personally concerned with technical adjustments he must keep close contact with the process, so that he knows what the player is worried about and working at; and also to ensure that any changes are not in conflict with his strategy. Occasionally, he may question the advice that the coach wants to give.

Boycott and Willis were both critical of my attitude to coaching during the 1979–80 tour of Australia (when we lost 3–0). Boycott wrote in *Put to the Test* that 'the nets were often organised in a lackadaisical fashion. Ken Barrington, as assistant manager, was supposed to be in charge of net practices, and he's a real expert at it. I'm not knocking Kenny, but he certainly didn't seem to exert the same influence as before (did somebody tell him not to?). He seemed to run the nets as a timekeeper rather than as a coach.' As one of the few in a position to 'tell him not to', I would deny any implication that I tried to diminish Barrington's role, nor do I know of such an attempt.

Willis, however, was more explicit. In *The Cricket Revolution* he wrote that I 'had my cricketing disagreements with Ken Barrington. Ken wanted to sort out the techniques of some of our young batsmen, an opinion I shared, but Mike would not allow it. He felt that if you are good enough to play for your country then you are able to sort yourself out.'

I am sorry if I gave Ken and others this impression as, like Willis and Boycott, I greatly valued his expertise and help. On that tour of Australia I remember him spending hours in the nets with Dilley, trying to smooth out his run-up. On the previous tour he worked a lot with Hendrick. He believed, as I did, that Hendrick's stock ball was a couple of feet short, and encouraged him to bowl a slightly fuller, more attacking length. This was the occasion of one of Kenny's *mots*: he was standing in the crease with a bat, trying to show Mike what he meant. 'If you pitch it *there*,' he said, pointing, and oscillating between playing forward and back, 'you put the batsman in two-man's land.'

What I meant to convey to him was my caution about the timing and extent of technical innovations, but perhaps this caution came across too strongly. Only once can I remember questioning Barrington's coaching directly, and that was for its timing rather than its content. On Brian Rose's first tour, in Lahore, Ken suggested that he should cock his wrists and open the face of the bat in pick-up. Excellent advice – but was this the moment for it? Such a radical change affects the whole of a man's technique, so that he may find his bat coming down much less straight when first trying to implement it. Brian would have few enough chances, outside Tests and One-Day Internationals, on that tour, and I felt that such an experiment would be risky. He had done well enough to be picked for England with his old pick-up; I felt that he should try to change at a less critical period in his career. The three of us talked this out thoroughly.

Oddly, Willis himself had been my mentor in this cautious attitude, for I have never forgotten his account of how his coach at Surrey in the late '60s tried to make him bowl with a classical action, left shoulder round. Bob literally could not bowl straight enough to avoid the side netting! And not only Willis, but Procter, Daniel, Croft and others have reason to be grateful that they never adopted the advice offered by

Taking stock: the nursery end

Willis's coach, or listened too admiringly to the prescriptions of a Trueman. Too many wish to turn others into imitations of themselves.

Equally crucial for the professional sportsman is the skill of the physiotherapist. Here too the captain must develop a healthy relationship. When a player is injured, or ill, any decision about selection has to be taken in the light of discussions between the player, the therapist and the captain. The latter needs to know whether a player is fully fit; and, if not, whether playing would involve mere tolerance of discomfort or the risk of recurrence; whether such risk is of a minor repetition or of a major aggravation of the condition. He has to formulate in his own mind the best approach to the player: is he over-anxious, for example, about the injury, and if so should one humour him or treat him bluntly? The captain needs to know how many reserves should travel to an away match; this decision will rest on a prediction of how the player will respond in a day or two's time.

Obviously, the player himself will have at least an equal interest in these questions: it is *his* body and *his* career that are at stake. As John Miller, the MCC physiotherapist, has written in an illuminating paper called *The Rehabilitation of the Professional Sportsman*, 'Treatment is rarely taken blindly, any more than is advice from the coach.'

There are many cautionary tales. One such concerns the Kent fast-medium bowler, John Dye. Dye had a hamstring injury, which he thought was cured, so he told the captain that he was fit for the county's next match. Kent lost the toss, and fielded. Dye marked out his run and, as is customary, came in for a practice run-up. Just before reaching the stumps, he veered away, limping. 'Sorry, Skip,' he said cheerfully, 'I'm afraid it's gone again.' And he hobbled off the field. We took the opposite line with Willis in the World Cup Final in 1979, and also with Edmonds in the Gillette Final in 1980 when he risked having a knee ligament give way.

Such calamities underline the need for accurate diagnosis and assessment. They also imply the necessity of a rigorous fitness test by the player before declaring himself fit.

In 1979 Mike Hendrick injured his shoulder during the Oval Test. A couple of months later he announced that he was fit for the tour of Australia. However, after bowling three overs in the first match, against Queensland, he broke down, and did not bowl again on the tour. Hendrick ought to have been put through a more demanding fitness programme, with the team's physiotherapist, before we accepted his own estimate of his fitness for the tour.

In India, three years earlier, it was only by playing in the game at Nagpur (rather than resting further) that Fletcher discovered that his broken foot was nowhere near mended for the Madras Test which was the next match on the itinerary.

Therapist and captain will always have to come to terms with those whose anxieties about failure present themselves in physical terms. I can think of several who could be relied upon to report some niggle or strain a day or two before a Test match. It must never be assumed that such symptoms are trivial. On the other hand, once the condition has been thoroughly examined a tough line may be the best method.

We used this approach with Old once, before a Test at Brisbane. He had been saying he was not fit, fussing about a strained back, and looking as though he would not be at all sorry if we came up to him and said, 'You're not fit and you shouldn't play.' But he had never actually left the field because of injury during a Test match. He had had injuries before Tests, but once he started a match he stuck it well. The difficulty was getting him into the right frame of mind to begin it. So, at practice on the morning of our selection meeting, I said, 'Look, Chilly, if we decide to pick you you've got to play as if it's the only Test you'll play in on the tour. And once you've started, you're staying on!' I reminded him of his tremendous effort in the Centenary Test, when he had bowled magnificently for two hours despite a strained groin. He looked relieved at this firm line, and duly performed well in the Test.

John Woodcock relates a story about Old which counteracts any tendency to dismiss his injuries lightly. In the Calcutta Test in 1973 Chris had hobbled off at a crucial stage. That evening, Woodcock happened to see him standing in his slippers at the door of his hotel room. He asked what the trouble was. When Chris showed him his heel John was struck by how horribly sore the foot looked, and all the more impressed by Old's flat-out spell after the rest day. Nevertheless, there is some truth in the acid pen-profile of him written by Russell Davies in the *New Statesman* in 1978: 'Left arm never fit at the same moment as the right shoulder, inner ear, bladder, etc. Would be wonderful player if all of him could turn up at the ground on same day.'

Physiotherapists must often, I think, allow players to follow their own hunches. Daniel used to rub his sore Achilles' tendon daily with acne cream! However, there may be occasional problems about the team physio's overall responsibility. Thomas, who has been England's physiotherapist on many tours, rightly became uneasy when the trickle of players who went for hypnotherapy with Dr Arthur Jackson in Sydney threatened to become a flood. As captain, I queried with a couple of players whether they were really sure that they wanted this help, and checked at the same time whether they were carrying out Thomas's recommendations with regard to preventive and remedial exercise.

The captain is often the recipient of confidential information about a player's physical (and indeed mental) state from the physiotherapist. This is, for the therapist, a difficult area of responsibility, as the information may have a bearing on a player's past performances and on his future prospects.

The captain may also have to use his influence to add weight to the therapist's advice. Sometimes he will need to insist that a player comes three or four times a day for the intensive treatment required for a speedy recovery; he may also have to discourage over-enthusiasm and premature violent activity. Occasionally, he will have to be a party to a decision to use pain-killing injections to help a player last out a crucial match; a decision that can be agonising if it could lead to physical damage and a loss of full function for a more extended period. Naturally, no such decision should be taken without the player's informed consent.

The captain will also use the physio's advice in his approach to training. I have already mentioned in this chapter Thomas's contribution.

It was at the instigation of the Middlesex players that ground authorities were urged to ensure that a doctor was available during the hours of play in any match. We were appalled at the chanciness of one or two survivals after blows from a cricket ball – Ewen Chatfield's in New Zealand (saved by Thomas's speedy intervention) and Roger Davis's for Glamorgan. We also arranged for a brief first-aid talk and demonstration from Miller and the club doctor before the start of each season. I think that *all* clubs and schools should make such a talk routine.

The most crucial element in any game of cricket (apart perhaps from the weather) is the pitch, and it is grossly unfair that the men responsible for it should still be such lowly figures in the hierarchy of the game. After a big match the sponsors sometimes strike a commemorative medallion for the head groundsman, as for players and umpires. At Lord's, the late Jim Fairbrother used to receive his medal not with the others at the official presentation on the balcony of the pavilion, but in a back room a few days later.

Yet a good groundsman can transform a ground, and hence the side that plays there. Harry Brind turned the Oval square from being – in the late '70s – notoriously dull for cricket, with its slow, low bounce, to providing a near-perfect pitch for the 1981 Test match. Tony Greig was fined for a newspaper article in 1977 in which he wrote that Old Trafford should be banned for Test cricket if the pitch did not improve dramatically from the standard produced in 1976, when Holding and Roberts were lethal, and even as hard a man as Close was reduced to a mere mortal, his legs tottering under the fusillade. But Greig was right in what he said. He based his views on the recent marked improvement at Hove, where he had been responsible for some straight talking to the county groundsman, Peter Eaton.

Players constantly complain about pitches. I suppose this is inevitable. My particular gripe concerned pitches that were still damp at the start of a match, particularly when the reason was the groundsman's fear. Damping down a pitch may take away some of its life, and it may ensure that a loose pitch does not break up before the end of a match; but such a remedy is often a last resort to cover inadequate preparation or a poor soil base. For such a pitch aids nondescript medium-pacers rather than fast bowlers or spinners. It puts a premium on accuracy rather than flair. And it flatters a moderate batsman, who thrusts his leg at almost every ball, while hampering a more accomplished player who looks to score

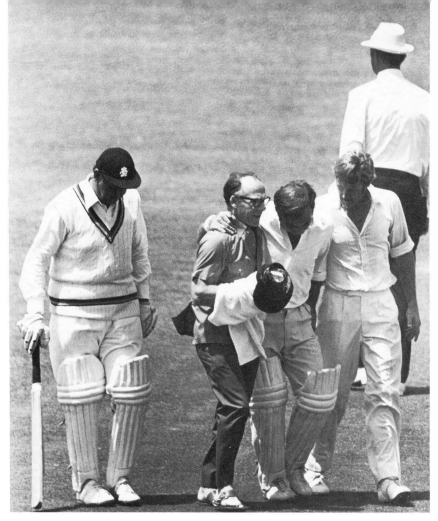

Fourth Test, Australia v. England at Sydney, 1975. John Edrich is helped from the field by Bernard Thomas after he had had a rib broken by a ball from Lillee.

off both front and back foot. Moreover, such pitches often get easier as the match goes on, thus making a draw too likely. In short, they are an anathema to class and they promote mediocrity as much as they reflect the mediocrity of the groundsmen who produce them.

I therefore admire those groundsmen like Ron Allsopp at Trent Bridge and Keith Boyce at Headingley who are prepared to take a chance by going for dry, hard, bouncy pitches that favour fast bowlers and genuine spinners, and make more pronounced the gulf between class batsmen and the rest. And I respect their efforts even when they go wrong.

It is a delicate question how far a captain should be able to influence the groundsman in the type of pitch he prepares. Certainly he should encourage him to avoid the slow, low ones, and produce the kind of pitch I have already described as being good for cricket. However, there is a blurred line between a pitch that favours attacking cricket and one which offers so much help to bowlers that a result is inevitable. Yet any county with reasonable bowlers will do better, overall, if they play all their home matches on 'result' pitches than if they play on easy-paced batting wickets. For suppose they are good enough to win twice as many matches as they lose: then, on rough pitches where they might have only three draws out of twelve matches they will win six and lose three, whereas on easy pitches, where nine may be drawn, they will win only two matches. The fact that they lose only one home match in a season will not entail a position high in the table, as draws bring no more points than defeats.

So a captain of any better-than-average side will have an interest in persuading the groundsman to veer towards pitches on which results are likely if not virtually certain. There is a smooth transition from an honourable attempt to produce fair and lively pitches via shadier efforts to favour one's own side to downright cheating. I thought that Illingworth's policy of shaving the ends at Leicester and leaving some grass on the middle was entirely fair, as the pitches were basically sound, and the end-result was not unduly favourable to bowlers. But Nottinghamshire's ploys to ensure results at Trent Bridge in 1981 were more dubious; nine of their eleven victories occurred in home games (though when we played there the pitch, despite being helpful to bowlers, was a fair one).

I have to beware of allowing my attitude to be influenced by Middlesex's peculiar position as tenants, rather than owners of the ground or employers of the groundsmen, at Lord's. He who pays the piper calls the tune; we had little say in which pitch, let alone what kind of pitch, we were to play on, so that we would constantly play limited-overs matches with ludicrously short boundaries – a particular handicap for sides (like ours) that depended on slow bowlers. Once, in 1974, we were allocated, as an experiment, a recently relaid pitch for a championship match against Leicestershire. Despite the fact that a perfectly adequate pitch was ready (it was being kept for a two-day match between MCC and Scotland a few days later), and despite the fact that both captains complained in advance, on the grounds that the pitch would be dangerous, we had no choice but to play on it. It was remarkable that no one was injured. In the aftermath of that game, the groundsman was forbidden to talk to me. Since then, there have been numerous conversations between Middlesex and MCC on what constitutes a satisfactory pitch for first-class cricket, and the fiasco of 1974 has not been repeated. However, it is unquestionably a drawback not to be able to discuss pitches for a particular match or for a whole season directly with the man who makes them.

There are, of course, many functionaries who influence the daily lives of the professional cricketer, most of whom he encounters with a directness and humour that characterise the game at this level. I cannot mention them all, but naturally the captain may, at some stage, have to mollify, persuade, order, appease, threaten or cajole any or all of scorer, cooks, dressing-room attendants, gatemen, secretaries, ground superintendents and administrators, ice-cream sellers and sight-screen movers.

The captain has a remarkable degree of power and freedom in running his team. On tour, however, and in some counties, these wide-ranging functions are divided. The man who shares them is the manager.

On tour, the manager and his assistant (if he has one) deal with all the travel and money arrangements – tickets, cars, hotel bills, meal allowances, laundry and the rest. The manager gives or withholds permission for newspaper articles or public appearances by players. He takes on many of the day-to-day media relations, regularly visiting the press-box around tea-time to answer any questions journalists might like to raise with him. As the TCCB's representative, he liaises with the home Board of Control. In 1979 many details of the playing conditions for the One-Day Internationals still had to be settled when we were already in Australia. More commonly, these contacts are mainly informal. On one tour the assistant manager took his social duties so seriously at lunchtime that he had to resort to a post-prandial siesta in the dressing-room, where his snoring irritated the players. The manager accepts or declines invitations to the touring party for official or semi-official functions, where he makes most of the speeches. He is ultimately responsible for discipline, and for dealing with crises. He is the chairman of selectors. He shields the captain from many irritating chores; he and the captain together do the same for the rest of the side.

On most of these matters he will consult the captain and other players before making his decisions. Ideally, he is also fully involved with the side in its cricketing problems or anxieties. The managers can be a help around the dressing-room, or a hindrance. If the former, the players come to expect them to be there during intervals, and find them both supportive and unobtrusive. If the latter, it is often because they hark back to days when men were men, and cricketers cricketers, and try to influence the approach to the cricket in unhelpful ways. The story is told of a Pakistan manager who strode into the dressing-room during a Test in England at a time when the visitors were in a bad position; he ordered one of the players to put his pads on and fight for Pakistan. 'But manager,' the player replied, 'I have already batted.' 'Never mind,' said the heroic official, 'do as I say, for the honour of our country.'

No manager that I came into contact with was remotely so foolish. In fact, they all knew the game well, and gave the players the feeling that we were all on the same side. The best, in my experience, was Doug Insole, who fulfilled all the roles: he was efficient; he gave excellent advice, sparingly; he was a friend, confessor, disciplinarian and solace to the players. He also created an easy and relaxed atmosphere in the team-room that was normally attached to his own bedroom. An insatiable fruit-eater, he supplied masses of fresh and dried fruit. And each night he washed the glasses up after the players disappeared.

Tours where manager and captain see eye-to-eye on most matters tend to be happy ones; where conflict exists at this level they are likely to produce a divided team. Such was the case on the 1970–1 tour of Australia, when David Clark and Ray Illingworth had very different priorities; on the perennial issue of how many social obligations should be accepted on behalf of the team, for instance, both were unwilling to compromise. Clark felt that the captain was churlish, while Illingworth thought the manager over-keen to commit the side.

Back in 1959, R.W.V.Robins managed the tour to West Indies captained first by May and later, when May had to return home because of illness, by Cowdrey. The latter describes the conflicts between manager and both captains, and implies that the team, 'puzzled by the manager's determination to administer military-style discipline', sided firmly with the captains. He describes Robins as harrying the team over tactics without prior discussion with May; says that he was so press-conscious that the journalists were 'never without a story nor the latest inside information'; and states that he gave the acting captain (Cowdrey himself) a public reprimand in the dressing-room for not making a quixotic declaration on the last day of the series when England were trying to hold on to a 1-0 lead.

In conversation, Illingworth has criticised the order of selection of manager and captain on overseas tours. He feels that the captain should be appointed first, and that he should have a say in the choice of manager. However, he also regrets the fact that when he joined Yorkshire as manager the captain had already been selected. This apparently contradictory attitude highlights the underlying problem of having managers in cricket: who is ultimately in charge? This issue is more prominent in county cricket, where there is far less administration than on tour. Captain and manager need to be clear about their roles, and the limits of their power.

At Yorkshire, for example, Illingworth as manager gave the captain a list of twelve names before a match, and discussed with him who should be twelfth man. In the dressing-room it was not always clear who decided that a player should be criticised for his play, or that he should be ordered to the nets. The idea that the captain has sole charge over what happens on the field may be unrealistic if his command stops abruptly at the dressing-room door.

To put it bluntly, the county side with a good captain has no urgent need for a manager; while no manager, however brilliant, can make up for a bad captain.

I was delighted to see, in 1982, the skills of captaincy so clearly improving a side's fortunes as Illingworth's did when, halfway through the season, he took over as captain. As Ted Lester, their scorer, said to me in August of that year, 'They're organised now, he's got them together. He doesn't set a field for a bad ball, and the bowlers do better for it.'

Being only the manager must have been purgatory for Raymond; like having the kid next door play with your train-set every day and being condemned to watch the derailments, collisions and general run-down of the assets of a life-long love. And the invitation to lead out the side at the age of fifty must have been an irresistible challenge, to be able to put his cricketing brain to work again and run his own train-set. He himself admitted that 'it's hard, from the dressing-room, to have an effect. You can suggest something, in an interval, but it has to be done at the right time.'

Apart from the cost (a manager's salary will probably be equivalent to that of one senior and one junior player combined) I have always been doubtful of the value, at county level, of a team manager. He could, of course, help the captain deal with chores such as petty discipline, minor administration, and organising practice. If all goes well between them, he may be able to offer useful tactical tips. If I had been able to choose a manager, Illingworth would have been high on my list.

But I should *not* like to be presented with the twelve on the morning of a match (as Chris Old was). I would rather be king of my own castle, and I would bet the same went for Illingworth. His success with Yorkshire as captain on the field may, paradoxically, have undermined his position as manager, though what sank him in the end was his daring to be involved with those who in 1983 advocated the sacking of Geoffrey Boycott, the idol of so many Yorkshiremen.

Long after Illingworth took his redundancy pay and departed the county under a cloud for the second time in his career, the unhappy saga over Boycott rolls on. But that is another story.

CHAPTER FOUR

'My God, look what they've sent me': the captain and selection

'My God, look what they've sent me,' was A. C. MacLaren's response on first seeing the names of the England team to play Australia in the mortifying fourth Test at Manchester in 1902. England lost by three runs, and the match became known as 'Tate's Test', since poor Fred Tate, in his only game for England, dropped a crucial catch and was last man out. For reasons that no one was able to fathom, the selectors had left out C. B. Fry, Gilbert Jessop and S. F. Barnes, despite the fact that Barnes had taken six for 49 in the preceding Test at Sheffield.

What most concerns me in this story – related by Neville Cardus in *Wisden*, 1965 – is the implication about the role, or lack of it, of the captain, MacLaren, in selection at this time. If he had a formal place on the committee it seems to have been disregarded, and it sounds as though his opportunities for informally influencing the make-up of the side were, to say the least, limited.

In this chapter and the next I shall discuss some aspects of the processes that determine who walks on to the field for the first over of the match. Who selects the party of sixteen or seventeen for a tour, or the twelve for a match? What place does, and should, the captain have in selection? Do any general principles exist governing sound selection? And what factors enter into the decision to bat or field on winning the toss?

The history of selection committees for England teams has shown minor variations; but since 1899 the basic rule has been that the captain has been co-opted on to the panel. Before that date teams for home Tests were chosen by the ground authority, with 'at least half an eye', Insole tells us in his article called 'Test Selectors' in *The World of Cricket*, 'on their crowd-pulling potential, and perhaps some local bias'. In those early days teams for overseas tours were chosen by the captains, with a little arm-twisting by the hosts.

If one is to judge by the accounts that come down about the shenanigans of 1902, the co-option of the captain was not yet firmly established.

Fred Tate, Sussex and England.

BELOW LEFT, Lord Hawke, Eton and Yorkshire, and BELOW, A. C. Maclaren, Harrow and Lancashire. Neither was noted for his tact.

'My God, look what they've sent me'

But nor, apparently, was the sovereignty of the official selection committee. For though, as I have said, MacLaren's opportunities for influence were limited, he had, in a way unthinkable today, resorted to subterfuge at Sheffield, where he had sneaked Barnes into the team only by a late telegram sent entirely on his, MacLaren's, initiative. It may well have been that the Tate selection was the upshot of a continuing squabble between MacLaren and the chairman of selectors, Lord Hawke, and that Hawke's twelve for Manchester was designed to dictate the final eleven to the captain: MacLaren could not sensibly leave George Hirst out, Hawke felt, rather than Tate. But MacLaren seems to have matched Hawke in bloody-mindedness. He *did* leave out Hirst, remarking that 'the selectors wanted to see Tate bowl on a wet wicket, and so they should'.

The most important point here is the principle of co-option, which embodies a compromise. The captain is not in sole charge (as he had been for overseas tours); but nor is he excluded from the process (as he had been, apparently, for many home Tests). How much say he then has depends on the respective persuasiveness of him and the other selectors.

The story is told (by Alan Gibson in his book *The Cricket Captains of England*) of how Fry got his own way in 1912. Fry was offered the job grudgingly, for the first match of the series only. He replied to Lord Harris (chairman of the relevant MCC sub-committee) that he 'would accept the job only if he was made captain for all the matches'. He added various conditions about the composition of the selection committee, and ended up with one that, Gibson implies, gave him exactly what he wanted; they 'agreed with Fry about the best side, and the best emergencies, and never met again'. G. O. Allen, also according to Gibson, acted in the earlier part of the 1936–7 tour of Australia 'as a University captain, choosing the sides himself, but later a selection committee was set up'. Gibson adds that he thinks it was 'the last time that a captain assumed such powers'.

No doubt there were also captains and selectors in which the balance of power was reversed, and captains kow-towed to what the latter decreed. Hutton describes his part in selection as follows: 'As I considered myself a stop-gap, I was at a disadvantage among selectors with amateur backgrounds and distinguished playing records . . . I felt rather like a head boy called to a meeting of housemasters and . . . I was mainly content to rely on their judgement.' Whatever arrangements are made for coming to decisions, individuals are bound to differ in respect of their personal ability to influence others.

In my view, it is right that there should be a sharing of the responsibility of selection. On one side, the captain must have a significant say, as he is often the one who is blamed when things go wrong. What is more, he is unlikely to bring the best out of Joe if he is constantly resenting the fact that Jim is not playing instead. The prospects are even more unfavourable when Joe gets to know – as he often does. MacLaren, for example, who was, it seems, supremely insensitive, made no bones about letting everyone, including the players, know how disgusted he was about the selection; and even a tactful captain would find it hard not to convey to the unfortunate Joe that he was there on sufferance.

On the other side, the captain needs help and at times contradiction, and not only from other players. For one reason, the captain generally sees only those players who take part in matches that he himself has played in. He may know that these players have shortcomings, but what about the others? National selectors can and do travel around to see those who are on the fringe of selection. In county cricket the person in charge of the 2nd XI (usually the coach) is in a better position to know about the potential and the form of these players than are the established first-team players. Of course, it is never enough to know *that* a batsman is scoring runs or a bowler taking wickets; the opposition and the pitches need to be taken into consideration too.

In the second place, the captain, like the other players, may become complacent. Cliques can develop. Nowadays a captain is more likely to have been, as it were, promoted from the ranks than to have been brought in from outside, or to stand apart from the side by virtue of class or even age. Such a captain may find it hard to be critical of his team-mates. So many Tests are played now that strong alliances and allegiances spring up from the regular winter tours, on top of the weeks spent together at home for Tests and One-Day Internationals.

All these factors underline the requirement that selection committees should contain people who are not too close to the current side. Not that this requirement is new: certain decisions must always have called for this measure of distance. For example, there are times when a club, or a national side, is in a position to take a longer view rather than attempt to pick the best possible side for the next match. A series may already be won; for the last Test, it may be helpful to bring in a newcomer. (In 1954, Bedser and Trevor Bailey were left out of the team for the last Test against Pakistan, and their places taken by Frank Tyson and Peter Loader. This was when Pakistan gained their first Test victory.) At this stage, the selectors may decide not to go for the eleven that they might choose if their own lives hung on the result.

A similar line may be correct towards the end of a county season, when the team has no chance of coming in the first three or four in the table. One may want to encourage a player who has been kept out of the side because of a particular strength in that department (as at Middlesex in 1984, when Hughes had been the unlucky one to have been kept out by Daniel, Cowans and Williams). In 1981, we left Downton out for the last match, to have a look at Colin Metson as wicket-keeper. Now, in all these situations captains are likely to feel a loyalty to the players who have been integral to the side so far, and be unwilling to experiment. Outsiders may see the overall position more clearly.

'My God, look what they've sent me'

Similarly, the players on the selection committee, including the captain, may be reluctant to take a difficult step. It is never easy to know precisely the right time to leave out a man who is on the decline in favour of a rising star. I remember a time in 1976 when we felt at Middlesex that Titmus was not quite the force he had been. We had been impressed by what we had seen of, and by what we were being told about, John Emburey. But it was extremely hard to bring ourselves to the decision that the time was ripe for a change; and rightly so, for such decisions are, in their context, momentous. I remember the selection meeting at which we were agonising over the matter. After some time, the chairman of selectors, Bob Gale, said something along these lines: 'I think that you're all saying that you feel Fred should be left out. I think you should have the courage of your convictions.' Without his influence I doubt whether we players – who had not only played with Fred for years, but had grown up as cricketers when he was in his prime – would have brought ourselves to make the change. Incidentally, we managed to lose the match in question, at Dartford, after making Kent follow on!

Gale's role in this process was typical of a good chairman of any committee. He had listened to the discussion, and was able to help the participants to see what it was that we were all wanting. He did not, in this instance, need to be closely in touch with the facts on which our views were based in order to have his effect.

The chairman can also contribute in another way. Having been a party to the decision he can help in its implementation. As far as I can recall, Titmus accepted the decision without rancour; he was always philosophical about his cricket, frequently saying, 'If you've got it you'll get wickets (or runs) and if you ain't you won't.' But no one likes to be dropped. The inherent sense of humiliation and anxiety is made worse by the publicity surrounding professional sport. Certainly, it is up to the captain to tell the player concerned that he has been left out, to offer some explanation and to give him a hearing. But in practice the opportunity is often insufficient; in the case in point, we were leaving for Dartford the evening of the meeting.

Gale's successor at Middlesex, Mike Sturt, gave me, as captain, invaluable support by being prepared to take on some of this task. It may involve sharing the odium which might otherwise be directed solely at the captain, or patiently reviewing the individual's decline over the past months. It may mean telling him that we felt it in *his* best interest to be rested, or to be taken out of the firing-line for the time being. It may, again, call for some blunt confrontation, if it is thought that a player is being a nuisance or disrupting the side or playing for himself at the expense of others. The chairman of selectors is often the right person to tell a player that his opportunities at the county may be limited, and he should feel free to look elsewhere; or that his contract will probably not be renewed for the following year.

I have said that I doubt the value of a manager for county sides.

Middlesex have been fortunate, in recent years, to have in Sturt a chairman of selectors who is both firm and sensitive, who knows the game thoroughly and can put in the necessary time to do this part of what would be the manager's job.

Australia may never adopt England's procedure with regard to including the captain in the selection committee, but for a brief period, between 1979 and 1983, they made a move in this direction. I say 'made a move in this direction', because what they did was to include their *last* captain on the panel. This policy seems to me illogical, as it leads to two undesirable consequences whenever there is a change in captaincy. In the first place, it may be embarrassing to have to ask the incumbent to leave the room whenever the other selectors want to discuss *his* tenure of the office. And, secondly, the new captain is then not involved in the selection of the team he is to lead for the forthcoming Test or even tour. This method incorporates the worst of everything.

They have now reverted to their old arrangement, according to which any sounding out of the captain is informal, and at the discretion of the chairman. At the time of writing, Greg Chappell and Rick McCosker are members of a three-man committee chaired by Lawrie Sawle. (From 1980 to 1984 the chairman was Phil Ridings of South Australia.) Greg defends this system on the grounds that being a member of the selection committee confuses the captain's role; he then becomes identified, in the eyes of players and public, with the committee's decisions. When a player is left out he is liable to feel that it is the captain who does not rate him highly; as a result, Chappell says, the relationship between player and captain can be spoiled by being made unnecessarily complicated. Far simpler, he maintains, to give the captain a side, so that he is in the same boat as the rest of the crew.

I can see the point; but I do not agree. Both Chappell and I accept that the captain's judgement and preferences must be taken into consideration; we differ in that my view is that the consultation should be formal, and should entail a vote, while he supports an informal involvement. Now, I imagine that even in Australia a dropped player may well suspect – and often rightly – that the captain was in favour of his omission. So the captain cannot avoid such feelings unless he is absolutely cut off from the decision-making process and is *known* to be cut off from it. But that, everyone agrees, would be ridiculous.

It seems to me that there are other advantages in the English system. If the captain is ex-officio a member of the panel he cannot be ignored. Moreover, he can hear the arguments and offer his own. A debate occurs, and there is the possibility of persuasion and modification of judgement on either side. If a change of mind occurs over one place in the side, this itself may lead to a reopening of the debate about other places. For example, if it is decided to pick as 'keeper a man who is also a front-line batsman (like Alan Knott, say), then one may also be able to afford to pick an extra specialist bowler rather than an all-rounder. Whereas if the preferred 'keeper is only a modest batsman (say, Bob Taylor) the balance of the side may have to be modified. Much of a committee's time is taken up, rightly, with such hypothetical questions, and it is only by being a party to the debate that the captain (or anyone else, for that matter) can in a full sense be said to be consulted. There are too many ifs and buts to do justice to them all outside the debate.

Anyway, the captain *is* in a different boat from the crew. His decisions about bowling changes, field-placings, batting order and so on constantly embody value-judgements about the individuals in the team. More radically, he has to wear a different hat in playing a part in the running of a club or a touring party. He is often the only spokesman for the players in discussions about pay, contracts, and a host of matters apart from selection. It seems much preferable for the captain to be a full partner of these decision-making bodies and for him to accept and face the complications.

A high level of confidentiality is crucial to many decision-making bodies, including selection committees; and this is particularly important, for the sort of reasons that Chappell mentions, when the captain is a member. When I was captain of England I found it extremely galling that certain leaks were made to the press concerning our deliberations. About one controversial decision, an accurate account of the voting (3–2) and a correct breakdown of the way each member had voted at the Friday meeting even appeared in a popular newspaper two days later.

'Leaks' are often a matter of guesswork by the press, whose job it is to gain an impression of what happened without necessarily having it spelt out in words of one syllable. So members ought to be on their guard. The need for confidentiality often makes it difficult for the selectors to justify their decisions to the world at large. Colin Cowdrey describes in his autobiography *M.C.C.* how he came to be offered the captaincy of England in 1967 after Close had had an altercation with a spectator after a county match at Edgbaston. At the press conference at which the decision was announced the chairman, Insole, was pressed to say who would have had the job if the Edgbaston episode had not occurred. Insole at last said, 'Close.' This disclosure not only hurt Cowdrey, it set off his captaincy, he felt, on the wrong footing. I am not sure that I agree; I am inclined to think that every time we get a job it is either because there is no one better or because the apparently better man has spoiled his copybook or is unavailable. So perhaps Cowdrey was over-sensitive. But being chairman of a selection committee can be difficult.

In other circumstances the duty to keep one's silence is plain. It is equally plain on the occasions where someone is left out of a touring party or not taken on to a county staff because of some major defect of character, such as persistent theft, or a liability to lose self-control and become violent, or because there is a fear that there are already too many players who are prone to selfishness or a damaging cliquishness. As a

Selecting the England team to tour Australia, September 1979. Left to right: Charles Elliott, Brian Close, author, Ken Barrington, Alec Bedser (chairman), Donald Carr, secretary TCCB. Also present was Peter May, chairman TCCB.

result, as Insole says, the committee 'must frequently be prepared to suffer in silence criticism based on an unavoidable ignorance of the facts'.

I have been writing about selection for Tests, tours and county matches. Perhaps it is worth describing, briefly, the make-up of the committees in the various contexts. Teams for home internationals in England are now chosen by a committee of four which co-opts the captain, who is therefore the only player involved. Meetings used, before Sunday cricket was introduced, to be held on the Sunday before a Test. The usual time has now been changed to Friday evening, at the most convenient place for the members. Often the venue will depend on the captain, as he will have a county match. When I was captain we met at Lord's, in a small room at the back of the pavilion. We would have wine, beer and juices available, and salads and cheese laid out on a trolley. We would rarely be interrupted, and would stay until we had finished the job. Occasionally the chairman, Alec Bedser, would go out to make a phone call, perhaps about someone's fitness. Before the Headingley Test in 1981 we were unable to contact Willis or Bernard Thomas on the Friday evening, and provisionally agreed that Willis should be left out because he seemed unlikely to be fit; but Alec was to contact him at the Oval next day (where Warwickshire had a championship match), and talk to me that afternoon before we announced the side on Sunday. In the event, Bob (and Bernard) felt that he would be fit, despite not having played on the Saturday. We included him in the twelve, but insisted that he play in a 2nd XI match on Monday, and bowl a good number of overs in the nets on Tuesday. But it was rare that the outcome of a selection meeting was left open in this way; and we tightened up on getting ourselves fully informed about the fitness of probable choices before the meetings.

The chairman was often the one who said, 'Come on now, we've got to settle this, you know.' And sometimes the only way to conclude a debate would be by a vote. I found that it was rare for me not to get what I wanted if I wanted it strongly, mainly because it was recognised that the captain is likely to get the best out of those he values highly. In fact, I would be as tentative as anyone on some of the fringe places, and it was usually in such circumstances, when each had to go on his hunch, that we had to vote.

Once the team has been chosen, cards and instructions for the match are sent to each player. These arrive on the Monday morning. It seemed to me, in my early days for England, to be an unnecessarily cruel way of discovering you have been dropped to hear the side announced on the radio at Sunday lunchtime. In 1976, when I arrived at Bath for a Sunday League game, the old dressing-room attendant said to me, 'Them've dropped that fellow of your'n, what they do call 'ee, that Brearley.' They hadn't, actually, though they did a match later, and then I heard it second-hand after the radio announcement. I introduced the practice of making sure that anyone who was left out was told, personally – usually by me, sometimes by the chairman – before the team was made public. Being included is not so difficult to take; newcomers to the side, along with those who keep their places, still hear the news over the radio.

We made a mistake in this area in 1981. We had brought Underwood into the twelve for the fourth Test at Old Trafford, but he had not played. The next Test was at the Oval, where we knew that the pitch was likely to be fast and bouncy and would probably not favour spinners. So we left Derek out of the twelve, though privately we had no doubt that he would be the man we would call on at the last minute if the pitch looked helpful to spinners. Since he had not played in the previous Test, and since he was, in our minds, still our second spinner if needed, we did not feel that he had, in any real sense, been *dropped*. So, though I phoned Gooch and Gower to tell them their bad news, I omitted to phone Underwood. Unfortunately, the announcement of the side at Folkestone, where Kent were playing their Sunday match, made mention only of Gooch's and Gower's replacement by Wayne Larkins and Paul

Parker. Everyone congratulated Underwood for keeping his place in the twelve, and it was not until his mother phoned him at teatime that he discovered the truth. This uncertainty was due to my oversight. One can scarcely *over*-communicate.

On the same theme, I remember that we decided to leave Graham Barlow out forty minutes before the start of the second Test in 1977. The players were practising fielding at that moment, so I asked for the team not to be announced until the session had finished. Unfortunately, this instruction was ignored, and Barlow's suspense was ended by the public address system.

I happened to be in the England dressing-room shortly before the start of the Centenary Test at Lord's three years later and was struck by the tension and misery on Robin Jackman's face as he still did not know whether he would be playing his first Test for England or carrying the drinks (he carried the drinks). Of course, the odd error is bound to occur. If it is rare, the captain will be forgiven: if common, it is a sign of inconsiderateness, and hints at unsuitability for the job.

Selection for tours follows the same pattern, with a slight difference: the chairman of the TCCB cricket sub-committee is added to the panel. Since there is, as a result, an even number, the chairman now has a casting vote (that is, he votes twice) in the event of a 3–3 split. Before 1977, the casting vote was the captain's. In fact, Greig had used it the year before to gain the recall of Close. Hutton, one of the selectors, had missed the meeting, and the vote was 2–2. Hutton remarks that, 'Bedser wisely made it his business to get the procedure changed.' Hutton had no time for Greig, describing him as 'a little too sure of himself for my comfort'.

The manager for the tour would also be present, but without a vote, as would a representative of the MCC, and the secretary of the TCCB. I presume that the presence of these extra people is due to the fact that somewhat wider issues can arise with regard to long overseas tours than for a single match at home; the team will be ambassadors for England, and it is slightly more likely that considerations other than purely cricketing ones will come into play, as had happened way back in 1958, when the MCC committee, then responsible for selection for overseas tours, withdrew the invitation to John Wardle on the grounds that he 'did a grave disservice to the game' in 'publishing in the press criticisms of his county captain, his county committee and some of his fellow players'.

In those days the selectors merely made a recommendation to the MCC committee, who had overall responsibility for the tour. Not until 1970 did this role pass to the TCCB, and it is for historic reasons that the MCC representative survives on the selection panel. Until 1977, the team travelled as MCC, and they still wear the club's colours.

In Australia, too, the selectors used to recommend a touring party to their Board, who might reject a player for non-cricketing reasons. Indeed, in 1951–2 the Board went further. Sid Barnes, who had already been selected for the third Test, at Adelaide, against the West Indies, was omitted at the insistence of the Board 'on grounds other than cricketing ability'. Barnes claimed £1,000 damages against the writer of a letter to a newspaper, but the writer withdrew his criticism in court and paid the costs. But the cricketer's Test career was finished.

At one time, I was told, the England selectors decided not to include, in any touring party, two particular players together; as a pair, they had apparently behaved atrociously on a previous trip. No one was excluded for such reasons, however, from any team with whose selection I was involved.

Once on tour, the officers of the tour – manager, assistant manager (if there was one), captain and vice-captain would automatically comprise the tour committee; they could, and usually did, add a fourth or fifth member. As a result, players would outnumber administrators on the body responsible for selection.

The same was true at Middlesex. The daily routine of county cricket, the amateur status of the chairman of selectors, and the frequent absence of the coach with the 2nd XI, tended to produce a situation in which the captain and his senior colleagues made most of the decisions over selection. It would take an effort for the people concerned to arrange a meeting, or even to keep in touch by phone, and during my middle years as captain, we did not have regular meetings once the season was properly under way. Sturt, however, played a more active role; so that the occasional failure, on my part, to consult him became a failure to keep my side of the bargain, of which his side was the commitment that I have referred to. Before Sturt, Middlesex worked (or failed to) almost like the Australians in reverse: the players ran things, for the most part, and consulted the chairman at *their* discretion!

We come back to the issue of formality, and the value of committees. Having meetings can be a nuisance, and committee decisions can be compromises in which no one is satisfied with the outcome. Nevertheless, for all its shortcomings I prefer this system, with its checks against whim and against personal grudges, to the autocracy either of the omnipotent captain or of the so-called 'supremo' manager.

Once a captain has been appointed, one of the next most important tasks will be to decide on a vice-captain. This may have been settled at the same time as the captaincy; but it may also be left until the new captain is installed, so that his views may be heard.

For home Tests there is no formal vice-captain. I do not know if this practice is universal, but when I was captain we would want to establish at our meetings two things: first, who would captain the side if I were injured before the match? And, second, who would take charge if I were off the field during it? Occasionally the answers to these questions would be different.

For a tour, a vice-captain was always appointed. Poor Cowdrey was vice-captain on no less than four tours of Australia, under May, Dexter, Smith, and Illingworth. At Middlesex, especially when the appointment of vice-captain seemed likely to cause disappointment, there was sometimes a call for doing without one, and allowing the team to be run either by the senior player or by an ad hoc appointee if for any reason the captain were not playing. I never liked that idea, preferring to have a clear statement of the responsibility, and in the event we always appointed a vice-captain.

The criteria for the job are mixed; some players are ideally suited on one criterion, less so on another. I suppose his primary function is to stand in for the captain: that is, run the team adequately when the captain is away, without feeling compelled to stamp his own mark on the side. Ideally, the vice-captain is able to suppress, if necessary, some of his convictions in the interest of the captain's priorities. Naturally, he must make his own decisions; but he is still subject to instructions or suggestions from the captain about the general policy of the team.

Like a vice-president, such a man may not be suited for the presidency. He may lack the personality to impose his will and style on the side. He may be unwilling or unable to take a firm line. He may, in short, be an admirable Number Two, able to give advice without sulking if it is not followed, and yet not be a Number One. But the vice-captaincy is often the best training-ground for the captaincy. The captain can bring on a younger player by involving him in his thought-processes. The latter can be an apprentice before standing alone. It is also an opportunity for the management (including the captain) to assess someone's potential for leadership.

In selecting a vice-captain, thought should be given to the candidate's ability to captain a side in the short-term; his ability to advise and help the captain; and his potential for captaincy and willingness to learn. Different qualities may be more desirable at different stages in the captain's career. For example, when I became captain of Middlesex in 1971 there was a division between the four or five senior players, all of whom had had success at Test level, and the rest. I felt that I needed the support of one of the old brigade as vice-captain – not only for his experience but also as a symbol of his, and even, I hoped, their commitment to me. So for two years Titmus was vice-captain. Later I became more confident, and the club (and I) thought that we should look to the future. Thus we made it a deliberate policy to try out, for a year or two each, the main potential successors to me. We explained the policy to Titmus and to the players as a whole; and over the next ten years the following were all appointed vice-captain: Mike Smith, Clive Radley, Edmonds, Emburey and Gatting. I believe that by this means we gained a fairly shrewd idea of their suitability for the captaincy.

Vice-captains are often chosen, then, with an eye to the future. In all cases, one hopes that the person will develop and win the confidence of the side. In certain instances, however, one may suspect that the opposite will occur, and yet feel that it is essential to make the appointment. At its most cynical, such a move consists of giving a man enough rope to hang himself before he has too much power. It is inevitable that certain people, because of their strengths but also because of their image, will at some stage be given authority; and it may be important that they be given it at a low enough level so as not to do too much damage.

As I write these lines, the individuals I have in mind are Boycott and Edmonds. But I want to make it clear that I never formulated the cynical view until after each had ruled himself out in the eyes of virtually all those close to them – that is, the players, the selectors, and, in fact, many of the press. In each case, I very much hoped, perhaps naively, that the better, more constructive side of the two men would emerge in their exercise of responsibility. I also thought that it might not. In either event, I wanted to have each as vice-captain, Boycott of England and Edmonds of Middlesex, for a variety of reasons. I wanted to have the benefit of their ideas; I wanted to know what they were thinking, including knowing when they disagreed with me; and I wanted to form a view of their tactical skills as well as their ability to lead and manage others.

In Boycott's case, a freak delivery from the medium-pace bowler Sikander Bakht which broke my arm gave him the chance to prove or disprove himself at the highest level. In the event he effectively ruled himself out by his performance as captain in New Zealand, not least by his attitude during the second Test at Christchurch. In one of his books, Willis, who was now vice-captain, describes how Boycott was unable to force the pace when England needed quick runs for a declaration in their second innings. Willis sensibly sent Botham in at Number Four. But when Boycott was run out 'by about sixteen yards' he came back to the dressing-room where he 'sat in a corner with a towel over his head. Edmonds asked him about the rest of the batting order and he said it now appeared to be the responsibility of the vice-captain.' Next day he was still sulking; for when Willis presumed that he would be declaring at the overnight score 'to give us a complete day to bowl them out and square the series', he replied that, 'having already lost one Test, he did not want to lose another'. He did declare, though, and Willis and Botham did most of the damage as New Zealand were dismissed for 105. Willis goes on to say that this tour ended Boycott's chances of ever captaining his country again.

It is also possible to get a closer picture of a player by involving him on the tour committee, as we did with Botham in 1979–80, or on the county selection committee. Botham impressed me with his confidence in exercising authority. He responded with a self-assured good humour to Boycott's jibes about his stripes needing a polish. I remember an occasion at Adelaide, a few weeks into the tour. We decided, as tour committee, to spend one afternoon seeing each player in turn. The aim was to hear from everyone how he felt the tour was going; whether he personally was getting a fair chance, whether he noticed any problems, and so on. I suppose it was not the easiest moment for a cricketer of Boycott's stature, especially as he was struggling at the crease. He started with a few cracks directed at Botham. I admired the way the twenty-four-year-old handled the situation. After some guarded conversation about the tour in general, we got on to Geoff's batting. And it was Botham who was perceptive and confident enough to point out that in trying to deal with the extra bounce of Australian pitches Boycott was becoming rooted on the back foot. The result was that he was unable to transfer any weight on to the front foot, so half-volleys were not being punished, and he was static and immobile in the face of bouncers. He had in fact recently been hit on the head by the Combined Universities' opening bowler, and several times on the shoulder by Richard Hadlee in Tasmania, both on slow pitches. We were anxious about what would happen in the forthcoming one-day matches against West Indies and the fastest bowlers in the world, let alone in the two series against them over the next eighteen months. Botham's advice was, I think, crucial to Boycott at that moment, who faced the onslaught with skill and courage.

It is possible to misjudge someone on the strength of his performance at a lower level of responsibility. For example, I did not suspect that the pressures of captaincy would affect Botham's play adversely, as I am sure they did – though he continues to deny it. Nor would I have predicted how touchy he would become about criticism.

My own experience of vice-captaincy was in India, in 1976–7, with Greig as captain. I enjoyed the job, and was struck by how simple it is compared with being the man who has to act and 'take the can'. I was a relative novice at the start of the tour (having played only two Tests, both against West Indies the previous summer). Naturally, Greig turned for advice, in the first instance, to Knott and Fletcher, both excellent advisers and highly experienced tourists. I had to learn, and to wait until he rated my opinion highly enough to consult me regularly. In the course of that trip, our mutual respect was much enhanced, and the upheaval of the months that followed, in which the idea of World Series Cricket was spawned and Greig lost the England captaincy to me, did not damage it. In 1977 he was willing, and able, to offer me in return the solid support of his advice and criticism.

I have said a good deal about the mechanisms of selection committees, arrangements and so on; what about selection itself? Is it possible to say anything general on the subject?

I will start with some old chestnuts. 'Never change a winning side.' As a blanket claim this is fatuous. If you have the chance to strengthen a side you do so whether or not it has won the last game. Conversely, you should resist pressures to change a losing side just because it has lost.

'Always pick the best wicket-keeper and the specialist bowlers. Your batsmen are there to score the runs, the bowlers to take the wickets.' (This was maintained by a national selector.) Again, this is an exaggeration. If your best bowlers and 'keeper are all like, say, Lance Gibbs or Keith

'My God, look what they've sent me'

Andrew (a brilliant 'keeper for Northants and England in the '50s and '60s who could not hit the ball off the square) with the bat, then once five wickets go down the team is as good as all out. The argument has some weight against modern trends, however. For one-day cricket has put a premium on what may be called 'bits and pieces' players, people who field well, can bowl a few overs, probably at medium pace, and are capable of a quick 50. Such cricketers are unlikely to do much at Test level. Vic Marks and Chris Cowdrey are cases in point. It would be more reasonable to put the argument in this way: one's top cricketers need to be able to perform one of the specialist skills at the level required.

'Always pick class.' This suggestion quickly leads on to the question of what is meant by 'class'. There have always been good-looking, stylish batsmen who never get any runs, and dogged, ungainly players who seem impossible to get out. On the other hand, one can say of certain techniques that they are too unreliable, or too limited, to succeed at the highest level.

At the end of one season I told a young county player that he had to decide on the level of his ambition: did he want to continue with his method, rely on his excellent eye and timing, and remain at his present level – a cowboy of a batsman and a moderate county player who might or might not make the grade? Or was he willing to work on his technique to give himself more of a chance? Another young batsman invariably planted his left foot down the pitch in front of off-stump, and used only his bottom hand; as a result, he was virtually incapable of scoring on the off-side, and was in trouble against really quick bowling. I was doubtful about the prospects of both these players because their batting lacked class. A good run of scores from them might well be misleading.

However, it is important to pick players when they *are* in form. What often happens is that there is a time-lag between a purple patch at county level and selection for a Test match. I think that the principle is: if you believe that a player has class, that is, that he has the technique and the skill to perform well at the level you are concerned with, pick him sooner and persevere with him longer than the man who lacks it. Both Test and county cricket are showcases of the game, so, all else being equal, there is an argument for picking the thoroughbred ahead of the carthorse. (Though one must beware of show-ponies!) At least this is a more profitable generalisation than one attributed to a certain Yorkshire and England captain: 'pink-faced batsmen can't play fast bowling,' though even this has more chance of being true than his other gem: 'black men can't hook.'

So much for old cricketers' tales. Selection calls for clarity about goals. For example, England tours are remembered and judged by results in Test matches. I would not want to say that the other games do not matter; such a view implies a lack of respect for the spectators and opposition, and the likelihood that the games will be played without pleasure or sparkle. Indeed, playing the minor games hard, and winning most of them, sets a pattern that may repeat itself in the Tests. Nevertheless they are secondary. So are the One-Day Internationals. It was Willis who most strongly pressed these arguments on me. 'You can't afford to pick players who *might* mature into Test cricketers,' he would say. 'On every tour there are at least two batsmen who are out of the reckoning through injury or total loss of form, and the same is likely to be true of fast bowlers.' Yet in 1982, when Willis himself led the side to Australia, he and the other selectors picked at least two players who would be strong candidates for selection *only* in the one-day matches (Jackman and Marks). The itinerary for this tour was unusual, moreover, in that the One-Day Internationals were to be played all together, after the Test series. So it would have been feasible to fly out additional one-day specialists if needed.

In 1981 Australia made a similar error. Instead of including the lively Mike Whitney in their touring side from the start, they brought him in at short notice for the fifth Test when injuries ruled out Rodney Hogg as well as Lawson. Graeme Beard's initial selection as an all-rounder was thus acknowledged to be a mistake, since the players on the spot clearly concluded that his slow-medium cutters were hardly likely to make an impact in a Test, however useful he might be for one-day matches.

Conversely, any review of a county staff must take account of the range of cricket played. The plethora of one-day cricket has tended to place a premium on fitness, agility and all-round skills. Success in the one-day game is based on attacking batting, but on defensive bowling and fielding; its proliferation has not made it easy for batsmen capable of building long innings or bowlers capable of taking wickets on good pitches to emerge. Cricketers probably take longer to mature now than they did. Sadly, the skill that is most difficult to master, and probably needs the most protected environment, leg-spin bowling, has almost disappeared from first-class cricket, at least in England. But my immediate point is that a county staff needs a range of players, and players with a wide range; and very different types of player may be selected for the different competitions. Both captains and players have had to become used to a first-team squad of perhaps fourteen or fifteen players rather than a 1st XI or XII.

I have mentioned clarity about goals as a prerequisite of sound selection. Overall strategy should also influence the choice of a side. Here I should like to mention Hutton's policy in Australia in 1954–5. Hutton had, naturally, a healthy respect for Ray Lindwall and Keith Miller. He knew full well that real pace wins matches. During England's previous tour to Australia, which England lost 4–1, Hutton had said to Cardus, 'When we come back here next time, we'll beat 'em with fast bowling.' So, in 1954, as captain, he was keen to take the virtually untried Tyson. I once asked Len at what point he really believed England might win that series. He replied, 'It was during the NSW match before the first Test. Neil Harvey was batting against Frank. The ball hit him on the pad. He had to take his pad off to rub his leg. It must have hurt. From that moment, I knew we had a chance.'

Chance or not, Hutton put Australia in to bat at Brisbane for the first Test, and lost by an innings and 154 runs. Tyson's analysis was 29-1-160-1. But Hutton stuck to his guns – and his plan. He acted with what Cardus called 'a firm-mindedness and shrewdness never excelled by any other captain'; he dropped Alec Bedser, for years the spearhead of England's attack, and retained the raw Tyson, who proceeded to take twenty-five wickets in the next three Tests.

Single-mindedness may, of course, degenerate into obsession and prejudice. I discuss the other side of the coin in Chapter Nine; it does seem that Hutton had a blind spot about unorthodox spin bowling that corresponded to his clear-sightedness about pace.

Another obvious factor is that teams should be selected with a regard for conditions. At Perth, a stiff breeze blows most of the time from one end. There one needs into-the-wind specialists, as well as downwind bowlers. On a dusty pitch, one might play an extra spinner; on a green, moist pitch an extra seam bowler. As a rule, a side picked for India or Pakistan would need more spinners than one picked for New Zealand or Australia. However, the rule needs to be applied with care. Good horses are versatile, and perform well over all sorts of courses. I think of Michael Holding's fourteen wickets at the Oval in 1976 on a pitch described by *Wisden* as 'slow and dusty'. Moreover, some bowlers (and batsmen) do better when conditions do not favour them too much. Imran Khan's record for Sussex was better at Eastbourne than at Hove; at the latter ground, the ball bounced and swung more, but Imran became over-excited, bowling shorter and with less control. Furthermore, on a slower pitch, the ball that beats the bat will be less likely to go over the top of the stumps.

Qualities of character are equally important. David Steele showed a truly British obduracy in 1975 and 1976 – a brilliant selection, conceived by Greig. The phlegmatic natures of John Edrich and Graeme Fowler have been invaluable to them and their sides. It is said that when Edrich scored 310 at Headingley against New Zealand, on a pitch that helped seam bowlers, he played and missed once an over on average throughout his innings; but he was utterly imperturbable, and would often hit the next ball for four. Bowlers, too, need similar traits of perseverance and great-heartedness. For there will be times when everything is against them – pitch, umpires, heat; even their own fieldsmen (who drop their catches) and captain (who puts them on at the wrong end and at the wrong time). There are many examples, but I could mention Botham, Lever, Underwood and Willis as bowlers who would always bowl their heart out for the side.

Two other factors that may, from time to time, enter into selection for tours: how homesick does an individual become? And how well can he adapt to the local conditions? Geoff Arnold, the Surrey, Sussex and

'We've got a chap called Tyson, but you won't 'ave 'eard of him because he's 'ardly ever played.' (Hutton talking at Perth, October 1954.) Three months later Frank Tyson leaves the field with Brian Statham (left) at the end of the Melbourne Test. He had just taken seven wickets in the innings and England had won the match by 111 runs. They had heard of him now.

Various Underwoods, Fletchers, Titmuses, Greigs and Amisses. Christmas 1974, Melbourne.

England fast-medium bowler, was a case in point; he rarely bowled as well abroad, or towards the end of a tour, as he did at home or at the beginning. This leads to the knotty problem of families on tour; knotty in more than one sense. For Alan Knott found it, increasingly, a wrench to leave his wife and son behind for four months at a stretch. One of the attractions of World Series Cricket for him was the welcome given to families; he was able to take a flat in Sydney, and keep that as his home base during the season, whereas I am afraid that England have been less accommodating, often laying down strict limitations on the length of time wives and girlfriends would be permitted to join players during tours. Other countries have gone even further. In the '50s Russell Endean declared himself unavailable for South Africa since wives were forbidden to accompany the team. I find such attitudes on the part of the authorities unforgivably blimpish. For the most part, the presence of wife or girlfriend makes a man happier and more relaxed about his cricket. It softens, agreeably, the too-male atmosphere of a tour. Besides, cricketers are, actually, grown-ups; if they choose to have one sort of company rather than another (or than none at all) that is up to them, provided they fulfil their obligations to the side.

That is not to say that there are never problems. One particular wife made herself so unpopular on tour, and was so demanding, that her husband's career may even have been affected. Denness's team, in 1974–5, had to make regular crèche arrangements. It cannot always be easy for players who are nervously immersed in a Test also to be immersed in a small hotel room with several jet-lagged, screaming children.

There is no simple, categorical answer. Like other problems of management, it is up to those in charge to approach each situation flexibly and sympathetically. However, the basic guideline must be that it is outdated and immature to insist on the separation of a man from his wife and family for four months at a time. Other considerations apart, the cost of travel and accommodation is likely to solve many of the problems, since most players cannot afford to keep wives with them for too long.

There are differences of opinion about the optimum number of players for a tour. In my view, there should be sixteen for a long trip. With fewer than this, there is precious little cover in case of injury or loss of form. With more, too many players are under-employed and get bored. This is a particular problem now that tours have been condensed and the proportion of internationals increased. Another change over the past thirty years has been the speed of travel; it is easy to keep players on stand-by whether at home or in the country of the tour.

In county cricket, it can be hard to know how many players to have standing by for a match. One may be taken by surprise by the pitch, or by late injuries or illness. Our last game at Lord's in 1982 was against Surrey. On the morning of the match, we discovered that the pitch was bare, loose and dry. We had our regular pair of spin bowlers at the ground, but no one else. As luck would have it, Titmus, then forty-one, who had already played an occasional game for us earlier in the season, looked in for a cup of tea and a chat. We decided to play him. As it turned out, Edmonds hobbled off with a bad back in the second innings, Titmus took three wickets, and we gained an improbable victory that was crucial to our clinching the championship a week or so later. Perhaps Ray Illingworth was right when he said I was the luckiest captain ever! The moral of the story is less than flattering: it was slack of us not to have learned about the pitch earlier, or at least not to have had Titmus available in case it turned out as it did.

The following season, Middlesex were not so lucky. At the beginning of July, they had a commanding lead in the championship table again, after winning six consecutive matches in June. On the morning of the next match, at Edgbaston against Warwickshire, both openers were forced to withdraw because of injuries that, the evening before, had seemed either trivial or mended. There was no spare opening batsman in the twelve. A reserve was summoned, but did not arrive until mid-afternoon. Being a batsman short, Mike Gatting put Warwickshire in on an over-dry pitch. The balance and assurance of the side had been ruined; Middlesex suffered their first defeat in the championship in twelve games, and this match started a minor slide the outcome of which was that they finished second to Essex.

Such a muddle can all too easily happen. No county wants to haul reserves around unnecessarily, not only because of the expense involved, but also because those left out often miss the chance of playing in other matches that are important for themselves and their careers. A team probably has to go through such a mix-up every decade or two to remind the players and captain of the need to be fastidious in reporting minor injuries early, and taking appropriate action.

Cricket, as I have said, is essentially a game of diverse skills. Selectors hope to produce a well-balanced side. This applies to batting as much as to bowling. Bradman has commented that the 'umbrella' fields used in the modern era at the start of an innings would have made him feel that many opportunities for scoring runs were being wasted. I, too, liked to have one opening batsman who preferred to attack from the start. He balances the steadier player at the other end, who has, as a result, less pressure on him to score fast. Combinations such as Boycott and Gooch come to mind. Even better balanced were those pairs which also had one left-handed and one right-handed batsman, like Keith Stackpole and Bill Lawry, or Bob Barber and Boycott. It is amazing that even at Test level bowlers often dislike bowling at left-handers, and lose their line not only against them, but against their right-handed partners.

Number Three is a crucial position, and often the hardest to fill. He has to have the qualities of an opener (as he may be in for the second ball of the match!); but also a certain versatility. He has to be able to come in when bowlers have settled into a groove, or in mid-afternoon, after several hours with his pads on; or when spinners are already operating on a turning pitch. Even a fine player like Allan Border, of Australia, has always looked vulnerable against a new ball. He is of more value to a Test side at Number Five rather than Number Three.

I cannot think of any general advice for selectors about filling this position. A defensive player, like Chris Tavaré, may do a useful job there. But if Boycott was at Number One and Tavaré at Three, as at various times in 1981 and 1982, it would have been disastrous to have had Brearley at Number Two. The innings would have been liable to become totally becalmed. The same principle applies throughout the order, of course. And a hitter in the middle or late order is a great asset.

Traditionally, the well-balanced side has had two quickies, a medium-pacer, and two spinners, one turning the ball from leg, the other from off. There is an added bonus for the captain when he has an inswing bowler as well as an outswinger; a seam bowler as well as a swing bowler. For certain conditions favour certain types of bowling; and some batsmen struggle when the ball leaves the bat while others prefer it.

As for spinners, various elements – as we shall see – have contributed to the decline in their role: the use of fertilisers, for example, and the higher seam on the balls. Captains like Hutton have dented the notion of a well-balanced attack. And the West Indies in the late '70s and early '80s may have altered it for ever. Why bother with spinners if you have the likes of Roberts, Holding, Marshall, Croft, Garner and Walsh, and can play four of them in your side at a time?

On one occasion, England went into a Test with four fastish bowlers and no front-line spinner – at Headingley in 1981. After the first day's play, I almost wished I had not come back to captain the side. Australia were 210 for three; that was bad enough, but worse was the thought that – before the match had even begun – I had been responsible for a glaring error: we left out Emburey. As I have written elsewhere:

In mid-afternoon, I had brought Willey on for a few overs. He is not in Emburey's class as a spinner and still had a bruised index finger, which necessitated his using his second finger to spin the ball, yet he had made several balls turn and bounce – on only the first day! Emburey would not only have been able to attack; he would also, on the day's evidence, have been more accurate than all our seamers apart from Old. Before tea, when Boycott and I found ourselves at extra-cover and mid-off to Willey, I said to him (not without a tinge of reproach, I fear, as he had advocated the extra quick bowler) that the pitch was already helping the spinner. He, more level-headed, retorted, 'This pitch helps all sorts.'

After play, Marsh did not help matters by asking, on his visit to our dressing-room, if our omission of Emburey had been a bluff to get them to put us in to bat. I suppose that it was some sort of tribute to our cricketing sense that our selection had caused Hughes to take Marsh and Lillee for a second look at the pitch, to reinforce their decision to bat first.

Back at the hotel, I could not sleep for a long time, brooding over the choice. I thought, 'They've not brought me back for my batting; and now, before the Test's even started, I've made a tactical howler.'

Next day I told Emburey I was sorry; we had been wrong to leave him out and the decision had been mine. John tried to reassure me, though I knew he was disappointed and guessed he was critical. By the end of Saturday's play, however, after I had seen the Australian pace trio operate, the initial selection seemed more defensible. In fact, on Sunday I phoned Emburey to hear about Middlesex's week-end, but also to tell him that I was not so sure now that I had been wrong. Ironically, there were times not only on Monday but even on Saturday when Hughes would have been delighted to have had a fourth seamer rather than his spinner. If we had had to start another Test a week later on the same pitch it is possible that Australia would have picked Hogg and we Emburey.

'My God, look what they've sent me'

In the heyday of their spin quartet, India have gone to the opposite extreme, and have picked sides with only one seam bowler. In 1972–3, Eknath Solkar would bowl a couple of overs at gentle medium pace to knock the shine off for the spinners; in the third Test, at Madras, India opened with him and Sunil Gavaskar. In their next home series against England, their selection followed a similar pattern, with Gavaskar once again bowling a token over or two with the new ball.

Apart from the balance of spin and pace, selectors must also weigh up the proportion of bowlers to batsmen. As a rule, the better the pitch for batting, and the more you need to take a chance for a win, the greater is the need for five front-line bowlers rather than only four. In 1981–2, England made a mistake in picking five specialist bowlers for the first Test at Bombay on a pitch of doubtful quality: they needed all the batting they could pack into the side. Chastened by this experience, they then erred in the opposite direction, picking only four bowlers for the next three Tests, all played on strips that suited batsmen.

Selection is, of course, a matter of making the most of whatever resources are available. Fortunately, most countries are unable to produce the unending supply of athletic fast bowlers that erupt in the heat of the Caribbean. As I will argue more fully later, I hope that everything possible is done to encourage genuine spin bowling, by groundsmen, legislators and even captains. It is essential, for instance, to continue the campaign against slow over-rates (which enable four fast bowlers to remain fresh enough to keep going unrelieved for the entire six hours), and to consider limits to the number of bowlers permitted to run in more than, say, ten yards.

Selectors, like captains and players, need luck, especially in the short run. In part, the luck comes in timing and the relative strength of the opponents. Nevertheless, selectors, again like captains, are entitled to congratulate themselves when an idea 'comes off' (and is therefore hallowed by the term 'inspired'). The most spectacular of these hunches was the recall of two veterans – Cyril Washbrook and Compton – and the part-timer, the Rev David Sheppard, to rescue England's batting against Australia in 1956; the Ashes were won 2-1 after the first Test had been lost.

The most notorious and controversial selectorial decisions concerned Basil d'Oliveira and the abortive tour of South Africa in 1968–9. They also had the most far-reaching consequences. The chain of events leading up to the crucial meetings was extraordinary. D'Oliveira had been dropped after the first Test against Australia in 1968, despite scoring 87 not out in the second innings. The problem was that he did not have sufficient penetration as a bowler to take the role of third seamer, while as a batsman he was competing against some fine players. Nevertheless, the decision was harsh. Over the next two months he lost form. By the time of the last Test, at the Oval, d'Oliveira was still not in the reckoning. He was, however, asked to come to the Oval after the captain, Cowdrey, had heard that the pitch there was favourable for medium-pacers. Even so, d'Oliveira was at this point third choice, behind Tom Cartwright and Barry Knight, for a place as stand-by! As it happened, neither Cartwright nor Knight was fully fit; but yet another stroke of fate was required before he actually made the eleven: Roger Prideaux, one of the openers, dropped out because of a virus infection, and d'Oliveira played.

So, on the first evening of the match, d'Oliveira walked to the wicket at Number Six, in Cowdrey's words, 'an utterly calm figure, betraying none of the huge tension there must have been within him. This, so far as he was concerned, was the innings which must decide whether he was to have the chance he had dreamed about for years – to return to South Africa as a free, equal member of an English Test team.'

If any innings demonstrated a man's coolness and ability to rise to an occasion, this was it. That evening, d'Oliveira phoned his wife. He was not out overnight. 'Don't worry,' he told her, 'I shall make a hundred all right. I have never played so well.' He did. Dropped at 31, he played, Cowdrey says, 'a superb innings, full of attacking shots and commanding presence'. He was out for 158.

And yet he was not picked for the tour of South Africa. The selectors maintain that the decision was based purely on cricketing considerations, and I have no doubt that this is what they set out to do. And yet, and yet. In such a situation could a man be sure that he had banished all other thoughts from his mind? Might he not unconsciously or partly consciously believe that saving the tour justified sacrificing d'Oliveira? Or might not his wider views tempt him to go the other way, and say that, whatever the cricketing points, he will *not* risk being branded racist for not picking d'Oliveira? As for cricketing grounds, the man had just scored 158 in a Test against Australia, standing up, as Cowdrey says, to more than customary pressures in so doing. His temperament at least must have recommended him at that time above all times.

The sequel is well known. The decision provoked a furore. Three weeks later Cartwright withdrew because of a shoulder injury, and d'Oliveira was chosen as his replacement. Now it was Dr Vorster's turn to believe that the selectors were not immune to political influence, and he announced that d'Oliveira would not be accepted. MCC cancelled the tour, and there have been no official tours between the two countries since then.

This was not the first occasion on which race had been of consequence. In 1896, MCC, who were responsible for the choice of team for the Lord's Test, had not picked Ranjitsinhji though his form had clearly warranted it. 'They took the view,' Alan Gibson tells us, 'that an Indian prince had no business playing in a Test match for England. But the argument against him arose from his colour, not the fact that he was not an Englishman.' However, the Lancashire committee invited Ranjitsinhji to play in the next Test, at Manchester, 'after consulting the Australian

'My God, look what they've sent me'

Three redoubtable England selectors, photographed at the Oval in 1962. Alec Bedser, chairman 1969–82, R. W. V. Robins, chairman 1962–4 and Doug Insole, chairman 1965–8.

captain, Harry Trott, who said they would be delighted to play against him'. The selection turned out to be something of a coup, at least pragmatically, as Ranji scored 62 and 154 not out.

Selectors have one resort when all else fails: to pick themselves. In 1926, Wilfred Rhodes, by then a forty-nine-year-old selector, was chosen for the Oval Test against Australia. He took four wickets for 44 in the second innings, and was none too pleased when the captain, Percy Chapman, took him off with Australia eight down on the grounds that it would be pleasant to share the wickets round a bit. In 1953, Freddie Brown, who was chairman of the selectors, was included in Hutton's team for the Lord's Test. He was a mere forty-two years of age, and he too took four wickets in an innings.

CHAPTER FIVE

The morning of the match: reading the entrails

We have arrived at the first morning of a match. Twelve or thirteen players have been chosen. What remains to be done, by the captain, before the first ball is bowled?

He will, we presume, already have arranged with the players a schedule for their pre-match activities. For county matches, I normally wanted players on the ground at least an hour before the start. For Tests, it would be one and a quarter or one and a half hours. We would usually have a timetable for training and fielding practice. On most Test-match days, and early in the season for county matches, both would be compulsory, and would be timed to end twenty minutes or half an hour before the start. Training was really a matter of stretching exercises and a little running. The idea was to prevent injuries, to establish a habit of stretching, and to have a short group activity to get everyone together early in the day.

Fielding practice would be divided into two groups: close-fielders and outfielders. Slip specialists would practise in the following way: one person would throw the ball at about shoulder height to a batsman, who would run or steer the ball to a ring of slips. We would stand, when possible, in the positions that we would typically take up on the field, so that we would get used to spacing ourselves. We would also use a similar routine for slip-fielding to spinners, but with underarm throwing from close range. This method is by far the most realistic simulation of slip-fielding, better than any slip cradle. The close-fielding group would also practise the sort of catches that might come to short-leg or silly mid-off.

The other group would do some outfielding, stressing quickness and sharpness of pick-up and throw. We would sometimes play fielding games with, perhaps, a batsman taking short singles, and fielders aiming to hit the stumps underarm. There would also be catching practice. Before one-day matches both groups would do some outfielding.

The emphasis on fielding and fitness is a far cry from the time of, say, Hutton, who told me that all they did in his day was 'knock a few balls in the air, and see if anyone caught them'.

Personally, I liked to delegate the organisation of the fielding practice to two others, one for each group; partly because it was one less occasion on which I was responsible for telling people what to do, partly because I would sometimes be engaged at the scheduled time with last-minute questions of fitness, or who to leave out of the twelve, or indeed with the toss itself.

The fielding practice was made a priority. I regarded it as being of great importance, and it was a routine that I reinstated with the England team when I was recalled in 1981. I would tell the players that nets, if they wanted them, had to be fitted in before or after the time specified for fielding; as indeed did visits to the physiotherapist except in an emergency.

As for nets, much depended on the state of the net pitches and the stage of the season. Early on, most batsmen would want the assurance of a knock, and most bowlers would like to loosen up there. It may be up to the captain to make sure that there are a few extra bowlers available. Later, those who are in form are unlikely to visit the nets frequently. Others may do so, but often later in the day, when there is less rush and they can quietly try to sort things out, whether by themselves or with the aid of a coach. I would, on rare occasions, try to persuade a player to practise, but some would stubbornly maintain that nets made things worse. Then I would cite Boycott as an example, or Titmus. I remember an example of the latter's procedure at a time in 1964 when he was not happy about the way he was bowling. The third match of the South African tour was at Benoni, against the South African Colts. On the first day, Titmus took six wickets, despite having several catches dropped. Next morning after play had started he went to the nets alone, taking half a dozen balls. He placed a couple of spare stumps on a length, one just outside off-stump, the other on middle. He then bowled, over after over, until he felt that his rhythm and control were right. He used to maintain that the main aim for a bowler was to be satisfied about the way the ball left his end, and not, at least at the start of a season, to worry too much about what happened to it at the other end. Once he was bowling well, Titmus liked to steer clear of the nets, except for a few deliveries, unless there was a gap of several days between matches.

Another factor that influences players' keenness to have nets is, as we have seen, the state of the pitches. On most county grounds, net pitches would be worn and either useless or dangerous for batsmen a few weeks into the season. Nevertheless, net pitches were usually adequate for Test matches. And some players had to be chivvied to use them. Botham was one. Once or twice I had to be willing to fend off a few bouncers from him in the nets – his form of protest at being told to bowl. His idea of batting practice before an important innings or match is simply to get his arms moving and feel the ball on the bat. He will then amuse himself with some big hits. In my view, his apparently flippant attitude is not entirely unproductive. Certainly it is better than nothing. At times, whoever is his captain needs to make him turn his arm over and swing the bat.

Fletcher discovered this to his cost in India in 1981. England had lost the first Test at Bombay. There were then eight days before the next Test. Reasonably enough, Botham, who would be batting at Number Five, and bowling a large number of overs, was not picked for the intervening game. The mistake was that he did not practise either. He batted well enough, scoring 55 in a total of 400. But England's one main chance of winning lay in taking some early wickets with the new ball. Botham, however, overestimated his control, his speed and his ability to swing the ball; he bowled a series of leg-stump half-volleys with only two fielders on the leg-side. India got off to a racing start, with Gavaskar and Srikkanth putting on 102 for the first wicket, and saved the match comfortably.

Early in my captaincy career, I think I made some mistakes in ordering net practice after bad team performances. The players referred to them as 'naughty boy nets'. I suppose that working at our game was a token of our intention to do better; but such events can easily degenerate into pointless self-punishment. Once I even had the bowlers in on a day off, without the batsmen. Then, too, I received a higher-than-usual proportion of bouncers.

I have praised Boycott's dedication to his craft. As captain, though, he tended to presume that others should model themselves on his method. In New Zealand Boycott had the team driven all over Dunedin before the game, at about nine in the morning, for nets on sub-standard pitches. The low confidence of several of the batsmen was even further reduced, and the bowlers were unable to do more than go through the motions, for fear of hurting the batsmen. Such excursions were worse than a mere waste of time.

The captain has, as I say, the main responsibility for the way the team approaches a match. But he also has, on the first morning, duties that are more directly related to the impending game. Briefly, these are to form a view on who should be left out of the twelve (or thirteen), and to decide what to do if he wins the toss.

One factor may be the weather. In the days of uncovered pitches, this was, naturally, even more relevant. But even now a captain may need to know what the prospects are. For instance, if the temperature is likely to be 100°F, he will be hesitant about fielding first. If the forecast is for a cloudy, humid day, on the other hand, he may expect the ball to swing and move about, and be keener to field. If rain is forecast, he may well decide to take the field in a one-day match, since any hold-up after the start which results in a reduction in the overs remaining frequently gives the side batting second an advantage. I'm

Geoff Boycott leads England on to the field for the first time: Karachi, 1977. Boycott and the rest of the team had threatened to refuse to play if Pakistan chose their three Packer players – Zaheer, Mushtaq and Imran – who had flown home from Australia in response to popular demand. The matter apparently went to the Head of State, General Zia-ul-Haq, before the Test went ahead with Zaheer and Co in the stands. The players in the picture are: John Lever, Mike Gatting, Geoff Miller, Phil Edmonds, Derek Randall (hidden), Boycott, Graham Roope, Bob Willis, Brian Rose (hidden). Bob Taylor and Geoff Cope made up the eleven.

afraid that I was not conscientious enough always to arrange to find out the weather forecast. At Brisbane I did not need to bother, as each captain is given a copy of the forecast before the day's play – possibly as a result of the famous 'sticky-dogs' that have in the past transformed Tests there.

His most pressing task, and often the most difficult, is to assess the ground. The state of the outfield may be of concern. If it is hard, dry and bare, he can expect the ball to lose its shine rather quickly; if lush and green, the ball will change less. He may take into account how wet the outfield is; the ball may run more freely later in the match, as in the Melbourne Centenary Test. If the surrounds of the pitch are saturated, they may hamper both fast bowlers and fielders.

But as a rule the captain's main focus of interest will be on the pitch itself. Past knowledge of a ground helps, as does its reputation. On the county circuit, rumours spread about little-used, or new grounds. In its early days, we used to notice how many players were taken to hospital from Abbeydale Park, Sheffield. It may be a help to know, of a certain ground, that its pitches play better than they look.

Reputations can, of course, also mislead. We had expected a brown, low pitch at Melbourne for the Centenary Test. Instead, there was a thick covering of the serpentine couch grass. At Bombay, for the Jubilee Test in 1980, we could hardly believe our eyes when we saw how green the pitch was; three years before, it had been a slow turner. In fact, we almost talked ourselves out of playing a third seamer in this match, on the grounds that the pitch *couldn't*, in India, be as green as it looked! It was, and our spin combination of Underwood and Emburey bowled between them a mere seven overs in the match.

As visiting captain, you may need to know whether a pitch is one of the recently relaid ones. At the Oval, alternate pitches had, in the late '70s, been relaid. The entire character of the game would be different, depending on whether it was to be played on a new and bouncy or an old and dead pitch. On some grounds, including Lord's, strips tended to vary at different places on the square. Information could be and often was available from the groundsman and even the home team, though each source could be misleading. Groundsmen are not prone to condemn themselves out of their own mouths; and, like others, they tend to see what they want to see. For example, I asked the 'curator' (the Australian name) at Sydney about the pitch for the sixth Test in 1979. The previous Test had been at Adelaide, where the groundsman, Arthur Lance, had offered a gentle rebuke to captains who complained, but had not taken the trouble to ask about preparation. 'They ought to learn when it was last watered and last played on,' he said. So I made a special point of asking the Sydney curator. He said it would hold together all right. Willis and I, looking at it on the morning of the match, found this statement hard to credit. The pitch was even barer than it had been for the fourth Test, on the same ground, when the ball had turned appreciably; this one had the extra drawback, for batsmen, that the marks from bowlers' follow-throughs in that match were clearly visible on a length just outside off-stump. We were right to be sceptical. The ball started to turn from the first day.

It will already be plain that the captain should come to his own conclusion, mainly on the basis of what he finds on the day. What then can he tell from looking at the strip? He will at once note how much grass covers it, how thick it is, and of what colour. On a hard pitch, with thick, green grass, the ball will fly through, and may well deviate. The drier and browner the grass, the less help will it give the faster bowlers. An even covering of grass is likely to hold a pitch together, that is, to prevent it crumbling and allowing spin. To confirm this view, the observer may test the strength of the roots.

One can sometimes tell how flat a pitch is simply by looking at it. If the grass shows strips of green, alternating with lighter-coloured strips, the chances are that the pitch undulates; the mower cannot cut as close on the valleys as on the hill-tops. I have already mentioned the bare patches at Sydney: the captain will be interested in their exact line and length; they may determine his decisions about which ends the spinners should bowl from, or whether they should operate round or over the wicket to left-handers.

Pitches vary greatly in the degree to which the surface is cracked, and in the effect of different types of crack. Pronounced cracks, when they occur in crucial areas, are bound to affect the bounce of the ball. For if it lands on a crack, the rebound will be less than if it hits the firmer patches in between. Such unevenness almost always becomes more pronounced as the match goes on, as the cracks themselves tend to widen and crumble. It is worth breaking a tiny flake of soil off from a crack, if you can: if it flakes and crumbles easily, the pitch is likely to take spin, and possibly even to disintegrate. If not, the cracks may have less effect than you think.

In 1974, Middlesex were bowled out for 23 in a Sunday League match on a Headingley pitch that I described as a mosaic. When our first batsman was LBW from a near-shooter, I advised the ingoing batsman to look to play forward; he was out a ball or two later to a delivery of similar length that brushed his glove as he dutifully followed my advice. I was puzzled by the degree of variation shown on this occasion; and have only been able to guess that it arose from the tinge of green on the 'mosaic' tiles which had such a different impact from the cracks that formed their perimeter.

Occasionally, the edges of turfs are visible; the risk of re-laying with turfs rather than sowing is that they fail, or are not given the time, to mesh in with each other. Such pitches can have explosive results.

The captain should not only *look* at the pitch. He is also interested in discovering how hard it is. For this purpose he may bounce a ball on it, to see how high it rebounds. (World Series Cricket produced an interesting gimmick, which consisted of a contraption which allowed a ball to drop from a certain height on to different portions of the pitch and measured the rebound.) Tapping the pitch with a bat also gives an indication of hardness; sometimes the sound offers a clue: a dull, hollow sound suggests a less hard pitch than a ring. At Lord's, and elsewhere, pitches tend to be harder near the ends than at the middle, which means that the good-length ball from a quick bowler will go through faster than a bouncer. (The reason, at Lord's, is simply that the middle of the square is lower than the ends, as can be seen, whenever a deluge covers the ground with water, by the long lake whose shores are the famous ridges.)

Moisture, too, is an important factor. A damp pitch makes the ball liable to move off the seam. A wet pitch, or a 'pudding', may play easily, but very slowly. Our Fenner's mentor, Cyril Coote, used to say, 'Get on the back foot, sir, and play it with a broomstick, sir.' As a wet pitch dries, it will, of course, take spin. The harder it is beneath the surface the more sharply the ball will turn and bounce. A hard pitch with a thin layer of moisture on top may turn out to be lethal. On the other hand, on a pitch that has merely become greasy with drizzle or light rain, the ball may skim through and make batting easier, especially as the ball itself will become wet and slippery.

When the surface appears to be dry, there may still be moisture underneath. Middlesex played Sussex at Lord's in 1976 on a pitch that had been watered too soon before the match. We knew this, because we had been practising at Lord's for the previous three days. The hot sun caked the top, so that it looked a benign light-brown; but the moisture was there, for all that. The Sussex captain, Peter Graves, might have discovered it for himself by scratching hard at the pitch (preferably near the edge!) with his spikes; and would thereby have avoided making the mistake of batting first when he won the toss. Sussex were all out for 90, and lost by an innings.

All England captains who had the pleasure of touring with Ken Barrington as a member of the management had the benefit of 'Barrington's Knife'. Inserting it at various points would give information about the hardness and evenness of the texture, as well as reveal hidden dampness.

The reader may have begun to feel that captains need the perceptiveness, and even the tools, of a Sherlock Holmes, and that I will next be suggesting that it is a necessary part of his equipment to carry a magnifying glass. The TCCB also felt that matters were moving too far in this direction; for in 1980 they introduced the experimental playing conditions for domestic cricket that made it illegal to bounce a ball on the wicket, or to tap it with a bat, before the start of play. They also introduced a ruling that, on wet days, the captain was allowed to take with him only one Dr Watson to inspect the pitch. I thought this a fatuous rule, as it could be vital to discover from your bowlers whether they felt that they could run in properly and stand up to bowl in safety. Besides, I often found that it was worth asking bowlers *and* batsmen to give their opinions; human nature being what it is, both groups veer towards putting off the moment of personal performance; thus batsmen are inclined to see a greenness in the pitch that is totally imaginary, if not hallucinatory, from the bowlers' point of view. At Edgbaston, in 1975, it was certainly the batsmen who advised Mike Denness to field first against Australia; as it happened, a storm flooded the pitch after Australia had batted, and England were bowled out twice on an unplayable pitch. It was Denness's last Test match. At Johannesburg, after the

Ken Barrington tests the Karachi pitch with his knife, 1978. Geoff Miller looks on. As manager in India and Pakistan, Barrington ('The Colonel', thanks to his father's military career as a sergeant in India before the war) kept looking for the batsmen's pitches that he had enjoyed as a player ten or fifteen years before; but he was often disappointed.

fourth Test in 1965, Bob Barber referred ironically to Mike Smith's green-tinted spectacles, after Smith put South Africa in to bat, and they scored 390 for six.

Indeed, one mark of buoyancy and optimism in a side lies in their joint eagerness to take the field. Conversely, a side full of 'old lags' thinks mainly of the opportunity to put its collective feet up; after all, when it is batting, only two of them are working as opposed to all eleven. Fielding, wicket-keeping and bowling are tiring. And you never know, it may rain after your own team has batted and you won't have to field at all!

The attitude also has more rational determinants. Back in 1899, K. S. Ranjitsinhji was arguing in *The Jubilee Book of Cricket* that dry pitches inevitably deteriorate, so the captain who wins the toss will have no hesitation in batting first. The dictum was, 'If in doubt, bat,' and the justification lay not only in Ranji's point, which is valid, especially when pitches are 'natural', but also in the risk of rain. Hutton's insertion of Australia at Brisbane in 1954, when they scored 601–8 declared and bowled England out twice on a rain-affected pitch, has ever since been quoted as a cautionary tale for captains in general, and for English captains in Australia in particular. When we were discussing our policy during the team dinner on the night before the Centenary Test in

The morning of the match: reading the entrails

Melbourne, Willis's reaction to Greig's remark that he was seriously thinking of putting Australia in was that it would be 'sheer lunacy'. (It is a mark of Willis's ability to criticise himself that he afterwards admitted that Greig's decision was absolutely right – the pitch gradually assisted batsmen more the longer the match went on – and used his 'sheer lunacy' phrase as a catchword to poke fun at himself.) Despite the changes in the rules regarding covering, and despite the tendency of groundsmen to use more water and more fertilisers, it is still irrationally felt to be more of a gamble to put the other side in; decisions to bat first, even when they have predictably catastrophic consequences, are rarely held against one.

As I say, a team that has come to expect to do well is, nowadays, more likely to be enthusiastic about taking the field. Against Australia at the Oval, in 1981, I had a nicely balanced decision to make. The weather would be hot later; but the pitch would be at its liveliest at the start of the match. The groundsman's opinion was that it would be easier for batting as the match progressed, though the ball might keep low later on. And his view was confirmed by Mickie Stewart, the Surrey manager, who knew these recently relaid pitches as well as anyone. He said he thought we should field first. Willis was, again, against it: 'Don't complain if it's cloudy,' he warned, 'when it's our turn to bat.' But I think that one of the main factors in my decision to field first was Botham's enthusiasm for the idea. When the score read 120 for no wicket, the sun was blazing and the pitch had eased, I wondered if I had done the right thing. The truth is that in such circumstances either option is a gamble and might have any sort of outcome. In the event, Australia went on to make 352.

Before the toss, there may be a few matters to sort out with the umpires. They may wish to confirm the hours of play and timings of intervals. They will state which clock (or whose watch) they intend to go by; and they will want to clear up in advance any ambiguity as to what constitutes a boundary. At Lord's, for example, the grass slope leading up to the pavilion fence is in play. At Canterbury, any ball striking the tree that stands inside the boundary line counts four; but fielders may field a ball behind the tree. The umpires may want to check whether the wires that run along the top of a fence must be completely cleared for a six, and whether any part of either sight-screen is within the field of play (in which case, only four is scored if a ball hits it without bouncing). Any later grievance may be forestalled if agreement is reached at this stage about whether drinks are to be taken, and how often.

In some countries, it is the practice to offer the captains a box of balls from which they may choose the one with which they wish to bowl. I always let the bowlers choose. They usually look for dark, small balls, on the grounds that they are harder to see and easier to grip; for some reason dark ones are believed to swing more, too. In England, the captains used to be asked to approve a particular brand of ball to be used in the Test. Despite the fact that virtually all top-class balls are made by a single company in a single factory, and are later distributed under different trade names, bowlers often have strong opinions about which brand they prefer. Indeed, the umpire Charles Elliott tells me that at Lord's, in 1961, Cowdrey insisted on 'Tworts'; while Neil Harvey (leading Australia for the only time, in Benaud's absence) pressed for 'Surridges'. So, despite some nervousness among the authorities about the propriety of the practice, the match went ahead on that basis: each side bowled with its preferred brand. As Elliott said, there was nothing in the laws to prevent it.

Most of this is, I think, superstition. The view of John Reid, captain of New Zealand for many years, was more sane. 'Are they round?' he would ask. 'And red? If so, they'll do.'

More important will be discussions about fitness for play, though these may arise at any stage in the match. Differences of opinion may arise because of the customs in different parts of the world. In 1967, rain fell at Dacca, then in East Pakistan, during our Under-25 match against Pakistan. A few minutes after it stopped, conditions were, by English standards, clearly fit for play. We were in a strong position, and were, naturally, keen to start. The umpires felt we ought to wait. The conversation went something like this.

ME: 'I think it fit to play.'

UMPIRE: 'We are doubtful about the footholds for the bowlers.'

ME: 'Please allow me to be responsible for that.'

UMPIRE: 'We are afraid the batsmen might slip when running between the wickets.'

ME: 'But if they wear spikes?'

UMPIRE: 'But they may not have spikes.'

ME: 'Do you mean to say that you intend to hold up a big match and disappoint 40,000 people because some players may not be properly shod?'

UMPIRE: 'We do not wish to discuss the matter further.'

We did not play for a couple of hours, until everything was bone dry; Pakistan saved the game.

Another interesting example occurred at Sydney in 1979–80. This was the famous occasion when the ground staff left the pitch uncovered on New Year's Eve, when they went off to their parties. Unfortunately, it rained heavily throughout the night. There were still three clear days before the Test was due to start, so in normal conditions the oversight would not have been too important. However, there was no chance to allow the strip to dry as the rain continued non-stop until the morning of the Test. The ground then dried fast; and soon after lunch the umpires asked Greg Chappell and me whether we thought the ground was fit to play. If we had both agreed, I believe the umpires would have gone along with us, whichever side we had come down on. My own view was that the conditions were marginal, and that although I might have expected to start a county match they were not really suitable for a Test.

The morning of the match: reading the entrails

Nevertheless, I said I thought that it was fit. We were one-nil down in a three-match series; we had Underwood on our side; if we were to win the toss, I thought we would win the match, while if we lost it, we might still be able to wriggle out. In short, I gambled – and lost. Chappell said later that he was never so keen in his life to win a toss as he was to win that one – rightly, as the pitch steadily eased as the match went on, and after a closer tussle than the eventual margin suggests, Australia won by six wickets.

A few months later, there was a justified outcry against a prolonged delay in play on the Saturday of the Lord's Centenary Test. On this occasion, Chappell, as captain of the batting side, would have been perfectly happy for play to start, whereas it was England's captain – Ian Botham – who was reluctant. The crowd's incomprehension at the lack of cricket turned to anger, which erupted on the steps of the pavilion when the umpires were manhandled by some MCC members as they returned from their fifth inspection of the pitch. The outcry in the press and elsewhere had some effect. Players, umpires and administrators accepted that changes were needed; crucial parts of the ground should be more thoroughly covered, players and umpires should consider fit conditions that would not have been thought so before, and more attention should be paid to public relations on rain-affected days. Efforts in this direction had already started. In the early '70s, Lord's experimented with a cover that protected several pitches at once, and initiated the covering of bowlers' run-ups. And in 1978 the authorities at the Oval borrowed extra covers that had recently been used for the tennis at Wimbledon which enabled us to have enough cricket for a result in the New Zealand Test after the ground had been flooded on the Monday. And Warwickshire have taken steps to install covers that keep most of the ground dry whatever the weather.

The furore of August 1980 was not the first of its kind. I remember another Test-match Saturday, at Leeds in 1979, when play was abandoned early mainly because of wet patches near the boundary. I went back to the ground at 5.30; it was perfectly fit for play, and I joined some spectators in a game on the outfield.

Sponsors, the media and the public have gradually forced us to realise that we were too finicky. Those who put money into promoting big matches were naturally dissatisfied when the vehicle of their sponsorship was stuck in a garage on sunny days. And public expectations have become more emphatic and vociferous. People no longer take it for granted that the 'expert' knows best. Doctors have to take out insurance against suits for negligence. Captains and umpires must steel themselves against the jostling, the heckling, even the hatred of frustrated fans.

What, then, are the problems? And whose is the responsibility? Disagreement is to some extent inevitable, as with any borderline case. And disagreement is likely, though not, with understanding, inevitable, between club cricketers and first-class cricketers. We have all seen village matches being played in quagmires, thunderstorms and Stygian gloom. If they can do it, why can't we?

The main reason is the degree of physical strain involved. Jeff Thomson puts more into his delivery stride than the average blacksmith, so he needs a more stable platform for his bowling, and has more to lose if anything goes wrong. (The village parson, too, would lose more if Thomson hit him on the nose with a short ball than if the blacksmith did.)

There is also a difference between cricket and many other games. In cricket, wet conditions usually hamper one side more than the other, whereas at football or tennis each side is equally affected.

So the first guideline that was accepted in the meetings held in the autumn following the Lord's debacle was that umpires should be satisfied that the run-ups and footholds are reasonably dry. All concerned agreed that some degree of mobility should be possible for fielders within, say, twenty yards of the bat, though even here isolated soggy parts should not prevent play.

What had been absurd was the feeling that equally stringent requirements should be met for the rest of the ground. From now on, unless water was actually lying on the ground, or coming up at every step, we should regard conditions as satisfactory.

We also discussed the question of responsibility. Whose decision should it be to start or delay play? Captains are sometimes accused of not recognising their duties to the public. This may be so, but to my mind a captain's first responsibility is to his team. The side in a stronger position usually stands to gain more by playing than the other; often the risk of injury is borne solely by the fielding team. Moreover, those who are closely involved are inclined to see what it suits them to see. In my opinion, the captains cannot ignore the interest of their sides in any specific situation. Their views, therefore, are at best merely helpful.

The sole arbiters of fitness for play, as of other issues, should be the umpires. I am even doubtful whether captains should be allowed to play when the umpires have decided that conditions are unfit, as this leads to inequality and unfairness. Many sides which are, for example, unwilling to play against a strong side if they have a choice in the matter will nevertheless happily take the field in precisely similar circumstances against weaker opposition.

Where umpires do need help from the captains and players is in the general attitude as to what constitutes fitness for play. It is hard for them to take the players on to the field if they strongly disapprove. It is this general attitude that is changing significantly.

Contrary to some beliefs, cricketers *do* usually want to play. There will be moments when delaying the struggle has a secret attraction, and there are a few players who look to the clouds (or to little injuries) to avoid being tested. But waiting is like hanging around at an airport – demoralising and draining. With half one's mind on the match, it is hard

The morning of the match: reading the entrails

Styles of tossing. FAR LEFT, 1938, Wally Hammond and Don Bradman walk out at Lord's before the second Test. Bradman's dress shows his attitude to pre-match practice. Hammond, who looks a bit hang-dog beside the chipper Bradman, presumably felt better at the end of a good day's work. NEAR LEFT For, having won the toss, he was himself 210 not out at the close of play. The match was drawn, with Bradman scoring 102 not out in the second innings. BELOW LEFT Bradman and Hammond again, at the Oval, in the same series. Hammond won again, and this time England scored 903–7 dec. Bradman fractured his shin bowling, and England won by an innings and 579 runs. ABOVE, 1980, the author and Greg Chappell have to answer banal questions from Channel 9 before tossing up for the one-day match at Sydney.

to use such time constructively, though in a wet May we would improve our squash and bridge more than our cricket.

The shift in approach was immediately evident the next season, in 1981. Umpires and captains faithfully paddled out hourly to the squares, water over their welts. We stayed longer at grounds on the off-chance of play (at Leicester, they bowled the first ball of one day's play at 5.45), and started on squelchier grounds. It was particularly galling for me to read of a local man's comments to the press on a match at Uxbridge that Clive Rice, the Notts captain, and I had shown a cynical disregard for the public, and should have been playing much earlier. In fact, we had agreed to play for several hours on each of the three days in conditions that the umpires thought unfit for play. Rice and I both felt that Middlesex had fielded in worse conditions than either of us ever had for first-class cricket. In addition, on the day in question the run-up and footholds had been flooded at one end, so we could use seam bowlers only from the other end. We risked injury, and played. As Clive said, 'We want to put on a show, but it has to be the right kind of show.' There are some who will never be satisfied.

Let us suppose, though, that on this day our captain has no such problems. He has decided on his final eleven, and now it is time to exchange teams with the opposite captain and toss up. When does the toss take place, and where? People may imagine that it must occur on the pitch, twenty or twenty-five minutes before the start. This is not always so. In county matches I have frequently tossed up in front of the pavilion (saying, 'You don't want to go all the way out there again, do you?'); or on the nursery ground, by the nets ('Shall we get it over with early, so that we all know where we stand?'); or even in the dressing-room (though that sometimes involves undignified crawling under tables to find the coin). In that same Sydney Test, I kept Greg waiting until nine minutes before the start, while we tried vehemently to persuade Boycott to play; stiff neck or not, he was more likely to score runs on that pitch 75 per cent fit than most others 100 per cent. He did play, but the anxiety and uncertainty was not an ideal lead-up to the Test. (What had happened was that as soon as we knew there was a possibility of play, I had told Boycott to have a net in the indoor school, and had asked a couple of players to watch his movements. They returned a comfortable half-hour before the start: but then the disagreements began. It could be that asking Geoff to play when he was unwilling to do so was likely to prove counter-productive; I was banking on his professionalism, his competitiveness, his instinct for survival, and his sheer technique to pull him through; in the event he scored only 8 and 18.)

There are occasional misunderstandings during the toss itself. At Lord's, against India, both Srinivasaraghavan Venkataraghavan and I thought that we had won the toss. Fortunately, I was bent on fielding first, and he on batting. He told me later that I seemed distracted; I felt that the mistake had probably been mine. When I tossed up with a predecessor of his, Ajit Wadekar, at Lord's in 1973, he appeared not to call until the coin hit the ground; I was about to put my foot on it when he said 'heads'. He seemed to have been watching it in a particularly hawk-eyed way. But the coin turned up tails. Yet another W.G. story concerns tossing-up with a 'greenhorn' captain. The Old Man, it is said, would call 'The Lady'. Whichever side the coin fell, Queen Victoria or Britannia, W.G. would grunt with satisfaction and choose to bat or field.

One final example. In 1975, Middlesex played Warwickshire in all four competitions. On each of the first three, David Brown won the toss, put us in, and we won. On the fourth, at Lord's, we asked each other if there was any point in tossing (as he knew that I would have batted first on each occasion). We agreed that there was not. The ground authorities would not accept that there had been no toss, but that 'the captains had negotiated, and Middlesex would bat'. According to *Wisden*, we won the toss! (We won the match, too, and for the fourth time David shook hands and thanked me for the game as he left the field with his pads on.)

Mumbo-jumbo and the heavy roller. Vital as it is in the long-term preparation of a pitch, the heavy roller rarely makes a difference in the short-term. Here Ron Allsopp (left) is engaged with his staff on the last-minute preparations for his pitch for the World Cup qualifying match between Australia and Zimbabwe, Trent Bridge, 1983.

I think it will by now be clear that I do not believe that all this peering at and agonising over the pitch is a sort of entrail-searching divination. There are good reasons for taking care. Sound judgement now will help you to decide on your final eleven. It will determine your decision on winning the toss. It will influence your aims and policy once the game starts; for instance, if you are convinced that the pitch is not good and will deteriorate, you may instruct your batsmen to bat as long as possible on it, regardless (almost) of their rate of scoring. Or, if you are certain that there is moisture underneath, you may try medium-pacers, or even spinners, earlier than normal.

In fact I think I was occasionally dilatory in my examination of the pitch, assuming too quickly that I had taken in what was discoverable – a fault Illingworth never committed.

What *is* often mumbo-jumbo, though, is the choice of a roller. Only once can I recall a roller making a discernible difference, at Maidstone

The morning of the match: reading the entrails

in 1981. The pitch was damp, and the ball seamed about. We had bowled Kent out for 120. I opted for the heavy roller, thinking that any slight undulations might thereby be flattened. What happened was that for twenty or thirty minutes the ball not only seamed, it lifted chest-high from just short of a length. Since it did not behave in this way at any other time in the match, either before or after, I could only infer that the heavy roller had brought up to the surface just enough moisture to suit the bowlers.

I suppose, too, that on a soaking wet wicket, the heavy roller may keep it placid for a bit longer. On dry pitches, however, the weight of the roller, or the use of any roller at all, seems to make no difference whatever. Yet, like other captains, I might bat on overnight simply to ensure that I could apply a heavy roller next morning. Every captain is advised, when about to declare on a wearing pitch, to use the heavy roller to 'break it up'. I do not believe that I ever saw a roller have any such effect.

CHAPTER SIX

Batting orders

As the captains walk away from the square after the toss, players who are knocking up on the outfield or sitting in the dressing-room pause or poke their heads through the windows, questioningly. The captain gestures to them, patting his leg to indicate pads (and therefore that the team is to bat) or turning his arm over to mime bowling. Then he returns to the dressing-room. It is now twenty to eleven. If the match is at Lord's, the tea trolley will just (only just, he hopes) have been wheeled in by the attendant, Roy Harrington. There will be thirteen cups, and packets of biscuits wrapped in cellophane. (Visitors are offered tea in a glass.) The captain pours himself a cup, looks for his favourite custard creams, and feels a sense of relief – mixed with nervous excitement, especially if he is one of the first few batsmen. At last the season can begin. No more weeks of training and nets, of preparation and anticipation only! Although professional cricketers, like comedians and other performers, often feel insecure, they are all pleased when the routine of competitive cricket starts in earnest.

The scorer, Harry Sharp, known as 'the Admiral' from his naval days, acts as a conductor of the anxiety: 'Had a net, Admiral?' or 'In form, Harry?' he will be asked as he sets off on his long walk to the scoreboard at the top of the Grandstand.

'What did he call, Rip?' Rhyming slang is commoner in the London clubs; a residue of the days when many of their pros would have been cockneys. 'Rip', 'ripper' and 'Jack' are all forms of 'skipper': part of the education for the graduate who plays cricket for a living will be the discovery that if he breaks his 'ampsteads fighting with the man who 'alf-inched his tifter, he has damaged his teeth (Heath) in a fight over a stolen (pinched) hat (tit for tat).

In 1983, the Middlesex players admired what they viewed as sang-froid in Mike Gatting when a spin of the coin was to decide whether they or Gloucestershire should go through to the National Westminster Cup

The dourness of post-war England and the exuberance of the West Indians shown in these dressing-room pictures of a long-sweater day at Trent Bridge, in the 1940s, and a warm one in Adelaide, 1980. Arthur Jepson, foreground (later a Test umpire), with other members of the Notts side, and the West Indians – notably Colin Croft, Desmond Haynes, Malcolm Marshall and Joel Garner – at the height of their success.

semi-final: having called heads, and won the toss, earlier in the day for an abortive ten-over match, and having intended to call heads again after several hours of 'trials' and 'practice' in the dressing-room, he had a sudden intuition when the coin was in the air that he had to call 'tails'. It duly landed tails side up.

This almost superstitious attitude extends beyond the toss. When the score is on 'Nelson' – 111 or 222 – everyone in the dressing-room has to keep his feet off the floor. During a long stand in Adelaide Willis would not allow anyone who had not been watching at the beginning to start doing so, in case it changed our luck. To revert to the first day of a Middlesex season, in his corner of the large Victorian room – by the window, furthest from the door – Clive Radley might be putting on the socks which brought him a run of success the previous year. And a few years ago Peter Parfitt's accent would revert to a broader Norfolk as, holding his Slazenger bat up to his face, he kissed and stroked its sand-papered surface, and murmured, 'What have you got in store for me today, my little beauty?' Gatting for his part would quite likely be annoying everyone by obsessively knocking a ball up on his bat. Batsmen handle a good bat lovingly, smell it, gaze at it, pick it up. Opening batsman Mike Smith would be having his last-minute 'net' in front of the dressing-room mirror. He clicks his tongue on the roof of his mouth to represent ball on bat as he plays an immaculate forward defensive shot. Someone else will be repairing his bat or pads, hurrying with tape, or conferring with the 'physio' about the best way of getting maximum protection without loss of comfort.

If the batsmen are pleased (and excited) to be starting, the bowlers also have mixed feelings about having to wait. Sides often like to begin a season in the field, where rust can be scraped away without an abrupt end to a man's day, and where the nervousness can be shaken off by a sense of togetherness. Now Wayne Daniel, sweating from the nets and his warm-up, towels himself down by his seat by the door before putting on tracksuit and T-shirt, hoping for a long, restful day. Later in the season, after several hard sessions in the field, the winning of the toss will bring more needed respite.

'Does the pitch look any different, Rip?' someone will ask. Early batsmen are discussing armour. 'It won't have much pace after the new ball, but I don't fancy a cracked rib at this stage of the season: maybe I'll wear a chest protector.' At last the bell goes (five minutes before eleven), the umpires emerge, the fielding side appears to a ripple of applause from the few hundred spectators. The twelfth man tells the openers, 'They're on their way.' 'Good luck.' 'Sock it to them.' The openers depart. Number Three is now buckling on his pads: Number Four has his gear laid out beside his case. If he is one of those (or do *all* cricketers share this nightmare?) who has dreams about being utterly unable to get changed and padded up in time, he may put on his box and thigh-pad now, so as not to be rushed later.

Batting orders

On the first day of a new season all the team will watch the start, sitting on the balcony if the weather is warm, or huddled at the glass doors or the large windows near the corner of the room when the usual early May north-easter is blowing. (And *that* will be another reason for being pleased to bat first!) Smith or Wilf Slack and I reckoned to get an audience of our colleagues for the first half-hour or so; less as the season went on, unless Imran or Sylvester Clarke were bowling on a lively pitch. But when Roland Butcher or Gatting were at the crease the dressing-room card school might well call a halt and watch.

If nothing untoward happens on the field, and the score mounts steadily without too much cause for alarm, the team will gradually fall into its pattern of behaviour for the batting days that lie ahead. Argumentative conversation is one thread that will run throughout. Tom Cartwright found that what he most missed in his move from Warwickshire and the factories of the Midlands to rustic Somerset and the gentility of Wells was animated discussion. The Middlesex team have never lacked that.

There are, too, the card-players; though the bridge school is usually kept for rainy days. Newspapers, magazines, and books are dipped into. Some, particularly the beneficiary, write letters, send autographs and make phone calls. Most days, at least one player will pay a supernumerary visit to Nancy Doyle in the kitchen, returning with rolls and coffee, possibly as a consolation for his low score. It is part of the twelfth man's job to find out which batsmen would like their lunch in the dressing-room, if they are not out at the interval; and to draw up a drinks list for close of play. He will also carry the lunches down from the dining-room later.

There will of course be in-songs and in-jokes. 'Strine' was popular for a time, and few days would pass without a Mike Selvey impersonation of John Arlott or Richie Benaud. If the match is being televised, though, the sound is always turned off. At an everyday county match the television may also be on for other programmes, especially for sport.

There are visitors to the dressing-room. A notice on the door reads: 'Strictly no admittance without permission of captain or manager', and players will normally ask the captain if it is all right for Eddie Dawe, say, to come in (he regularly brings the team fruit or toiletries), or a friend from overseas. One visitor who is welcome is the assistant secretary, Len Wynne, at least when he brings the travelling expenses for recent away matches. He might also tactfully remind us that the sponsors would be pleased for a visit to their box. One of the team would be responsible for twisting arms in this direction; a thankless task, as no moment seems quite right.

There are interruptions to this idyllic leisure. Wickets fall; the dressing-room too falls silent – in respect for the dead – as the batsman returns, and there is a scuffle of movement as the next man in gets his pads on, and his successor changes out of shorts and T-shirt. The twelfth man puts a statutory glass of squash beside the incoming batsman's seat. Sometimes everyone knows that there will be an explosion of invective, or even a bat preceding the batsman. Keith Fletcher once accidentally set a fire-extinguisher off with his bat after a dubious LBW decision at Southend; and when a team-mate lobbed the extinguisher into the corridor that separated the two dressing-rooms most of its contents emptied themselves into ours. Some batsmen sit silent, head in hands, for five minutes and then revive. Others seem unconcerned; John Murray used to return whistling lightly. Yet others always have an excuse – notoriously Brian Close, who once blamed the twelfth man for giving him chewing gum of the wrong flavour after getting out second ball. Even W. G. Grace alleged that the glare dazzled his eyes, and that was why he was bowled for o at Brighton one day. And there are batsmen, of whom Boycott is one, who need to go over and over their dismissal with anyone who saw it (or even didn't), in order to reconcile themselves to the enormity of the catastrophe.

But what has the captain to do with this little world? Has he any responsibility for how those in it behave?

In the first place, he must, I think, be aware of what goes on. He watches, and listens, as well as participating. He may need to intervene in respect of any detail of the scene I have described. He is the one who tells Harrington when to bring the tea, and who decides whether to act on Emburey's regular complaint that it's stewed. Cricketers have never been obsessional about their diet (unlike a hawk-eyed Rhode Island athletes team coach who hovered over the team as they lined up at a self-service cafeteria for lunch and bellowed repeatedly, 'Remember, it's roast beef and NO GRAVY'). Indeed, the opposite is true, especially at Lord's which provides the best meals on the circuit (though Sheffield runs it close). I was once driven to call a team meeting to suggest a limit to the number of roast potatoes being consumed between sessions of fielding, and to offer to ask Nancy to keep salads in the refrigerator, so that those who were batting or bowling at lunchtime need not miss their meal. During a One-Day International at Headingley I asked a selector not to smoke his cigar in the dressing-room; it was a cold day with all the doors and windows shut, and the clouds of cigar-smoke were irritating the eyes of a player who still had to bat.

During the football world cup in 1974, Middlesex were playing Yorkshire at Middlesbrough. We were batting during an important match between Scotland and Yugoslavia. The entire team, except for the two batsmen, were intent on the football. Those departing to the middle tended to return a couple of free kicks later, more concerned about the score in Frankfurt than that in Middlesbrough. This was not the only episode of its kind, and they all prompted me to insist on a more discreet use of the television during play, if not its disuse.

The dressing-room can become so cosy that a man forced to leave it to go to the wicket may long to return, as to the womb. To counteract this, and to feed his competitiveness, Phil Edmonds decided one year to sit apart from the rest of us when he was next in.

I have always felt strongly that the dressing-room is the one place in the ground where a player can be totally frank about all sorts of potential *bêtes noires* – umpires, pressmen, opposition. Therefore, if he wants to throw his bat or slam a door in disappointment or disgust, this is the place for him to do so. I may prefer him not to; but he should feel free to act as he wishes here, as opposed to on the field. Consequently, I tended to guard the privacy of the dressing-room, especially in Test matches, where every action is scrutinised. Fletcher was, I noticed in India in 1981–2, more generous to outsiders than I was; while Benaud, a pressman himself, made a point of making writers and broadcasters welcome in the dressing-room. I clung to the idea that the dressing-room was a sanctuary for players in which they could let off steam, however unreasonably or even maliciously, without risk of unwelcome publicity. On tour, or in Tests at home, there were precious few such places.

Possibly my attitude was resented in some quarters. In 1977, in Bahawalpur, we were honoured by an unannounced visit by a top Pakistani general, complete with extended family and entourage. It was perhaps fortunate that our manager, Ken Barrington, whose father had served in an earlier army in the Indian sub-continent, intuitively realised that we were on thin ice if we tried to eject the Martial Law Administrator for the province.

Some of these visits, however unwelcome at the time, are a source of amusement in retrospect. Many years ago, we used to have tea-time calls at Lord's from a retired bat-maker. The players treated him kindly, in the way people sometimes have with those they adopt or make an exception for, and we used to draw up a comfortable armchair for him in a favourable place for watching the game. But he became proprietorial about his chair, and once asked the then England captain, M.J.K. Smith, to give it up to him. He also liked his tea, but was prone to spilling the entire cupful into a nearby cricket bag.

Nor are outsiders always tactful in what they say. They are inclined to ask you breezily what *you're* doing here, or comment in an infuriatingly bland tone that 'you're back early', when you have just been dismissed for a low score.

Obviously, it is no part of a captain's role to be petty or bureaucratic. He should intervene only if the happy balance of his team is upset; and the point of his intervention should always be to improve performance on the field. To that end, he can be a facilitator of attitudes that are mutually helpful rather than cantankerous, selfish or casual. With regard to batting, for example, the team will benefit by a free pooling of views about the opposition's bowlers. It may seem unbelievable that they should be unwilling to do so but there is the sad story of an England batsman who once retorted, about an unusual bowler who was causing problems for his colleagues, 'Figure him out for yourselves: I had to.'

One of the great captains, Richie Benaud learned much from playing for New South Wales under 'the best captain never to lead Australia' – Keith Miller, a fierce competitor who never allowed any game to atrophy. The same can be said of Benaud.

Bill Lawry. A delightful and amusing man, 'Phant' set out to be orthodox but ended up over-defensive and dull. The way he was dropped entirely after the third Test against England in 1971 – without any prior word – may have encouraged Ian Chappell, his successor, in his suspicious attitude towards administrators.

Peter May. One of England's best captains, he kept a certain reserve which enabled him to crack the whip when necessary. Tactically he was sound but tended to be slow to move on to the attack.

Ted Dexter, BELOW, was a pioneering tactician in one-day cricket, leading Sussex to victory in the first two Gillette cups. Keith Andrew, *left*, was a marvellous, unobtrusive wicket-keeper for Northants who played twice for England. His captaincy approach, with a poor county side, was to try to give his team the experience of *not* losing – which often meant playing for a draw.

Brian Close was a character. He was shrewd *and* naive, stubborn *and* flexible, single-minded yet erratic. Perhaps in the round he lacked tact, but he was an engaging man, a fine tactician, and a courageous leader who earned the – sometimes amused and occasionally fearful – respect of his players.

Colin Cowdrey was not a good captain, though he had many of the attributes of one. He was intelligent, charming and had generosity. Against India at Manchester in 1959 he announced over the weekend that as the forecast was fine he would not be enforcing the follow-on if, as was likely, he had the choice. I am not sure that there is not something condescending in this; if I had been an Indian, I should have preferred the coup de grâce. Cowdrey's problem was himself; he lacked decisiveness, and was too concerned about how things (and he) looked.

Ray Illingworth with Ian Chappell, LEFT and Ian and Greg Chappell BELOW, and Tony Greig, OPPOSITE. Four of the best captains of my time, all strong characters and all determined to win.

If Illingworth was an archetypal Yorkshireman, Ian Chappell was many Englishmen's idea of an Aussie. His grit, courage and competitiveness were the main elements in Australia's revival in the '70s, but a price had to be paid in loss of fun and generosity.

I have known Greig to go to unpleasant lengths on the field with comments directed at the batsman. But he was in essence more open to self-criticism than either Illingworth or Ian Chappell and he lacked their shrewdness.

Greg Chappell was as tough as anyone but less flamboyant and outrageous than his older brother.

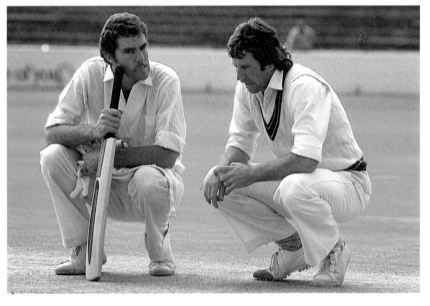

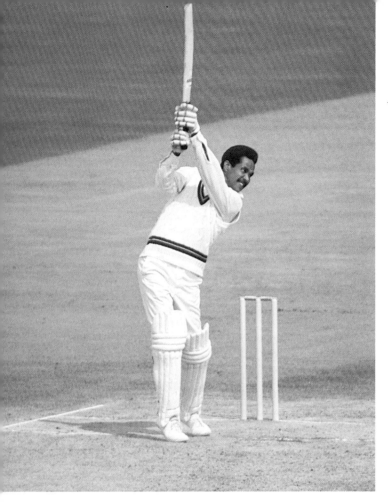

Gary Sobers was indeed the 'King', the 'Four in One', as his fans called him. But the four did not, in honesty, include captaincy. His leadership depended mainly on his own cricketing skills.

Clive Lloyd, like Sobers, is a delightful man, but he allowed West Indies to become cynical in the exercise of power. On the field, he had one quality he shared with Frank Worrell: his restraint and steadiness were important factors in the growing maturity of the West Indies team. But I never felt he had a cricketing brain, as was shown by his lack of ideas when handling the ordinary Lancashire attack.

Kim Hughes is one whose
playing performance and
peace of mind alike were
ruined by his tenure as
Test captain. His
departure was as sad as
his appointment was
cruel. Tossing him the job
in post-Packer Australia
was like inviting the
Darling children to take
the place of Captain Hook.

RIGHT, Sunil Gavaskar
and Kapil Dev, *left*,
represent the different
power-bases in Indian
cricket – Bombay and the
North. Their rivalry as
super-stars became
public and bitter in
1984–5.

The sharing, when it does occur, is often informal. It can become out of date. In 1969, when I was a part-timer for Middlesex, the county asked me to open the batting against Lancashire, two days after I returned from a holiday in France. I was under-prepared, to say the least. Moreover, I had never faced Peter Lever, the opening bowler. I asked Clive Radley about him. 'He swings it in, if anything,' Clive said. I faced the first two balls of that innings, both bowled by Lever: both swung out, and off the second I was caught behind. As Mike Smith used to say, you can never trust bowlers: they develop something new each year.

Advice may be misleading in style as well as in content. Alan Butcher Surrey's opener, was picked for his first and to date only Test at the Oval against India in 1979. Wishing to avail him of the benefit of Boycott's experience, and to get them talking, I asked Geoff to give him a word of encouragement before they went out. Only later did I learn that Geoff had told him that Test cricket was utterly different from county cricket, that you should cut out risky shots, and so on. My – and his – wish to help had only further frozen Butcher into his nervous, new-boy feeling.

New boys suffer most, though, at the hands of the opposition. As in any walk of life, most people take time acclimatising to a new environment, but professional sport with its confrontations offers unusually direct opportunities to exploit such nervousness. Weaknesses of new players are rapidly passed round the circuit, and played on – not maliciously, but because of the natural competitiveness of sportsmen. (Hence the common phenomenon of the setback that strikes many young players in their second season.)

Bob Willis, Ian Botham, OPPOSITE ABOVE, and David Gower, LEFT. It is hard for me to write objectively about these men, who are not only friends and ex-colleagues but also successors. Let me start with some criticisms. Willis was blinkered as a captain, and had an abstracted air, especially when involved in a bowling spell himself. Like many Warwickshire captains he had little idea of how to use spinners. And he allowed his role as leader to be taken over by a committee on the field. He was particularly susceptible to Botham's persuasiveness. Perhaps I was too; for I backed Ian as my successor in 1980. In the event, his own performance declined and he became highly sensitive to criticism. Gower like Botham was thrown in at the deep end, and like Willis appeared to be bulldozed by Botham.

Yet on the credit side, Willis was highly respected for his courage, will-power, and straight-forwardness. Off the field at least, everyone knew who was in charge. To an even greater extent Botham was a powerful figure, and his ideas were often inventive and sound. Gower, too, is an intelligent cricketer; in India, in 1985, he seemed more active and aware of his responsibility to take charge.

Willis has retired, after a distinguished career. But Gower and Botham have many years ahead. They have both, now, the opportunity to learn the job of captaincy at county level – an opportunity they both lacked when first chosen as captains of England.

Benaud says that captaincy is 90 per cent luck and 10 per cent skill. A large part of the 90 per cent consists of the players on your side, and I was immensely fortunate in these three.

Batting orders

Teamwork between batsmen is most clearly called for in the matter of running between the wickets, where there is a need for awareness of each other's speed, or lack of it, and a concern for one's partner's safety as well as one's own. At best, a level of understanding may be reached, as between Jack Hobbs and Andy Sandham, at which no words at all are needed; simply a look and an instantaneous response.

No one enjoys batting with a man who frequently runs others out or who looks for a single at the end of an over whenever he fancies the bowling and at the beginning of the over when he wants to get away from it. Len Hutton is reputed to have said, when Jack Ikin had bravely faced a ferocious spell of bowling from the South African quickie, Cuan McCarthy, 'but a better player would have been at the other end.' One may acknowledge his point without approving of the sentiment. However, partnerships between sadist and masochist are more promising than between pairs who each want to have the same toy at the same time: when playing Gloucestershire one's best chance of separating Zaheer Abbas and Mike Procter was a run-out on the sixth ball!

For many batsmen, short singles form a vital part of their repertoire, so having a nimble partner who is alive to such possibilities may make all the difference to their performance. But considerateness is not limited to running. During the tour of Australia on which Boycott was struggling against fast bowling, he and Derek Randall were batting together in the match against Tasmania when Richard Hadlee, their only quick bowler, came on after lunch for what was likely to be a short spell. Randall took almost every ball from Hadlee, turning down easy singles in the process. His selflessness – none of the other bowlers was remotely threatening – helped Boycott make a century and so regain the confidence through which his batting blossomed soon afterwards with a series of magnificent innings, especially against fast bowling.

Randall and I contrived an unusual aid to survival when we were up against it in the Centenary Test in Melbourne. We needed a massive score, 463, to win, and had lost an early wicket. We decided to face the afternoon session by thinking of it as made up of fifteen-minute segments that we had to get through. At one point, Derek said, 'Stick at it, Skip. In ten minutes there'll only be fifteen minutes to tea.'

Two batsmen can also agree to face one bowler each, as Alan Knott and John Emburey did when saving the sixth Test in 1981. In the following year, against Pakistan at Lord's, Gatting took Abdul Qadir for several overs to protect first Ian Greig and then Derek Pringle, both of whom had previously been utterly bamboozled by the leg-spinner. Amazingly, John Edrich preferred facing the fearsome pace of Lillee and Thomson during the tour of 1974–5 to the spin of Terry Jenner; the arrangement that he would take as much as possible of the fast bowlers suited several of his partners.

The captain must foster these kinds of co-operative spirit, and may well urge the side to keep talking to each other while at the crease, whether for encouragement, reassurance, or caution. Similarly, he will himself be alive to the batsmen's needs for reassurance and praise – during intervals, for example, or after an innings. It can be demoralising for a batsman to walk into the dressing-room unnoticed after his hard work in the middle. Careless remarks can hurt, too. When we played Worcestershire in the Gillette Cup semi-final in 1980, we needed only 125 to win. It was not an easy pitch to play strokes on, and the main danger bowler was Norman Gifford, the left-arm spinner. I was much tempted to hit him over the top, but dutifully and doggedly resisted the temptation. At tea, after 25 overs, we had scored only 50-odd runs, and I was 17 not out. But we had not lost a wicket, and several of Gifford's overs had been used up. I was miffed when one of the team looked up from his card-game and asked, 'Is that all you've got?'

The captain has, too, more definite contributions to make while the team bats. Sometimes he has to give instructions to the batsmen. 'Have a look and then push the score along,' he may say. Or, 'Whatever happens, we don't want to lose a wicket tonight.' In 1983, after most of the cricket in May had been washed out, Gatting told the Middlesex early batsmen to play exactly as it suited them in the first innings of a match. His priority was for them to find confidence and rhythm by a long innings.

On a pitch that helps bowlers, a captain may, as we have seen, say that it does not matter how long it takes to compile a big score; that if we make, say, 300, we should win. In contrast, R. W. V. Robins led Middlesex to the county championship in 1947 with a team that had tremendous batting but limited bowling. Robins knew that they needed to have as long as possible to bowl sides out, and that therefore Middlesex had to score fast. '350 by 5.30,' he would order. And, more unkindly, to Jack Robertson, who might be 60 not out at lunch, 'Get on with it, Jack. They haven't come to see you bat, anyway.' The worst instruction I have heard of was given to a young batsman in his first Test. He had scored a duck in the first innings, and as he was going in to bat in the second the captain is alleged to have said, 'Play for a draw, but make it look as if we're trying to win.' This captain was more concerned about his own image with the press than with a necessarily anxious moment in the life of one of his players.

How specific should a captain be about the target? The answer depends in part on the individual batsman. Some players will carry out the spirit of an instruction, and it may well be sufficient to say, 'Maximum runs in the next hour.' Others would always find excuses not to take risks in such circumstances, and to them it may be better to insist that you want at least 80 runs in the hour, which means 5 an over; which in turn means that after eight overs we should have at least 35, and so on. (But you cannot score the runs for him!) The players should be confident that if they throw their wicket away in such situations they will not as a result lose their places in the team. One instruction should not need to be

David Gower reflects on the situation at Lord's during the second Test against West Indies, 1984. He was rightly criticised for not appearing on the balcony on the fourth evening of this match to make a decision, and to communicate it to the batsmen, on whether or not to come off for bad light. England had done marvellously well that far, gaining a first innings lead, and getting near to the point at which they could declare and go for a win. In these circumstances it seemed unduly pessimistic of Allan Lamb and Derek Pringle to march off when the light was not too bad. The responsibility was the captain's, and he could not deflect the blame by pointing to the outcome: on the fifth day, Gordon Greenidge scored a remarkable double century as West Indies raced to a nine-wicket victory.

made explicit; at the fall of a wicket batsmen should, wherever possible, cross on the field of play. It is of course the captain's responsibility to ensure that they do so, just as on the field he must try to keep the tempo brisk.

Occasionally it is necessary to convey a message directly to the middle. The captain may have to whistle or clap his hands to attract the attention of the batsmen, especially when they are aware that a change in policy unwelcome to their personal interests is to be expected. At other times the batsmen themselves look up to the dressing-room for instructions. 'Are we still going for the target?' they may need to know. Or the umpires are debating about the light: 'Should we come off if they offer us the option, or stay on?' When umpires are debating about the light, the captain must always take responsibility for at least part of the decision. He must make it absolutely clear to the batsmen whether as a matter of policy he requires them to stay on or come off, or whether the decision rests with them and their personal confidence or lack of it. Clear signals are essential in all these cases.

The Botham grin during his century at Leeds, 1981.

Sometimes the captain can even convey a subtle message. In the Headingley Test in 1981 the pitch favoured the bowlers. Having allowed Australia to score 403–9, we lost wickets cheaply. Botham went in to bat, and started to play shots. He tried to force Lillee off the back foot and missed. He looked up to the players' balcony and saw me. I grinned broadly, and gestured that he should have tried to hit it even harder, thereby conveying, I hoped, my pleasure at his uninhibited approach and an unqualified approval of his continuing in an extravagant vein. Or a captain may wish to suggest to one batsman that he restrain or indeed unleash the other. It is worth having a signal that means that one batsman should talk to the other at once, for either purpose; the one I favoured was a rapid movement of thumb to and from fingers, like a glove-puppet.

All these broad gestures are necessarily public. If the plan calls for secrecy the time-honoured means of delivering it is with a batting-glove taken on to the field by the twelfth man. However, this ruse takes nobody in, especially when the batsman himself has to be informed by the fielders that the glove is on the way; and though they will not know the content of the note (unless he tells them) they know that it *is* a note, and will soon infer its import.

Not all such semaphore and note-carrying is about tactics, incidentally. Jack Simmons of Lancashire is more likely to be concerned that the twelfth man gets him a double portion of fish and chips for lunch. And notes may convey assignations, exam results, even the birth of a baby.

During the Adelaide Test of 1955, Hutton was alarmed to see Cowdrey play one or two reckless shots not long before lunch. So he sent out the twelfth man, Vic Wilson, with a message. In Hutton's words: 'To the surprise of all, Wilson in flannels and blazer walked calmly to the middle and, under the curious gaze of fielders and umpires, produced and offered two bananas to Colin. "What the hell are these for?" he demanded. Wilson replied: "Well, after seeing a couple of wild shots from you just now, the skipper thought you might be hungry. It rather suggests he is keen for you to stay out here batting and get your head down."'

In South Africa in 1965 I was acting as twelfth man while England batted in a Test at Johannesburg. Bob Barber and I happened to be in the middle of a chess game. When he called me on to the field during his innings, ostensibly for some dry gloves, his purpose was to inform me that his next move was Queen's pawn to QB4.

It was on this tour that I learned how differently players react to the stress of Test cricket. Barber affected a magnificent *belle indifférence*, while Barrington would be a picture of nervous tension as he waited to bat, face screwed up, smoking non-stop, watching each ball and talking to no one; until, at close of play, he would totally relax, play the big drum on a tin tray, and bubble with humour. The rest of the side come to respect such habits. When India are to bat, they all know not to talk to Sunil Gavaskar once he has put on his box. For the few minutes that remain Gavaskar likes to get himself into the right frame of mind without interruption.

The attitude of the team as a whole, and of influential individuals, can affect the way batsmen approach their task. In 1971, Middlesex scored only 76 in a forty-over match on a wet pitch at Northampton. At tea, Jim Stewart, who had recently joined the county from Warwickshire, was strapping on his pads ready to open the innings when he noticed that everyone was looking glum. 'What's the matter?' he asked. The reply came, 'Who's going to get these runs for us, then?' Northamptonshire were dismissed for 41 in 36 overs.

Bowlers enjoy seeing wickets casually tossed away by their own batsmen as much as rugby forwards who have battled into their opponents' '22' take pleasure in having to slog back to their own line as a result of fancy play by the backs. Randall once threw his wicket away after scoring a century against New South Wales; I remember how irate Willis was at this sheer waste, especially when Derek's only comment was that he was tired.

Gower's apparent laxity also irritated Willis in those days, almost as much as Tavaré's forward defensive stroke enraptured him. 'They need to be spoken to,' Bob used to say. We did speak to them about being more ruthless, about the chance, too, to learn to enlarge one's own range when totally relaxed with a large score to one's name. But too much caution can inhibit; people want it both ways, the solidity of a Tavaré combined with the elegant stroke-play of a Gower: which is like wishing a tortoise could jump like a gazelle.

Boycott was right to stress, as he often did in pre-Test team talks, how easily a side can slide from, say, 180–1 to 200–4. 'Always add two wickets on, and imagine how healthy the score looks then,' he would say. But the opposite attitude also needed stressing. West Indies batsman Seymour Nurse once exhorted me, 'If it's there, knock it, man.' And when Botham went into his shell after a couple of escapes from mishits and eventually played on to Bishen Bedi in the Lord's Test in 1979, Richards, who was watching, asked him why he had stopped trying to hit the ball, a point of view that Ian found immediately persuasive.

The New Zealand batsman Glenn Turner was one who utterly changed his own style of batting. When he first came to England at twenty-one his aim was, as he told me, to occupy the crease all day and continue the next. He came to realise that he could both enjoy his cricket more and offer the side more by playing strokes.

Cautionary advice can produce over-cautious batting. Even sensible remarks, like, 'Get forward on this pitch, because the ball is keeping low,' may be complied with so relentlessly that the bowler can feel confident that he will never be scored off if he bowls short. I am not advocating a casual or unthinking approach to batting. Players learn by experience – and sometimes by advice given at the right moment – when to take chances and when not to. This applies particularly to certain strokes, like hooking, sweeping and hitting over the top. A few players may play these strokes instinctively: they include some great batsmen and some very ordinary ones. But most need to *set* themselves to play the shot or set themselves not to.

Hooking fast bowlers as soon as one comes in is, for most, too risky, especially in a long match, for it is a stroke that cannot be played with complete control at any time, let alone before one has assessed the pace of bowler and pitch. Most players need to make a judgement about the likely value of the shot to them. On a bad pitch, for example, where they will find survival difficult, the hook shot may be well worth the risk. On a flat, easy pitch, however, with ample time to bat, such risk-taking may be foolish. Or again, a particular bowler may, with the new ball, be too fast for a batsman to hook with confidence; later on, when the ball is softer and the bowler tired, the batsman has the whip-hand. Similarly with sweeping: on an excellent pitch it would be folly to play the cross-batted sweep when runs can freely be had by driving; but on a 'turner', or a pitch where the ball does not 'come on' for the drive, the sweep may be the most effective, even the safest shot. Much of this can be assessed in the dressing-room: certainly the captain must be prepared, at times, to criticise batsmen for having failed to sum up the situation sensibly.

Such failure may stem from lack of confidence. For example, in 1978–9 Emburey, a capable lower middle-order batsman, got out a couple of times to the Australian leg-spinner, Jim Higgs, as a result of terrible cow-shots. The problem was that he felt that his defensive technique was not adequate to keep the leg-spinner out, and that he would prefer to go down with guns blazing. We were sure that he could, with practice, gain this confidence, and several nets against Barrington's leg-breaks enabled him to do so. In his next Test innings he made an invaluable, career-best 41.

Again, the captain is not alone in being responsible for constructive suggestions; but he should look out for shortcomings in the team – and for methods of rectifying them. Sometimes batsmen need to practise one particular stroke. If a man has lost confidence against fast, short-pitched bowling, he may regain it by having someone throw short balls at him from halfway down the pitch and by setting himself to stand up and play them defensively or let them go by, swaying to one side or the other. By this means, he can sharpen both reflexes and technique without risk of injury.

I always admired Knott's professionalism, part of which was a willingness to carry through a policy that he thought likely to be productive for him, regardless of whether its unorthodoxy could elicit ridicule. Like Edrich and Turner, he realised that he had a better chance of playing a steeply lifting delivery with a defensive bat if he changed his grip so that he had his top hand behind the handle of the bat, rather than mainly in front of it as in the orthodox way. It is a physiological fact that the unorthodox method enables a batsman to lift his hands in front of his face while keeping the bat straight. He also reckoned that, when he first came in, his best chance was not to aim to play forcing shots at all but to stand square-on and let everything go that would miss the stumps (and him). His grip, stance and technique were totally different from that which he adopted against medium-pacers or spinners. On the England tour in 1976–7, we flew from India and Sri Lanka to Perth in Western Australia. Apart from jet-lag and culture-shock, we also experienced cricket-shock, for the conditions could hardly have been more different. Knott's batting practice, in the first few days, consisted simply in having short balls thrown to him, and rediscovering his method against speed.

Now Knott is a cricketer who made idiosyncratic use of all his talents. The team, considered as an individual, should do the same, making use of its talents in the most appropriate ways possible. Why, then, are most first-class captains so loth to be flexible about the batting-order? No good captain sticks rigidly to a routine when it comes to the order in which he uses his bowlers; yet, apart from the strange institution of night-watchman (to which I will return), day after day batsmen follow each other in the same automatic succession. Why?

One reason for conservatism is that the players do not, on the whole, like the order to be fluid. To continue the metaphor, they do not wish to float or, for that matter, to sink. Part of the resistance derives from whim or superstition. 'I never get runs at Number Five, only at Four or Six.' So people think themselves out of success. Another part stems from the fact that most of us like to know 'where we are'; we become, for example, less anxious when we have found our seat on a plane, and less anxious still when we have sat in it for a while and taken in our surroundings. Batsmen get used to a certain routine, and when this is changed they feel, as Ranji put it, 'like fish out of water'. At Number Five, you relax while the openers are together; when one wicket falls, you may take the first steps towards getting dressed for batting; but when the second wicket goes down then *your* period of expectancy begins and, according to your style, you screw yourself up, or start to watch, or consciously relax; in short, you prepare for batting in your particular way. If you are unsure that you will be next; if the captain has two or three players padded up at the same time, any of whom may get his nod, this rather exhausting period of waiting becomes extended.

Moreover, whenever the captain changes the order he implies a shortcoming in the man 'demoted', especially if both players are specialist batsmen. At Middlesex, we agreed that as professionals we should be sufficiently flexible to be able to play according to the needs of the side; as a rule, for of course no one would grumble at changes in exceptional circumstances. Players also feel that it is fairer to keep to an original order; that changes often require someone to go in to take risks for quick runs, or to 'hold the fort' when conditions are difficult. They prefer to take the smooth with the rough.

Sometimes a captain's designs in 'promoting' a player are forestalled by that player's attitude. He may be perverse; or he may abandon the style that has been so productive at, say, Number Eight in favour of a more dignified (and less authentic) mode of play which he feels suits his image of a Number Four. Knott himself recognised that his idiosyncrasy was permitted partly because batting was for him a second string. Coming in at Number Seven, his cheeky chips over mid-wicket off a slow-left-arm bowler on a turning pitch are not greeted with howls of protest if they get him out as they would be in a 'proper' batsman. Hitters sometimes get the idea that steady accumulation of runs brings more success in the long run; but in their attempts to ape the 'grafter' they look as uncomfortable as a navvy in a dress suit.

In the World Cup in 1983, the West Indies, in the matches leading to the final, had normally played Larry Gomes at Number Four, between Richards and Clive Lloyd. Richards, with 334 runs and Gomes with 251, had scored heavily, while Lloyd, with fewer chances, had totalled only 104 runs. Gomes, moreover, was an ideal foil to Richards, quick as a whippet between the wickets and happy to give his partner most of the strike. In the final, when West Indies needed only 184 to beat India, Lloyd came in ahead of Gomes. It was hard to avoid the conclusion that he desperately wanted to have a chance of a score himself on what he, and everyone else, believed would be a serene third triumph. The result was quite different: Lloyd was out for 8, Gomes for 5, and West Indies lost by 43 runs.

India themselves had come close to a historic win four years before when I set them 438 to win in eight hours at the Oval. Thanks to a wonderful innings of 221 by Gavaskar, they needed only 110 in the last 20 overs, with nine wickets left. When we at last took a wicket, Viswanath, who was a difficult player to contain and who was in excellent form, was kept back, behind Kapil Dev and Yashpal Sharma. One after another their batsmen made mistakes, and the match finished thrillingly with India nine runs short with two wickets in hand. It was not merely second-guessing that made me think the change in their order had been a mistake.

However, I did mention the special circumstances that fully justify a fluid batting order. It is far more likely to be good tactics in one-day cricket, where a few blows can transform a match. Moreover, in a short match there is more of a case for keeping two stodgy batsmen apart, as many felt that I should have done in the World Cup Final in 1979. In fact, we did adopt this policy the following winter in Australia, where either Gooch or Randall went in first with Boycott, and both Peter Willey and I were prepared to bat at Number Three. The plan was that if Boycott was out in the early stages I would go in; if his partner, Willey would be Number Three.

During that tour, Botham was Number Six in the Tests, unless he was still tired from bowling. In the first innings, at Perth, he had bowled 35 overs, taking six for 78. When in reply we slumped to 41 for four, this was a situation which demanded that I should go in ahead of him, in the hope that he could have a little more rest. In the event, the respite was brief, and his stay at the crease even briefer.

I felt sorry for Hadlee who found himself in a similar situation at the Oval in 1983. Having taken six wickets for 53 to dismiss England on the first day, he was forced to come to the crease himself early next morning with the score 41 for five. He scored a magnificent 84: but hardly had time to change before he was racing in again with the new ball.

One almost sacred rite in cricket is the appearance of the night-watchman, though on occasions he must feel more sacrificial than sacred. In 1976 MCC played their traditional fixture against the tourists at Lord's. West Indies batted first and scored a modest 275. I think that the bowling I faced in the last hour that evening was the quickest I ever experienced. Michael Holding and Andy Roberts bowled flat out, on a pitch fortunately without much pace. At ten past six, Amiss was hit on the back of the head by a ball from Holding. He was helped off. I wondered who would replace him. Apparently the most likely candidate for night-watchman (Pat Pocock) had prudently found reason to leave the dressing-room; the man selected by captain Richard Gilliat was Phil Carrick of Yorkshire. As he approached the bloodied crease he looked pale. I remembered the line from *Beyond the Fringe*, and greeted him with: 'The time has come, Perkins, for a useless sacrifice.' Carrick was not, at that moment, in the mood for witty repartee, but has ever since called me 'Perkins' whenever we meet. Somehow he survived, physically and technically, until close of play.

Night-watchmen are usually on duty for the last twenty minutes of a day, though sometimes only for ten. Middlesex once had a lunch-watchman, though that was before my time as captain. The ritualistic element is reflected in the fact that it is almost unheard-of for a night-watchman to go in to protect an opener, even if there is time for only one over, which one watchman could arrange to face. I suppose openers regard it as part of the job; perhaps they are felt to be happier going in at once than having to wait in the dressing-room with pads on. Yet the convention applies even when the opener himself is makeshift, or has only just moved there from the middle order.

There is one drawback to this practice, a drawback which to my mind almost always rules out the use of *two* watchmen, if two wickets fall in the last few minutes; if they bat at Numbers Three and Four, say, specialist batsmen move down two places, so that there are two less bulwarks against a batsman being left high and dry, without reliable partners, later in the innings.

This picture of a team 'at bat', as the Americans say, will have shown, I hope, how the captain's focus shifts between the tactical and the personal; between monitoring the progress on the field and keeping an eye on the morale off it. Apart from rare, and brief, excursions into semaphore, his activity is off-stage and non-public. He has, however, just one other opportunity for his moment of drama: the declaration.

A captain's approach to declarations must vary according to the status of the match. In league cricket, a defeat has much the same impact on a team's final position as a draw, except when the opponents are close rivals. In the county championship, for example, each team is in the long run competing against sixteen other sides, not against one. Test series are, by contrast, one-to-one contests in which the aim is to win overall; so a single defeat may be more damaging. To my mind, this difference justifies a difference in declaration – and run-chasing – policy. A captain should be far more willing to take a risk in the average county match than in a Test.

In 1968, Gary Sobers made a game of the fourth Test in Trinidad after the first three had been drawn. The scores so far in the match had been massive – West Indies 526 for seven dec., England 414. Sobers's declaration left England 165 minutes or, as it turned out, 54 overs, to score the 215 needed, and he had only himself to bowl above medium

Iqbal Qasim, night-watchman for Pakistan at Birmingham, 1978, hit in the mouth by a bouncer from Bob Willis. Graham Roope and Ian Botham look on, while Phil Edmonds picks up the ball. The Pakistan team manager described our tactics as 'unfair'. The TCCB 'bitterly regretted' the incident, and 'reminded Brearley of his responsibilities'. They also encouraged captains to exchange lists of non-recognised batsmen. I thought that the fuss was out of all proportion and the exchange of lists a farce.

LEFT Derek Underwood displays his famous jumping duck shot against Michael Holding, Old Trafford, 1976. This was the game in which West Indies descended to ferocious intimidation, especially against John Edrich and Brian Close on the evening of the third day. Even Clive Lloyd admitted that 'our fellows got carried away', but he himself did nothing to stop them. Underwood was a plucky batsman who frequently endured punishment as night-watchman for England. Here, however, he was batting at his normal position, Number Nine, and failed to score in either innings.
RIGHT Close during the onslaught.

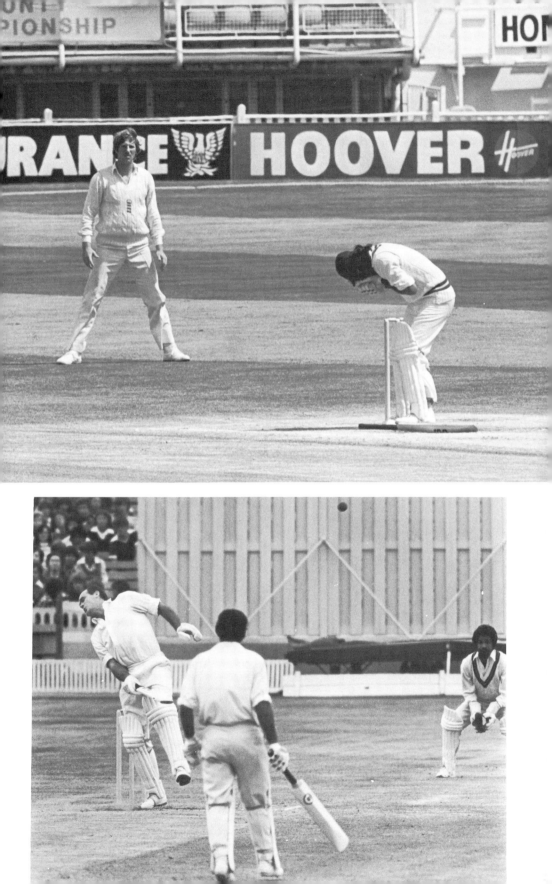

pace as Charlie Griffith had been injured early in the match. Had I been a disinterested member of the public I would no doubt have welcomed this injection of life into a dying game. As a member of his side, or a West Indian partisan, I would have felt differently. Though it may seem churlish to criticise such generosity, I do think he was wrong, for he gave England a far better chance of winning a game than West Indies themselves had; for the target was so low, and the time available for taking wickets so short, that on that pitch the side batting last would have had little difficulty in surviving for a draw whenever they might choose to do so. England were not handed the series on a plate; Cowdrey and Boycott batted well for them to win the match by seven wickets with eight balls to spare. But the odds were against them losing; and the outcome clinched the series.

There are exceptions, of course. Once a series is won a captain can afford to be magnanimous, and treat each Test in isolation. Or in a cricketing showpiece, like the Centenary Tests, where nothing is at stake except the pride involved in a single match, captains should not allow caution to rule their approach.

In the Centenary Test in Melbourne, I thought Chappell was unnecessarily ruthless in allowing Rick McCosker, his face ballooned and mummified beyond recognition because of a broken jaw, to bat at Number Ten in the second innings: I felt their lead – 396 with Max Walker still to come in – was already adequate. How wrong I was! McCosker's 83-ball stay enabled Rod Marsh to reach his century and Australia to set us 463 runs to win. Thanks to Randall's wonderful innings, by tea on the last day we needed just 110 with five wickets in hand. At that stage we were unlikely to win and if we kept going for the runs all the way down the order we would undoubtedly enhance Australia's chance of winning. Yet my advice to Tony Greig was to forget about trying to save the match. We had recovered our pride: the game was already a jewel in the crown of Test cricket. What would it matter if we lost? And to win, by reaching such a target on such an occasion, would thrill generations of cricket-lovers. Even the Aussies would only half-begrudge us such a victory.

I would give the same advice again, despite the outcome. Similarly, I believe England were wrong in *not* going for the target of 370 in 350 minutes in the 'Return' Centenary match. But my advice would have been different had either game been the first in a series.

In matches scheduled for two or more days, most declarations occur before the stage of a challenge to score so many runs in so much time to win. They are part of the jockeying for position early in a race. And although they do not call for such nicety of judgement and prediction as in the timing of a burst at the bell, these early-match declarations can make or mar a game.

Let us consider the side batting first in a three-day match. What factors will influence their decision to declare – or not to – before close of play on the first day? As a rule, and assuming fine weather, the captain will hope, or expect, his batsmen to have made this feasible. For if they bat the whole day one third of the time allotted has been used up in transacting one quarter of the business; whereas a declaration, say, fifty minutes before close of play both gets the game under way and offers his bowlers two bites of the cherry. No batsman really likes the prospect of twenty, fifty or sixty minutes' batting late in the day, against bowlers who are fresh.

There are exceptions. Sometimes the side batting first has failed, simply, to score enough runs. A premature declaration might tempt the opponents to go for a massive lead which would, if it were achieved, leave only one side with any chance of a win. There may, though, be a more positive, more enviable reason for batting on. The captain may be confident that his bowlers will be able to bowl the other side out twice cheaply, so that the primary task is to score as many runs as possible in the first innings. To this end, he may continue the innings into the second day. Such action makes most sense when carried out by a strong bowling side on a deteriorating pitch. In 1982, Middlesex adopted these tactics twice in two weeks against a Nottinghamshire team much weakened by injuries, and won both matches by an innings. Such measures require a high percentage of successful outcomes if a captain is not to get a bad name on the circuit. The question he must ask himself is, 'Do I back us to dismiss them twice for not many more than we amassed in a day and a bit?'

A similar problem may face the captain of the team batting second – let's call them Zshire. At some stage on the second day, Zshire's score is approaching Xshire's. Z's captain has three options:

A: to declare behind or level with X and hope for a fair declaration;

B: to tell his batsmen that he wants a big lead, and hope to win by an innings; or

C: to play it both ways; that is, to aim for a moderate lead, large enough to be useful if X are dismissed cheaply, but not too large to preclude a declaration if X bat well.

Option C is the each-way bet.

In choosing, the captain will have to make various assessments. Will the pitch assist his bowlers enough for them to have a reasonable chance of dismissing X cheaply? (Or again, are X so weak in batting as to make this likely?) Does he have confidence in his remaining batsmen to score the runs he requires, and at a good enough rate? If he decides on course B the last thing he wants is for his batsmen to scratch around, wasting time. Another consideration may be the character of X's captain; is *he* prepared to take risks? Do the two captains share a positive attitude, or are there grudges between them or their teams that would make Z's taking course A pointless?

Every captain will at one time or other adopt each method, though each man will by his nature veer one way rather than another. I took course A against Somerset in 1980, when we declared at 300 for five, one run behind. I could not be sure that we would gain a substantial lead, the pitch was easy enough to make it unlikely that we would bowl Somerset out and time was short. As it happened, we *did* dismiss them cheaply, for 128, and knocked off the runs for the loss of two wickets.

Course A is often dictated by rain. At Lord's in 1982, Derbyshire batted until lunch on the second day before declaring at 228 for nine, after three hours had been lost on the first. Conscious of our opponents' traditional caution, I decided that our best chance of points on this slow pitch lay in declaring a long way behind. Then Derbyshire would be able to set us a long run-chase on the last day. (It is an irrational fact that many sides are prepared to set 330 runs in 300 minutes when they would hesitate to set 270 in 200 minutes.) So I declared at 89–0, 139 runs behind. In the event, their declaration was none too generous; we were asked to score 348 runs in 247 minutes. Nevertheless, we ended only eight runs short, despite losing two crucial overs because of rain, with one wicket left.

Whenever possible I chose option B, aiming at an impregnable lead and trusting our bowlers to win the match. A championship-winning team will win most of their matches by bowling sides out twice, not by relying on declarations.

In some circumstances the tactics are obvious. When we had bowled India out for 96 in the Lord's Test in 1979, no captain in our position would have had any doubt about tactics – to make a big score in the first innings. If the team bat well, the only question will be the exact timing of the declaration. One of my guidelines here was never to leave it so late that, if the opposition scored in their second innings at their slowest, they would still not have come level with us by the end of the last day. For there is no point in having a stack of runs in hand if you still lack the odd wicket. Other factors will be fear of rain, a slow rate of scoring by your own batsmen or the chance of bowling at a time that suits and encourages your own bowlers – for example, during the last hour of a day.

More difficult was my decision to bat on against Kent at Tunbridge Wells in 1982. Kent had been all out for 276. Thanks to a brilliant century from Gatting, we passed their score with only three wickets down. My policy then was to go for a lead of 200 or more. However, Gatting was unluckily run out and our middle order found runs hard to come by. I was in a quandary: should I take course C and declare, say, 80 runs ahead, at a time when Kent could be level with us at close of play? Or should we soldier on – B – and count on bowling them out on the last day? With some misgivings I opted for the latter course. We continued batting for an hour on the third day before declaring at 438–9. To my relief and surprise, everything went our way, and we bowled Kent out for 90 in only 30.5 overs.

Sometimes I took course C. At Basingstoke in 1981, we led Hampshire by 111 runs at tea on the second day, with four wickets still in hand. This was, I felt, the latest moment for a declaration that would allow Hampshire in turn to declare should they bat well in their second innings. Had we gone on beyond tea we should have had only one chance of winning: to bowl them out. Besides, our tail could easily have crumbled ineffectually. As it happened, rain intervened: we dropped some catches, and Hampshire hung on for a draw.

In 1980, the playing conditions for first-class cricket were altered to allow discussion between captains over declarations: a good move, I think, for it did away with the nudge-and-wink methods that had from time to time obtained. The change permitted a frankness that could only benefit the game. My first experience of such collusion arose in a match against Warwickshire at Edgbaston, a match which had been spoiled by rain on each of the three days. We had scored 301–9 declared. On the rain-affected pitch, we had reduced Warwickshire to 136–7 on the last afternoon; but time was getting short. If we could have taken the last three wickets cheaply we could have enforced the follow-on, but we would then have had little more than two hours in which to bowl them out. Our better chance was to invite Willis to declare; to forfeit our second innings; and hope to take advantage of the risks they would have to take in chasing a lowish target on a drying pitch. I went off the field to negotiate with Bob. After some brisk horse-trading – in which I agreed to give up our remote chance of victory via a follow-on, and he agreed to keep attacking provided that we bowled mainly spin – we struck our bargain. Willis declared, we forfeited, we cancelled the tea interval, and Warwickshire needed 166 to win. The result of all this endeavour was a draw; they finished on 76–7. But it was a better contest than would have occurred without negotiating when both sides would have pressed on, each hoping primarily for one more bonus point. With the scoring system currently in effect in the county championship (in which sixteen points are gained for a win, plus a maximum of eight bonus points for runs scored and wickets taken in the first two innings of the match) the chance of winning should be sixteen times more remote than the chance of gaining another bonus point for it to be logical to opt for the latter.

My most satisfying first-innings declaration came against Surrey at Lord's in 1977. Only eight overs' play had been possible during the first two days, and Surrey's score was 20–1. On the last day, our seamers found the damp, green pitch to their liking. The ball deviated alarmingly; all went well, and we dismissed Surrey for only 49. As their wickets fell it gradually dawned on us that an outright win was on the cards, despite the eleven and a half hours lost to rain. It was, I think, Clive Radley who suggested that we forfeit our first innings to force Surrey to bat again while the pitch was still damp. None of us knew whether forfeiting was permitted by the laws of cricket, so I sent a message asking this question to Donald Carr, Secretary of the Test and County Cricket Board, whose office is at Lord's. The reply came that a side could not forfeit its first innings, only its second. (No one knew why: this law was subsequently changed, thanks to our attempt.) So we had to bat for one ball (which meant a waste of eleven minutes). Our fortune (and skill) continued. We not only bowled them out again for 87, but Geoff Arnold, their most dangerous bowler, was hit on the foot by a yorker and unable to bowl. The final scores of this dramatic match were: Surrey 49 and 87, Middlesex 0–0 dec and 137–1. If only things always worked out like that!

The exact timing of a declaration is tricky and inevitably involves guesswork. An additional anxiety for the captain can be a conflict between the team's interest and that of an individual batsman. In 1981, we believed that Kim Hughes delayed his declaration in the Oval Test while Dirk Wellham was stuck on 99 for twenty-five minutes. Kim was in an impossible dilemma. It was Wellham's first Test: yet our openers were dreading the prospect of thirty to forty minutes' batting before close of play. Australia's opportunity slipped away. By the time Wellham scored his elusive run the light had deteriorated so sharply that it would have been pointless for Hughes to declare, as we would not have had to face a ball.

How should a captain deal with such situations? The routine method is to convey to the batsman that he intends to declare by a certain time at the latest; so the batsman has, say, fifteen minutes to score the few runs he needs for a century. I did once declare (at Worcester in 1974) when Radley was 96 not out, but he was not unhappy about it, as I had warned him. And in 1982 Gatting and Butcher got out for 192 and 197 respectively, at a time in their careers when neither had scored a double century, largely because they knew we needed quick runs pending a declaration.

But should the interests of an individual ever take precedence over the needs of the team? It might seem that sentiment is out of place in a hard, professional game. Well, no one can specify within a few minutes precisely the right time for a declaration, and illogical as it may appear it is a fact that a century can transform a young player's confidence and hence his contribution thereafter. Nevertheless, most of us already err on the side of caution; fielding is hard work (so postponements are tempting); and we enjoy watching our batsmen demolish the bowling. Applying the closure (in the quaint 'Strine phrase) spoils the fun. So any further delay while everyone waits for a batsman to reach some wretched milestone can ruin a match as well as infuriate the fielding side. And, on the other side of the fence, it went against my grain as captain of the fielding side kept waiting for this purpose to smooth the path to a century, however much we resented the time wasted. Yet I imagine that even the Warwickshire fielders must in 1983 have felt for young Neil Fairbrother of Lancashire, who had reached 94 not out in his maiden first-class innings, when acting captain John Abrahams declared. Lancashire were 140 runs behind, it was tea-time on the second day: but an agreement had been struck between the captains, and Abrahams was as good, and hard, as his word.

Most cricket matches are scheduled for one innings a side, so captains do not have to concern themselves with the problems of when to declare in other than the penultimate innings. Indeed, the proliferation of limited-overs cricket means that the whole art of declaration has been removed from the repertoire of many captains. This is a sad limitation – though I acknowledge that many a match has been ruined by ultra-defensive declarations. Before moving on to the area that overlaps school or club cricket and first-class cricket (namely, setting a target) I should mention an unworthy episode in the history of declarations: Somerset's against Worcester in a Benson and Hedges qualifying match in 1980.

The logic of Somerset's captain, Brian Rose, was impeccable: they would qualify for the quarter-finals of the competition even if they lost at Worcester, provided that their wicket-taking rate did not decline unduly. To rule out this remote possibility Rose declared at 1 for no wicket, a score which Worcestershire overhauled in ten balls. The entire match lasted twenty minutes. This action turned the game into a charade, and was an insult to spectators and followers. It was within the letter but not the spirit of the laws; and the TCCB acted swiftly by disqualifying Somerset and altering the rules by prohibiting all declarations in limited-overs cricket. My only regret about this new rule is that it precludes a bold stroke of captaincy, whereby a team could sacrifice some of its overs in exchange for the opportunity to bowl in favourable conditions.

Such a scenario would be rarely, if not never, employed; but ruling it out of court does constitute a minor impoverishment of the game. And it has an analogue within traditional cricket – or had one when uncovered pitches meant that rain was always an element to be reckoned with. One dramatic example was the Brisbane Test of 1950. England's bowlers had done well to dismiss Australia for 228, only for our batsmen to be trapped on a 'sticky-dog' after a thunderstorm. (Australian sticky wickets were more lethal, on the whole, than the English variety, as the former started harder and would usually be dried by a fiercer sun.) Extreme conditions call for extreme responses: first F.R.Brown then Lindsay Hassett declared (at 68–7 and 32–7 respectively), both hoping to force their opponents to bat in impossibly difficult conditions. In their second innings, England had sixty-eight minutes remaining before close of play. Next day, the pitch would certainly be easier. So Brown held Hutton and Compton back. I have never forgotten my chagrin, at the age of nine, at hearing over a scratchy radio the commentator's description of Arthur McIntyre's incongruous run-out as he went for a fourth run. What a waste! The result was that Hutton had to go in that evening, with the score 30 for six; and ran out of partners next day when his glorious 62 not out could not prevent an Australian victory by 70 runs.

Such opportunities for the dramatic and unconventional declaration are rare, but they appeal to our imagination. The majority occur in more

Brisbane, 1950. Captains Lindsay Hassett and Freddie Brown inspecting the pitch. This was one of the most dramatic of Tests, with England declaring at 68–7 and Australia at 32–7 on the sticky wicket. Brown's tactic of saving Len Hutton until the pitch became easier – he went in at Number Six and Number Eight – failed because no one could stay with him. Hutton was undefeated in the match, with 8 not out and 62 not out, but England lost by 70 runs. E. W. Swanton reported that 'the friendship existing between the captains was reflected throughout their teams which fraternised in a way not known since before the Bodyline series. "Fergie", the Australian baggage-master to every MCC and Australia side since 1905, thought that this was the easiest and most contented side with which he had ever travelled.'

humdrum situations, when a captain curtails the penultimate innings of the match in the hope of ultimate success. The most straightforward case occurs when he is convinced that his opponents cannot reach the target, but wishes to allow his own side time to dismiss them. Such calculations may, of course, be shaken by events: Chappell (Centenary Test) and I (in the last Test against India in 1979) had our confidence in a favourable outcome rudely shattered by Randall and Gavaskar respectively. (Perhaps I should have paid more attention to Sunil's remark, when he came for a meal at my flat a few days before this Test. I asked him if there were anything he planned to do in London, before going home to Bombay. I was thinking of shopping, or St Paul's Cathedral. 'Yes,' he replied, 'there's one thing I came here for but haven't yet got. A century.' He acquired two at the Oval.)

On other occasions a captain courts defeat in his search for a win. He tempts the opposition, hoping that their wickets will tumble as they take the risks that the required run-rate will involve. On a tricky pitch he may be willing to offer a relatively low target, as in August 1982, when we set Surrey 161 to win in 135 minutes. This sounds, on the face of it, over-generous. In fact, the pitch was so suited to our spinners of whom, thanks to the remarkable coincidence of Titmus's social visit on the first morning of the match, we had three, that the declaration gave an equal chance to both sides.

There was another factor, too, in that declaration. At the time we were neck-and-neck with Leicestershire for the Championship, and needed the points more desperately than Surrey. Degree of desperation, as in other transactions, governs the concessions that one party will be prepared to make and the other demand: in a similar situation a year later Gatting was forced to set Northamptonshire, with their strong batting line-up, a target of 275 in 250 minutes on a friendly pitch, a bargain necessarily tilted in favour of Northants, who ended up comfortable winners.

In general, the easier the pitch the harder will be the task set. Invariably that also means that the run-chase will have to be over a longer period, so that the team fielding last have some scope for a concerted attack against the tail if the batting side lose wickets and give up the chase. Occasionally it will be necessary to keep the latter interested by not being too rigorously defensive. Personally, I hate actually *giving* runs away, and cannot abide pusillanimous captains who must always make the game safe for themselves before ostentatiously 'feeding' runs. I prefer a more realistic initial declaration, and a more subtle balancing of the equation between time, runs and wickets.

I also admire captains when they time their declarations on a different presumption. Instead of attempting to lure their opponents to defeat by errors of recklessness they prefer, in some conditions, to set a target which does not require an out-and-out assault. In Ray Illingworth's early days as captain of Leicestershire, his team-mates were astonished on two occasions when he called the batsmen in at least half an hour earlier than they expected. Illingworth's argument, in each case borne out by the result, was that he himself, and the other spinners, would be more likely to keep control *and* take wickets if the batsmen had at least half an eye on defence.

Similar reasoning may at other times lead to an opposite conclusion. On the same premise – that it is preferable to bowl against a side committed to defence than to all-out attack – the captain may decide to delay the declaration until such time that the side batting last has no option but to play for a draw. Then, too, the bowlers can keep close catchers in throughout. Brian Close followed this line in the match between Somerset and Middlesex in 1971, when he set a steep target. Somerset won the match by 98 runs.

Tom Cartwright always forcibly advocated this policy. He was our main bowler for the MCC team playing East Africa in a three-day game at Nairobi in 1974. I was toying with the idea of a declaration that would have left East Africa around 300 runs in five hours. Cartwright was scathing. 'Do you want us to be worn ragged and utterly frazzled by mid-afternoon?' he demanded. I waited a bit longer, until East Africa could only play for a draw. Cartwright kept his attacking field, and took five for 30. We won by 237 runs.

The timing of a declaration should also be influenced by the speed of scoring in the rest of the match. If the run-rate has never exceeded 2 runs an over in the first three innings it seems, in general, absurd to set a target of 6 runs an over in the fourth. When Middlesex played Yorkshire at Headingley in 1971, runs were always hard to come by on a saturated pitch, and I set Yorkshire 215 to win in three hours, a target that would amount to less than 4 runs an over. The pitch had become easier than I thought; Boycott scored a superb century, we dropped a crucial catch when Yorkshire were 71–2 and we lost by eight wickets with almost six overs to spare. Boycott had tears in his eyes as he thanked me for the game. 'If ever we have a chance to make a game of it with you, Mike, we will.' In the next ten years, Yorkshire never risked anything in a declaration against us.

It will by now be clear that a captain must take many factors into consideration in his decisions on declarations, among them:

the relative strengths of *his* bowlers and *their* batsmen;
the time available;
the nature of the pitch;
the styles and attitudes of his bowlers;
the degree of risk that the competition, and his team's standing in it, permit.

In order to make his assessment, he needs to take advantage of all possible sources of information: in particular, his own assessment of the pitch and the reports from his representatives at the front – his batsmen. Illingworth records that one of his openers at Leicester, Micky Norman, was especially reliable as a judge of how many runs a one-day pitch would yield, so Illy made a point of consulting him as soon as he was out. The same use should be made of such experience in deciding a declaration. Sometimes, of course, everyone is taken by surprise. In the World Cup Final in 1983, I went to the Indian dressing-room when their score was 180–9. I asked Gavaskar, quietly, what his feelings about the match were. 'We would have liked 280,' he said. Three hours later, West Indies were all out for 140.

Gavaskar's assessment was, I thought, right. His judgement was less sound in 1985 when captaining India against England at Calcutta. In this match he failed to declare the first innings of the match until after lunch on the fourth day – one day having been lost because of rain. India's score was 438–7; by that time Edmonds was reading a newspaper at square-leg, Gower was bowling, and the crowd were getting so restive that, according to a report, the obdurate Gavaskar called his batsmen in only when the chief of police told him that there would be a riot if India batted any longer. The report was later denied; but the crowd had a right to be incensed, as Gavaskar's high-handed and quixotic attitude was an insult to them.

Other captains have also had personal though inoffensive reasons for declaring when they did. W. G. declared once when his own score stood at 93; it was the only figure between 0 and 100 that he had not previously tallied.

One final point. In order to gain all the evidence he needs a captain must watch the play. Tony Greig was a captain I admired; yet he rarely watched the cricket when his team were batting. By contrast, I watched almost compulsively, finding it hard to tear myself away. One result was that my mood could swing too much with our fortunes, sometimes perhaps in a way that was unhelpful to ingoing batsmen! But I do believe that Greig captained well in spite of, rather than because of, his ability to switch off from the game in the dressing-room. It is, as Ranjitsinhji says, a captain's duty to 'identify himself entirely with the whole play of his side'.

CHAPTER SEVEN

Taking the field

The art of captaincy culminates in the team fielding. Seeds sown in the depths of winter, stirring in the April nets, come to fruition – or fail to – when the team takes the field. Plans outlined months before, elaborated in the days and hours leading up to the match, are put to the test. Earlier, the captain's duties have been continuous, but scattered and diverse. Now he must concentrate and be in charge every moment.

While there is no limit to the possibilities of tactical subtlety, bluff and motivation when the team is in the field, this is where, too, a captain's most basic tasks lie. He has to get the team on to the field to start with. Once there, he must convey his instructions to them. Third, he influences, by his example and expectations, the tempo of the game: he must see that it does not flag. Finally, he must think, at least minimally, ahead.

Captains reveal shortcomings in all these areas. I used to have problems in persuading the players to leave the dressing-room at roughly the same time, and to make a disciplined entrance on to the field as a unit rather than spread out, untidily, like dots in a morse message. There are some players who will always find an excuse for delay. One has forgotten to put a ticket on the gate for bank-manager or girlfriend and is hurriedly scribbling a note for the twelfth man to deliver to the offended party. Another decides to change his boots at the last minute. Several peel off for nervous or precautionary visits to the toilets (where – at Lord's and on many grounds – they may have to join a queue of members if it is a big match). Urgent telephone calls arrive. Commoner is plain procrastination, born of anxiety or perversity. Even superstition plays a part: Viv Richards likes to leave the pavilion last – except when he is captaining the side himself.

My successor at Middlesex, Mike Gatting, had in this area a greater impact than I; attributable, I observed, to sheer volume of vocal and mechanical arousal from the dressing-room door. I would sometimes make a point of waiting for stragglers by the pavilion exit, but that was unduly fussy if repeated too often.

Eventually, however, the team makes it to the middle, even if the last two dash out after the batsmen. The captain's second basic task is to be able to move his fielders wherever he wants. This often involves arm-waving signals. I remember a captain at the club where my father played when I was a boy whose podgy hand, flapping like a pigeon's wing, meant, to the distant fielder, that he was to move smartly to the left or to the right, closer or deeper. But it was never clear which. A loud voice helps, but can achieve little against 60,000 baying Australians, for example; and a captain may have to soldier on with laryngitis. For these reasons, and others, the captain must instil in his players the discipline of looking at him several times an over; and he must respond with clear gestures.

Regular eye-contact has other advantages. The captain can move a player without overt gesticulation; he can easily suggest a ploy – I remember sensing from time to time that Greg Chappell was becoming edgy about being kept quiet and might try one of his characteristic methods of breaking free – a quick single between cover and mid-off – and I could intimate all this to Gower or Randall at cover, moving them a yard to their right in the process, simply by a look and a minute head-gesture. Again, constant eye-contact keeps the players alert; they know you know whether they are on the ball. Glares of disapproval like glances of praise or shared delight can be condensed into momentary looks, not brandished for all to see. In a well-trained side, the captain can also, by a gesture, convey advice or instruction by means of an intermediary; from first slip I would often let mid-off know that he should talk to the bowler.

The aim is to keep in close touch with the fielders; the captain will find this easier to achieve if he himself has a regular fielding position. Many choose mid-off; a place which offers ready contact with the bowler and a natural chance, between overs, to talk to the wicket-keeper and slips as everyone changes end. It is also a good place for a synoptic view of the game. If you can catch, first slip is perhaps even more ideal, as you have a view of the movement of the ball, and are well-placed to sense the pace a bowler is generating from the pitch. It is not, however, advisable to try to watch the bowler's technique, especially in his follow-through, from first slip.

Having said that the team likes to know where to find the captain in the field, I will now say that it *may* be helpful to switch. I would sometimes move out from slip, maybe for a rest from that kind of concentration, perhaps to talk to the bowler between balls. I have even, for a time, moved from slip in case the sight of me there with my supposed critical attitude was putting the bowler off.

I have been told of theatre directors who have never mastered the fundamental requirement of timing and organising the actors' entrances

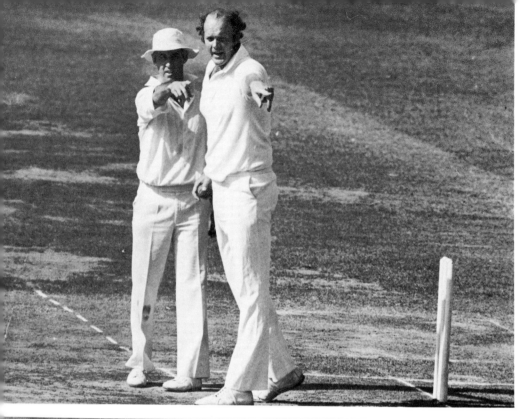

The captain needs to use clear signals and gestures. Sometimes, ABOVE, he and the bowler have the same idea, sometimes, LEFT, they don't. The author with Vintcent van der Bijl during the Gillette Cup final, 1980.

in such a way that they can be seen by the audience when they start to speak. Some captains never give their fielder-actors the chance to play their roles adequately.

The third basic rule is to keep the tempo of the game going. Hutton is alleged to have been the first to slow down the over-rate for tactical reasons – to give his fast bowlers extra breathing-space. The steady decline in over-rates since his day has not, however, been primarily tactical. Rather, a certain tempo has become habitual. I remember in 1965 being appalled and embarrassed when England under M.J.K. Smith bowled only 29 overs in a two-hour session in the Port Elizabeth Test. Yet twenty years later, at Calcutta, adverse comments about slow play on the fourth morning were restricted to criticism of the Indian batsmen; the fact that they received only 26 overs – half of them from spinners – in the two hours seemed hardly worthy of comment.

Captains have some responsibility for this. Interminable consultations with bowlers and ponderous returns to position are very dreary. Time-wasting is deplorable, though we have all been guilty on occasions. A good captain will expect a liveliness of step in line with a positive and, whenever possible, attacking approach.

That is not to say that he should allow himself to be rushed into decisions. Home crowds harry the visiting captain, and at times he has the right to be deliberate.

In the mid-'70s, when fines were introduced to penalise teams whose over-rate slipped below some stipulated level – rough justice, often, but it had an effect – Yorkshire introduced the practice of running between overs. Other sides viewed this unseemly haste with incredulity; but within

I found first slip the best place from which to captain the team. The problem is, catching them. My best series at slip was 1976–7, in India and Australia, before I became captain. Total concentration on the ball is easier when you aren't anxious about tactics or at odds with an awkward member of your side.

a few months most of us had copied them. About the same time, cricketers began running on to the field rather than strolling out like their more tranquil predecessors. I think Greig introduced the habit for England, and I continued it. Commentators would remark on the team's purposeful air; but I saw no lack of menace in the relaxed look of a West Indies team as they walked coolly out, led by the elegant Sobers or the hunched, cat-like Lloyd. The new urgency was, perhaps, a mixed blessing. It was, at any rate, a symptom of the times; more frenetic and less leisured, but in many ways also less productive. The over-rate remains far below what it was in the '40s and '50s.

My fourth basic duty for the captain was that he should think ahead. This is obvious, too obvious, perhaps, to say; except that I have known a county captain who never failed to be taken by surprise when the incoming batsman, on taking guard, was discovered to be a left-hander; not because, as happens occasionally, he was an unknown newcomer, but because the captain had not bothered to look! (Whereupon this same captain used to switch the field round, more often than not, so that it was a mirror-image of the one he had had for the outgoing right-hander.) I shall return to the fascinating topic of how far ahead the captain should look later; my immediate point is simple: it must be done.

Let us imagine that our captain has paid attention to these four basic requirements: he gets the team on to the field. He moves them around on it. He runs a brisk ship. And he thinks ahead. What else can a fielding team expect of their leader? And what should he ask of them? (The two questions are closely connected, as the team members will also come to expect their captain to expect a lot from them.)

I have already stressed, in the chapter on selection, the importance of respect. A captain is more likely to bring the best out of a player if he believes in that player. Naturally, he will not feel the same confidence in all his players. However, I think that the team members are entitled to expect from the captain a respect for their ability, and, even more, a respect and consideration for them as people. Much of what follows stems from this fact.

For example, I have already mentioned that Ted Dexter's main fault as captain was that he was more concerned about theories than about people, and when the theories became ineffective, his own interest waned. The story was told of a county match between Sussex and Hampshire which was heading for a draw. Dexter, the Sussex captain, summoned the substitute and left the field himself; before the match had ended he was seen by his players making for his car, portable television-set in hand.

Lack of concentration is as much a failing in captaincy as it is in batting or bowling; and in the captain it can imply lack of consideration. M.J.K. Smith was an example of the reverse. Usually calm and phlegmatic, he reserved some of his most biting comments for non-bowling fieldsmen who thoughtlessly left unnecessary work to those who had to bowl. If the ball had to be fetched from the boundary, he expected a non-bowler to make the effort to retrieve or chase it, rather than a similarly-placed bowler. Common sense also demands that, wherever possible, a batsman rather than a bowler should field where there is some risk of injury – say at short square-leg or at silly mid-off.

The considerate captain does not, without good cause and a word of commiseration, ask a fielder to go from one end of the field to another between overs. He thinks ahead to the field that he wants to set for the next over, and plans where each fielder will have to go. There is often a conflict between this consideration and the aim of keeping key fielders in key positions. For example, I saw Pat Pocock run, between overs, from deep fine-leg to deep third-man and back in the Test match at Delhi in 1972–3; the captain, Tony Lewis, wanted to keep a specialist at cover and himself at mid-on. He had no mid-off, so Pocock had to make his long trek in the heat. I am not saying that Lewis was inconsiderate; but he would have been had he not appreciated what he was asking of Pocock.

Ten years later, Sunil Gavaskar, the Indian captain, was to use a similar ploy on the same ground for a totally different purpose: to waste as much time as possible. Greig, likewise, went from long-off to long-off at Trent Bridge against West Indies in 1976. As he was trying to prevent the openers (of whom I was one, playing in my first Test) from having to bat that evening, I was more grateful than I should have been. (Anyway, I was out for 0 in the morning.) That same evening John Snow provided a more ingenious method of slowing things down. He came out from tea with a pocket full of cake crumbs, which he deposited behind his run-up mark. The seagulls, swooping and jabbering, distracted the batsmen and caused yet another hold-up.

I have mentioned the importance of having one's best fielders in particular positions in the field. There have always been specialist fielders: Hammond at slip, for instance, or Hobbs at cover-point. Left-handed fielders like Lock and Edmonds have often become experts at backward short-leg, partly because with a right-handed batsman one is inclined to start slightly fine and be more ready to move to one's left for a catch than to one's right. (This is a mirror-image of the approach of most first slips, who tend to stand fine to ensure that most of their chances either go straight to them, or to their right.)

Another reason for having left-handers at short-leg is the chance of run-outs. The batsmen may look for a short single from a ball turned just behind square, and backward short-leg is then well placed to pick the ball up left-handed and aim at the bowler's stumps. Again, this is the converse of having a right-handed thrower in the gully. For similar reasons, left-handers have traditionally fielded at square-leg or mid-wicket to right-handed batsmen, looking for a run-out when the ball is played between mid-wicket and mid-on. Don Wilson, of Yorkshire, was a fine example of this. Hobbs or Gower would, similarly, expect to get most of their victims by swooping to their right, picking the ball up one-handed, and shying at the bowler's stumps. A corollary of all this is that the left-handed mid-wicket specialist should stay at cover for the left-handed batsman, and one's right-handed cover-point stay on the leg-side.

Now all this has been well-known for decades. A more recent tendency, one which makes additional demands on the captain, has been to extend this principle. Much more thought has been given to where one's best fielders, and fielders with specific skills, should be for different bowlers and in different situations. Much of the impetus for this development has come from one-day cricket. For example, Alan Ealham, of Kent, was a fine all-round fielder, deceptively quick for a stocky man, with a hard, sharp throw and a wonderful pair of hands. Kent spotted that batsmen had got into the habit of ambling a single from a push wide of mid-on. (Mid-on has, traditionally, been a resting-place for ageing seamers, or for the totally unco-ordinated.) Suddenly, Ealham turned up at mid-on – with devastating results. Kent also used him in that part of the outfield where catches were most likely to go. It was Kent, too, who under Cowdrey's leadership experimented with putting their *least* agile fielders – like Cowdrey himself or Norman Graham – at short-cover or mid-wicket in the last few overs of a limited-over innings; the argument being that they needed their fast fielders in the outfield at that stage, and that Cowdrey or Graham might still gain a run-out from the suicidal single. In one-day cricket, third-man and fine-leg are often crucial positions, especially with really quick bowlers. I often put John Emburey, who was a good fielder with a powerful throw, at third-man for Daniel.

In longer matches, too, more flexibility is called for than was previously recognised. When captaining England, I would sometimes put Randall at deep square-leg for the spinners; there he would be able to cover ground prodigiously to make a catch from a mishit sweep; and he would also cut off many runs. Our other brilliant fielder, Gower, was less flamboyant and more controlled: he would quietly patrol the covers, or perhaps mid-wicket for the off-spinner. The captain should try to sense what shot a specific batsman will resort to in order to break out from a stranglehold – and have an appropriate fielder in the vicinity when he does.

In Australia in 1978–9, we gradually arrived at a more relentless approach to the left-handed Graeme Wood. Before the fifth Test, at Adelaide, Boycott said, 'We sometimes bowl three or four balls wide of the off-stump, which he lets go. Then we get bored, bowl a ball around middle-and-leg, Wood clips it to mid-wicket for two, and the pressure is off.' So after Wood had survived our opening assault, we kept a man backward of point to cut off one of his favourite strokes; we denied him his pull-shot by putting a man halfway back to the mid-wicket boundary (an unusual position, this); and when Emburey bowled, he kept Wood quiet by concentrating on his off-stump. We knew that his likeliest break-out shot against the spinner was the sweep. If he swept from the line of off-stump, the ball would have to go almost square, so Emburey and I agreed to risk a boundary if he bowled a ball down the leg-side (for then the sweep shot would go finer, to a more orthodox deep backward square-leg), and placed Randall twenty yards closer and twenty yards squarer in that general area. Everything worked. Emburey kept his line, pinned him down, until Wood – in desperation – went for the sweep and was caught by Randall.

To return to considerateness. Like an army commander, the captain will have to expose his men to danger and hardship. It is his duty not to do so unnecessarily or recklessly. For instance, he should never keep a man at short square-leg if the match is quietly fading away to a draw; or if it is as good as lost; or if the other side are about to declare. If he is in doubt about the need for such a fielder, he should probably err on the side of caution and safety. He should not allow fielders to stand there unless he has – and they have – some confidence in the bowler's accuracy. He should vary the precise location of the short-leg according to the batsman's predilection. For instance, some players either push forward against spinners, bat and pad together, or sweep fiercely. In some circumstances, it may be essential to have close fielders for bat-pad catches against such a player. If so, the forward short-leg will be much safer if he stands a few feet straighter – that is, towards silly mid-on – rather than square. From this batsman, the danger comes from the sweep. On the other hand, a different type of player may pose a different threat against the same bowler on the same pitch – say a driver or hitter, who rarely sweeps. For him, the short-leg should be square. There may be little difference between these two options in respect of potential catches from the defensive shot; the difference lies simply in the danger posed by the choice of attacking shots.

Some might argue that the captain should act like the junior officers in the First World War and never ask of another what he is not prepared to do himself. Close acted on this principle, and part of his charisma as a captain derived from it. However, such a policy may be simply silly. Willis would have ruined his knees squatting down for each ball and he was not mobile enough for the task. Besides, there are disadvantages in captaining the side from short square-leg; you do not easily get a detached overview of the game from that position! Moreover, players will respect the right of any man to opt out of fielding at forward short-leg after a reasonable stint of duty. Close's commitment to it was supererogatory – except that he happened to enjoy nothing so much as grovelling around the feet of the batsman in constant danger of being hit! He was also a master at the job.

Such a man, who revels in the danger and shrugs off the innumerable blows, is a godsend to a captain. Brian Hardie has made a tremendous contribution to Essex's success by his courage and skill there. And to

West Indies v. Australia, third Test, Trinidad, 1973: Keith Stackpole being led from the field by team-mate Ian Redpath, while Ian Chappell and Kerry O'Keeffe look on. He had been struck in the face while fielding close in. The captain must always weigh the degree of risk to the fielder against the purely tactical value of having a forward short-leg.

his and Keith Fletcher's credit, Hardie has taken the trouble to have a substantial set of protective equipment made.

The Closes and Hardies of the professional cricketing world are rare, however; so there often has to be an element of press-ganging, or at any rate sharing of the task. For Middlesex, Clive Radley and I for many years shared it, doing a couple of overs each in the hot-spot and alternating with the relative safety of silly-point. This was before helmets arrived to minimise the chance of serious injury. As a young man, I confess to having enjoyed the job, though I was lucky never to be badly hurt there. I did object, however, when Colin Drybrough, the county captain, removed himself from the position after a ball had narrowly missed his head; proceeded to have an argument with Fred Titmus, the bowler, who wanted to keep him there; and chose to change places with me! I preferred Titmus's own more directly sardonic method of finding a candidate when he took over from Drybrough a year later: 'Who's expendable?' he would say. 'Come on, Brears, you'll do!'

So the fielders can expect the captain to consider their safety; and not force them to run all over the field between overs. They can expect him too to be exact and exacting in his demands while at the same time acknowledging their experience at the job. For example, it would be ridiculous to tell Bobby Simpson where to stand at first slip, or Colin Bland to come in closer at cover. The 'keeper and the slips should usually be trusted to know how close and how spread out to place themselves – but not always. There is a widespread tendency to play safe; in the slips, this means standing too deep and too fine. If the ball drops short, no one criticises you for missing a catch, while if you field closer the chances will all be sharper. So there is often a real issue about how near to the batsman the 'keeper and slips should stand, especially on pitches where the bounce is unreliable. Pitches with low but quick bounce cause the greatest problems to slips as they have to stand uncomfortably close for the ball to carry.

I spent much of my captaincy career – both before being a regular first slip and after – exhorting 'keeper and slips to stand closer in and wider apart, rather as the Australians deployed themselves during Simpson's captaincy. I would much prefer to see a higher percentage of chances missed if a higher percentage of edges carry and thus become chances. Kapil Dev, the Indian opening bowler, has told me that he finds it hard to persuade India's slip fielders to come in as close as he likes to have them. Also I cannot subscribe to the mindless view that the ball should *never* travel in the air between slips, or between first slip and the 'keeper. It is equally galling if the cordon is too narrowly spread, so that an edge goes at a nice catchable height just beyond the reach of the widest slip. Moreover, I prefer the slips to feel that they should go for anything – a positive approach that actually makes it less likely that the ball will go between two slips, for it can happen that if they are too close each leaves it to the other. I may say that bowlers often disagreed with me on this, preferring a tight ring with minimal gaps; in which case a compromise was the most satisfactory outcome.

Another factor in the positioning of slips that is often totally – and culpably – ignored is the question: how deep should they be for *particular* batsmen? Boycott has always been master at playing his defensive shots with a loose grip. If the ball found the edge it would not carry far. Gooch, by contrast, rarely plays a purely defensive shot. His heavy bat is always moving towards the ball, and his grip is firmer. The result is that an edge from Gooch will carry yards further than an edge (to the same ball) from Boycott. Yet how few captains insist on making the necessary adjustment in the placing of their slip fielders!

Captains, slip fielders and others should also ask themselves another, related question: are we anticipating an edge from an attacking or from a defensive shot? The answer will influence their positioning. Gully too may be up for the thick, defensive edge or back for the slash or sliced drive.

Nor are such considerations limited to the close-in catching positions. It is often tritely said that the fielder in the deep must be right on the boundary, and that it is always an error in field-placing if the ball clears him but lands inside the boundary. The argument is that it is easier to

Alan Davidson and Richie Benaud miss a chance
during the Australian tour of England in 1953 as
a result of standing too close to each other in the
slips. As a rule it has been English teams who
have made such mistakes; the Australians have
tended – rightly, in my view – to stand further
apart from each other.

ABOVE RIGHT Ian Botham's extraordinary
position close in at second or third slip. This was
all very well on a dead slow pitch, but in normal
conditions his presence so near their line of
vision must distract the other slip fielders, and
too many of the chances that come his way will
give him too little time to react. Nevertheless, I
prefer Botham's gambling to the safety-first
attitude of many slip fielders, who stand too deep
so as to avoid dropping possible chances; and I
have seen him make many breathtaking catches
close to the wicket. His (and Allan Lamb's)
hands on knees are not to be recommended.

RIGHT Max Walker bowling to Colin Cowdrey,
second Test, Perth, 1974. The four slip fielders
are nicely spread to cover a wide area. Ian
Chappell is wider than most first slips would be,
especially to an inswing bowler like Walker, who
is likely to wrong-foot the 'keeper and have him
moving towards the leg-side. His attitude reflects
his confidence both in himself and in Rodney
Marsh. Ashley Mallett is in an interesting
position at short, squarish gully. I imagine that he
was hoping for a chance from high up the bat on
a defensive stroke. Cowdrey had only recently
arrived from England as a replacement; early in
an innings he would not be looking to play
wristily outside the off-stump or indulge in
ambitious cover-drives; and the Perth pitch
allows extra bounce.

run in to make a catch than out, away from the batsman. I agree with the last point, but I do not think that it supports an invariable conclusion. On a big field, with a slow outfield, the man in the deep may need to be twenty yards in from the edge in order to cut off two, especially if a man with Javed Miandad's speed is at the wicket; and occasionally the captain may feel that a particular batsman is unlikely to hit the ball all the way. Moreover, a fielder can cover more ground if he has space behind him as well as in front of him. The adage is often trotted out in the interests of safety rather than of attacking and thoughtful cricket.

Even at the level of county cricket, mid-off and mid-on are often badly positioned. How close they should be depends on which side of the stumps the bowler is bowling; for a right-arm, over-the-wicket bowler, bowling to a right-hand batsman, mid-off should be much deeper, as a general rule, than mid-on, as the ball has to be hit firmly enough to evade the bowler in his follow-through before the batsmen can commit themselves to a single. Mid-off should stand deep enough to invite a single from an off-drive, and close enough to challenge it by an aggressive pick-up and throw to the bowler's stumps.

As with slips and gully, how close the ring of one-saving fielders should be varies with the batsmen. Compare, again, Gooch and Boycott. It is rare for the former deliberately to play a ball short for a quick single. The latter rarely blasts the ball through mid-off. So it is absurd to have the ring of fielders in the same place for both.

At the level of professional cricket, or good club cricket, the captain, fielders and bowlers are constantly involved in interplay about such details. Most of the decisions will be made by consensus; and with an experienced bowler, the captain who insists on every little alteration in the field being implemented by himself invites ridicule. I remember an occasion in 1974 when Jack Bailey, who was about to become Secretary of MCC, was captaining an MCC side in a minor game at Nairobi. David Acfield, an experienced county bowler, moved his mid-wicket a yard or two squarer; whereupon Bailey barked out from deep mid-on, 'Through me, David, please!' Jack had to put up with some teasing as a result. But occasionally the captain will have to override either the bowler (and order a fielder to move to a certain position) or the fielder (and tell him exactly where he wants him). In general, the captain should expect his fielders to keep their positions, and not to wander. He will demand that they are tidy in their work, taking trouble over how they throw in, say, or toss the ball to the bowler, even when sloppiness does not cost runs. I used to be annoyed by 'flash' fielding, when, for example, a fielder used one hand to pick up the ball when he had time to use two. Another bête-noire of mine was the fielder who failed to back up, or the short square-leg who did not, as a matter of course, go to the stumps when a run-out was on the cards and the wicket-keeper was standing a long way back. But I think my most acid tongue was reserved for those who opted out of difficult catches, preferring to take the ball comfortably on the bounce rather than risking making a fool of themselves by going flat-out for the catch.

In this chapter, I have so far discussed the needs of the fielders and the expectations that the captain may legitimately have of them. But what about the bowlers? Like M.J.K. Smith, I believe they are owed additional consideration, though this must not be construed as mollycoddling. They have a right to be consulted about ends, length of spell, fields and so on; but as in all other areas of captaincy the captain must accept that it is his responsibility to take decisions which sometimes conflict with the wishes of the players.

On Smith's tour of South Africa in 1964–5, England scored 531 in their first innings in the second Test at Johannesburg. Ian Thomson, the Sussex medium-fast bowler, shared the new ball with John Price. Watching from the dressing-room, I was amazed that Thomson's off-side field included only one slip. As it happened, South Africa's opening batsman Eddie Barlow early on in the innings edged Thomson at catchable height through the vacant second slip position. Now, I do not know if the ultra-defensive field was Smith's idea or Thomson's. I should not be surprised if it came from the latter, as I noticed that in county matches he would become disheartened – with good cause – when Dexter would not allow him a mid-off even when the ball was hardly moving. *If* Thomson asked for the third-man and the mid-off when England had a massive score and the ball was new, then Smith was, I think, wrong to defer to him.

Bowlers have a right to reasonable fields. They should not be forced to bowl with ridiculously attacking fields; nor should they be refused the appropriate close-in catchers. I am often struck by the extent to which bowlers earn their attacking fields, and thus their wickets. Too often they deplore their bad luck when the edged shot misses the solitary slip; they forget that if they bowled fewer half-volleys and long-hops they could have had a whole ring of slips.

Some bowlers hate to depart from their normal field-settings. During the Old Trafford Test in 1977, I was keen to persuade Derek Underwood to try bowling over the wicket to exploit a long stretch of powdery rough just outside the leg-stump. I recalled a conversation I had had ten years before in the old Sind Club in Karachi. Intikhab Alam, the Pakistani leg-spinner, and I had signed the visitors' book, ordered drinks, and sat in one of the big, panelled rooms that remained from the years of the Raj. Intikhab, bowling round the wicket (which is in effect similar to the left-arm Underwood bowling over), had troubled us, and now he explained his views on that tactic. The benefits, for the bowler, of such a ball bowled into the rough are, of course, that the batsman has trouble judging both the height of bounce and the sharpness of turn. The thing you must *not* do, he said, was to pitch on or outside the off-stump, because that would give the batsman too much room to play his shots. Intikhab was clear that you must have more fielders than usual on the leg-side, and we went through some of the possibilities in detail.

Now, on the Monday morning before Australia's second innings, I asked Alan Knott what he thought Underwood's response would be to the idea of bowling over the wicket. I sensed some likely resistance and wanted advice on how to play it; I also hoped for support from Knott, who had kept wicket to him for virtually every ball he had bowled over the previous decade and more. Knott was not very hopeful. '"Deadly" doesn't like his fields tampered with,' he said; and my mind went back to the spectacle of Underwood during the Calcutta Test, seven months before. Despite a match analysis of four for 74 from 45.5 overs, there was a brief flurry of boundaries scored off his bowling during the second innings. Greig, the captain, had then quickly moved several fielders into the outfield. I still have a vivid mental image of Underwood, burned red, sweating, his trousers dusty, sagging and stained, his feet splayed Chaplin-like, standing forlorn at the end of his run-up while Greig, towering beside him, imperiously directed the men to far-flung outposts of the field.

Underwood had not enjoyed this sudden departure from orthodoxy. I sympathised with him at the time, but I also discovered how uncertain he can be, for so great a bowler, about what field he does want when he has to deal with the unusual, so that I could also see how Greig felt – that if he didn't take charge completely the ship would be directionless.

I was aware of all this as I listened to Knott, who went on: 'The last time I remember him bowling over the wicket was during the tour of India in 1972–3. Norman Gifford was much better in this style, and Underwood was left out of the next Test.'

I realised that I had better start working on the resistance early. After my net, I talked with Derek about my idea, and about the fields we might have, and drew diagrams of them on the back of an envelope. I reminded him that he could always revert to bowling round the wicket. I wanted to excite him about the thought of bowling over the wicket to Greg Chappell, who I thought would not enjoy the prospect. As we talked, Derek became more enthusiastic.

By the end of the day, he had taken six for 66 in 32.5 overs. He took three of these wickets (including Chappell's) bowling over the wicket to right-handers. It would be wrong to think that this tactic won us the match since, by the time he was bowling this way, we had already taken four wickets and the Australians were still behind our score. However, from a tactical and psychological point of view it was, for me, an interesting episode.

It illustrates, too, an important aspect of the captain's job: to remind, or even teach, bowlers that they have more resources than they give themselves credit for: that they have more strings to their bow.

Emburey and I always respected each other's ideas: if we differed, I would generally let him try his way first, suggesting that he give mine a go if his was not successful. (I might, for instance, be in favour of his

A superb shot of Richie Benaud's action – head and eyes steady, left shoulder round, wrist cocked. Note also the drag-plate on the right toe. The date is significant too: 1 July 1961, the last day of the Old Trafford Test. Soon after play began, Australia, on 334 for nine, were only 156 runs ahead. The last wicket added 98, however, and England needed 256 to win in 230 minutes. Thanks to a brilliant innings by Ted Dexter, England were 150 for one with 107 minutes remaining. But Benaud had started bowling round the wicket, into the rough, and he now dismissed Dexter, Peter May, Brian Close and Raman Subba Row for nine runs in nineteen balls. He took two more wickets after the tea interval, and England collapsed to 201 all out. Benaud's was a feat of captaincy, as well as of bowling.

bowling slower to a certain batsman, inviting him to hit over the top.) With Edmonds, by contrast, there was rarely this productive willingness to differ. I think we both felt that the other failed to appreciate our point of view. What I interpreted as contempt for my idea he experienced as uncertainty about his ability to put it into effect. He thought that I was unwilling to give him a long-off because I saw opposition batsmen too much in my own pawky mould; while I felt that he expected opposition batsmen to play him in *his* style – which in antagonistic moods I would characterise as a mindless combination of blocking and slogging.

So Edmonds rarely felt that I helped him or that my thinking enlarged his sense of his own ability. He and I were able to discuss our mutual difficulties. He felt – rightly, I think – that he would have done better, with his own Zambian upbringing, with a more abrasive, extrovert and physically tough captain, like Ian Chappell. Possibly Geoff Boycott got more out of him than I could. I noticed that Edmonds reacted well to

Taking the field

Boycott's jibes in the nets. Each time he bowled a bad ball Boycott would leer at him, saying, 'Anoother fower!' And, in the few Tests in which Geoffrey was captain, Edmonds performed well. He himself had a high regard for Majid Khan, his captain at Cambridge; but then Majid had a weak attack, and needed Edmonds to bowl virtually unchanged in every match. Whatever the reason, I am glad to see that at last, on the 1984-5 tour of India, Phil appears to be maturing into the consistently Test-level bowler he has always promised to become.

To return to my point: a captain should constantly be thinking of alternatives, and encouraging others to do the same. These may be schemes for individual bowlers, or plans for dealing with dangerous opponents, or indeed quick appraisals of unknown players. Incidentally, G.O. Allen rated Pelham Warner the best captain he had seen for such assessments; he was apparently remarkably skilful at getting an immediate picture of a new batsman's strengths and weaknesses from a first sight of stance, grip and movement at the crease.

When confronted by the well-known maestros, on the other hand, there is a danger that once they have played themselves in, a team virtually gives up against them. Yet there are always options open to the fielding team that are less likely to end in disaster than others. Take Viv Richards: I soon appreciated that all the one-saving fielders should be both deeper and straighter than usual (for instance, cover should be closer to extra-cover, and mid-off nearer the bowler than for, say, Gordon Greenidge). We knew, too, that it is often worth trying a bouncer or two early on. But what to do when these limited ideas do not succeed? It took me too long to try the simple expedient of bowling wide of the off-stump to him. In one-day cricket, that seemed, for a while, to induce more errors. And even Richards is human, and has patches in which he feels that he will never score another run – as during the second half of 1984, in England and in Australia. Such periods should simply be enjoyed with gratitude by opponents; they do not last!

It is also important not to be carried away by the power of one batsman and fail to revert to normality for his partner. Our task of scoring 202 to win the Gillette Cup Final in 1980 was boosted by a small mistake by the Surrey captain at a crucial stage. Gatting came in to join me with the score at 64-2, and for a while we both struggled on the slow pitch. Eventually Gatting hit out at Intikhab – he was missed at mid-on – then clubbed him to wide long-on for four. Surrey rightly posted a man at long-on; but wrongly failed to bring him in when I had the strike. This error enabled me to score eight runs from sweep shots to the now empty fine-leg area, shots that were both safe and productive with the new field that had been rearranged to deal with my partner's more muscular style.

I have said that the captain should encourage all the team to think about the game from a tactical point of view; he must also insist that each member of his side plays a part in encouraging and motivating the others. I shall have more to say about this topic in a later chapter. Now

I will simply add that anyone can help the bowler with ideas, support or criticism, though the captain must be aware of, and approve, the type of advice on which he acts. The wicket-keeper is crucial here. Bob Taylor would constantly and energetically encourage the England fast bowlers. He and I would often take turns in running to Willis at the end of an over, scuttling along beside his giant strides. Despite his glazed, distant look and his air of being wrapped up in his own fervent world, Bob welcomed any help we could offer, whether it was general encouragement when he was struggling to find his rhythm, tactical suggestions for particular players or comments on his run-up or action. He would ask if his hand was 'behind the ball' in delivery, or if he was falling away. He wondered if he was running in too fast, or too slowly. He would seek our ideas about going round the wicket to a left-hander. Such help was tactically and psychologically invaluable.

The captain must, of course, know his bowlers. One aspect concerns length and frequency of spells. Only in exceptional circumstances should they be bowled 'into the ground'. After the Melbourne Test of 1954–5, Hutton was asked if Tyson and Statham had not been exhausted by the end; was it not the case that they would have been unable to bowl the next day? 'Next day?' replied Hutton. 'They couldn't have bowled again for a week!' To win a Test, Hutton could afford to drain his fast bowlers. Carrying on with them so long was, naturally, a gamble, for they would have had no energy to come back later. But taking them off would have been a different and greater gamble.

Over a season or a tour the captain has to bear in mind the fatigue of his bowlers, and especially of the strike bowlers. At Middlesex we were well aware of Wayne Daniel's value to the side ('The Black Diamond', Mike Smith christened him, and 'Rent and Rates'), so we would not bowl him when a match was tame, or flog him on an unhelpful pitch. By contrast, Surrey's key fast bowler, Sylvester Clarke, used to complain that he was expected to charge in at almost any time.

Inexperienced bowlers must be nursed too, for different reasons. The captain should try not to let them lose confidence by being taken apart, but instead give them when he can the encouragement of a chance of bowling against the tail.

With some bowlers the captain must be firm about when to take them off. I am thinking of players like Willis, who was inclined to want to keep going beyond his peak, so that if he continued as long as he felt he could he would become ragged and less capable of lively spells later in the day.

On the other hand, many bowlers, especially medium-pacers and spinners, need to bowl in long spells to find their best rhythm. They thrive on hard work. Like many batsmen, they need time to probe an opponent; they can only rarely hope to operate as strike bowlers whose wicket-taking rate will normally be higher. John Lever is a case in point. For Essex, Fletcher will almost always use him in long spells of eleven or more overs. Even if he is below his best at the beginning, he then has time to sort things out, and can be relied upon to do so. He is fit, athletic and versatile. For England, on the other hand, he would usually be the third, if not the fourth seamer, and his opportunities for staying on were fewer.

The captain must also know which of his bowlers are capable of very short spells. You take a wicket fifteen minutes before lunch. The new batsman is known to be vulnerable to pace. Should you give your fastest bowler one or at most two overs before the interval? Obviously, many factors are relevant to the answer, but one is: can your strike bowler get into his stride quickly? There is no point in making the change if he will have stiffened up since his last spell, and will take an over and a half to get loose. The difference is often a matter of age.

Bowlers expect their captain to give them a chance to perform at their best, by being aware of their capacities and preferences. They also have a right to a *fair* chance. The captain should avoid favouritism. Quick bowlers should, on the whole, be given the wind. On completely un-responsive pitches, the sheer hard work should to some extent be shared. Unselfish bowlers should not be exploited by being loaded with all the donkey-work. Change bowlers should not always be taken off when a batsman comes in. And so on.

Yet true fairness is hard to assess. It is simply foolish not to give your best bowlers the first chance on a helpful pitch. And you are bound to keep them going for longer before taking them off when you know how reliably they have taken wickets in such conditions in the past.

I remember a conversation with Kim Hughes at the Australian High Commissioner's house on the second evening of the Oval Test in 1981. Dennis Lillee had not bowled at his best during the previous five Tests, due to pneumonia contracted early in the tour. Terry Alderman, on the other hand, had exceeded all expectations, and often looked more penetrative than his illustrious partner. At the Oval, Lillee opened the attack with a breeze coming from mid-on. This breeze was exactly what he wanted; but it would also have suited Alderman. I wondered if Alderman had not 'earned' the good end. Kim said that he had had the same idea; but Lillee's seniority and qualities had made him think again, and he had gone for Lillee. With our score standing at 100 for one overnight, I thought Hughes had not been vindicated. But next morning, and for the rest of the match, Lillee proved him right by taking 7–89 and 4–70 in the two innings.

Fairness is harder to arrive at for the captain who is himself a bowler. Illingworth once remarked that he thought a spinner should almost never have to bowl on the first day of a Test in England – which seems to me absurd, and probably made in self-justification. For Leicestershire, the other off-spinner, Jack Birkenshaw, bowled far more overs than Ray himself on easy batting pitches. I once asked a team-mate, Barry Dudle-ston, how Illy got away with it with the rest of the team; how did he maintain their respect when his under-bowling of himself was a joke throughout the county circuit? Dudleston's reply revealed much of Illingworth's strength as a captain – though the charge sticks. In the first place, he told me, Illingworth had grown up in a hard school, in the Yorkshire side of the '50s, when you earned the right to bowl in helpful conditions only by unrelenting achievement in a competitive environment where four Test match bowlers would all be itching to get their hands on the ball. Second, Birkenshaw was a fine good-wicket bowler, a master of flight, but hardly relentless enough to run through sides cheaply. Third, Illingworth almost never failed to take wickets on a turning pitch. Dudleston told me of a match against Glamorgan at the end of May, 1976: until then Illy had bowled only 53 overs without taking a single wicket, but on the drying pitch at Swansea he took 8–38.

I have already mentioned John Lever and his limited opportunities for England. In the late '70s England had a range of talented seam bowlers to choose from: Willis, Old, Hendrick, Botham and Lever. In terms of sheer ability, at Test level, I always felt that the first four marginally had the edge on Lever. They were slightly more likely to dismiss top-class batsmen, especially if there was a little help in the pitch. On the other hand Lever was a man of unquenchable optimism; he never broke down, and he would bowl for hours on unresponsive pitches. He was utterly reliable. The result was, in a way, unfair; or at least hard on Lever. For he would tend to be selected to play in conditions that least favoured fast bowlers. For instance, in 1977 he was preferred to Old for the Test at Hyderabad, a fast bowler's graveyard: his figures – 1–103 in 36.6 eight-ball overs – do not sound impressive, yet he had done a good job for the side.

The same thing may happen with batsmen. In 1976, Dennis Amiss had been hit on the head by a ball from Michael Holding in May. The question of his ability against the fastest bowling was again raised. As a result he was not picked for any of the first four Tests. He was recalled for the fifth; the selectors knew well that the Oval pitch was at that time the slowest and gentlest of the Test pitches. Amiss then played a remarkable innings of 203, batting with a changed technique that involved him playing back on his stumps, open-chested, to most deliveries. I do not detract from this courageous and skilful performance when I say that he would have been unlikely to play like this here had he struggled through the earlier Tests on less easy-paced pitches. These examples show, incidentally, how Test averages can in the short run mislead.

More generally, there may be problems for a captain in having five front-line bowlers; problems which are, paradoxically, most acute when the side is performing well. Then the fifth bowler is scarcely needed. He is often under-bowled, feels undervalued, and ends up under-performing. Such vicious circles cannot altogether be avoided; the team can only hope that the captain and the bowler involved have sufficient mutual respect to mitigate the bad effects.

Certainly the captain can never please all his bowlers all the time.

Consider, for example, the wind. I used to find it a great problem – it *never* suited everyone, and often suited no one. It was too strong – it blew bowlers off balance. It was too weak – there was no air. It was freezing cold – and the slips hoped to heaven that the ball didn't come their way. Whenever he takes the field Boycott lets his handkerchief hang in the breeze, to see its direction. As batsman or as tactician, he wants to glean all he can from this small but salient fact. If it comes from long-leg, the quicker bowler may be more able to swing his outswinger, and the off-spinner drift the ball towards slip. If straight down the pitch, everyone will want to bowl with it. (I recall a match in the '60s at Cambridge during exams, when a slow left-arm bowler called R. Carter-Shaw played a single match for us against Glamorgan. Richard Hutton, our quickest bowler, was not amused to be asked to bowl into a gale as 'Carter-Shaw always bowls with the wind.')

It is a fallacy that spinners and medium-pacers inevitably prefer bowling into the wind. At Port Elizabeth, in 1964, Titmus and David Allen bowled out Eastern Province on a turning pitch. Both wanted the wind behind them, and I remember Titmus, in mock-complaint, joking that walking back to his mark was terribly hard work. (On a less responsive pitch, where he would need to rely more on curve and flight, he might prefer to bowl against a breeze that came from the leg, but never against a gale.) In the match against East Africa mentioned in the last chapter, I asked Tom Cartwright to bowl a few overs into the wind. Tom never minced words. 'Michael,' he said, 'if you want me to float up a few half-volleys, of course I'll bowl into the wind. But if you want me to *bowl properly*, and keep going for you, you'd better give me the other end.' He took one wicket, rather against his better judgement, bowling into the wind; then I gave him the end he wanted, and he finished up with five.

Sometimes I would say: if batsmen have to bat at each end, why not bowlers? *Someone* has to bowl uphill, into the wind. Mike Selvey reckoned his nose got flatter year by year. And of course, he, like others (Alderman at Perth, for example) could make good use of a wind that's against him, though he would much prefer it to be from fine-leg than from third-man. Prevailing winds can, as we have seen, influence selection, particularly at Perth or Wellington or any other ground regularly exposed to strong winds.

Bowling changes are also influenced by its direction. Middlesex have played several home matches in recent years at the pleasant Uxbridge ground, which is on a plateau and thus particularly exposed. Against Derbyshire, in 1980, our two spinners were Edmonds and Titmus. A stiff breeze blew throughout the match from one end, dictating that Daniel and Vintcent van der Bijl should bowl most of their overs from that end. In the first innings, the wind came from fine-leg; in the second, from third-man. It therefore helped Titmus (who drifts the ball out) in the first innings and Edmonds (whose natural swing is in) in the second.

I suspect that many spectators, and even perhaps some players, failed to understand that this was the main reason for Titmus bowling nearly 22 overs in the first innings to Edmonds's 14; as opposed to 7 in the second to the latter's 32.

I have argued that an essential ingredient in good captaincy consists of a captain's respect for his own team. I will end this chapter by remarking that the complete captain also shows respect for the crowd, the umpires and the opposition. I have some sympathy for the 'old pro' remark attributed to Bill Lawry, the dour Australian batsman, on getting the bird from a crowd. 'If they want to see park cricket, let them go to the park,' he said. The public often criticises inappropriately. Nevertheless, the public deserves consideration from a team, and especially from the captain.

Second, the umpires. Captains should respect, and insist on their players' respect for, umpires and their decisions. I do not believe in appealing when you know a man is not out, though I am equally opposed to the reticence of not appealing when he may be out. I do not like the practice – sometimes born of self-deception, as well as plain deception – of giving an umpire the impression that he has made a glaring error, even when he has. I insisted that bowlers and fielders, like batsmen, snapped out of any such expression of emotion at once.

Third, the opposition. However fierce a contest, I think that cricketers owe each other respect in the face of the ignorance of many spectators. Of course one must expect to be the butt of the odd joke, as when Dennis Lillee pretended to be stung by the ball when I played yet another delivery defensively back to the bowler, or when he applauded, sarcastically, the dramatic occurrence of a single. I was able to enjoy, too, Ian Chappell's concrete joke at my expense when, in a visual parody of my well-known opposition to a restriction in the number of fielders allowed on the leg-side, he put all nine fielders on that side for an over during my innings against South Australia. But sledging – the use of language to abuse or intimidate an opponent – is a totally unwelcome aberration in the game, inane, humourless and unacceptable. The public taunting of an opponent falls into a similar category. Once, in a One-Day International at Sydney, Lillee and Ian Chappell invited the lower elements of the crowd to jeer at me when I missed the stumps in trying for a run-out.

Not that they needed much encouragement at the time. I was scarcely more popular than Jardine had been. But English captains have a tradition of arousing Australian crowds.

Since Chappell and Lillee retired, my impression has been that the spirit of England v. Australia Tests has reverted to that of earlier post-war years, of which Lindsay Hassett has said, 'During my time I never heard a single player of either side swear at another.'

Not that previous generations of cricketers were without blemish. In *Cricket Punch*, Frank Worrell describes the behaviour of some of the

Taking the field

Surrey team in a match against the West Indies touring team in 1957. Peter May had declared, setting the visitors a reasonable target on the last day. The trouble started when the fielding side claimed a catch off Nyron Asgarali and the appeal was turned down. 'From that moment onwards,' Worrell writes, 'the Surrey players kept up a constant stream of belly-aching. The objects of the belly-aching were the batsmen and the umpires . . . Throughout the innings we had to put up with this barracking from the Surrey players . . . We were abused when the players were changing ends . . . The incessant talking even went on among the close-in fielders while the bowler was running up to bowl . . . The Surrey players appealed for anything and everything . . . True, Peter May tried to pull his side together, and more than once he told his men to "steady on". But the captain who handles the England side so well did not appear to get the same response from his own county on this occasion . . . We all got the impression that Surrey want to be appellants, judges and jury in their own cases. The whole West Indian party was shattered by this experience. We never knew cricket could be played like that . . . Judging by the way they played us, Surrey are no longer capable of playing the game to enjoy it.'

No doubt there are examples of such sledging and general bad sportsmanship from every era of the game.

CHAPTER EIGHT

Placing the field

In the sixth Test at Sydney in 1979, we needed only 34 to win on a pitch that had taken spin from the start, and had deteriorated. As I was padding up to open the innings, umpires Tony Crafter and Don Weser knocked and entered our dressing-room, together with Graham Yallop, the Australian captain. Crafter was holding a used ball. Did I have any objection, he asked, to Australia opening the bowling with this ball? I said that I certainly did object, as it would be to Australia's advantage not to have to bowl their faster bowlers to knock the shine off: they would much prefer to start with a ball that their spinners could easily grip. The umpires were not impressed. They asked Yallop if he still wanted to use it. He said he did, and the umpires assured me that there was nothing in the laws to prevent him doing so. I was certain that there was, but could not quote chapter and verse. I also said that if Yallop could use a newish ball, what was to stop a fielding captain turning a Test into a fiasco by using a rank, old, soft ball with the string hanging out? This argument made equally little impact on the umpires. I did not want to get too worked up immediately before batting, so I shrugged and carried on padding up.

While Boycott and I batted against the Australian spinners, our manager, Doug Insole, read hurriedly through the laws. It was not until the score read 12–0 that he discovered the relevant passage – Law 5, which states, 'Subject to agreement to the contrary either captain may demand a new ball at the start of each innings.' That is unequivocal enough; but Insole wisely reckoned that he should let us carry on rather than complain. For if the complaint had been upheld, we would have had to restart our innings; and neither Boycott nor I would have thanked our manager had we been dismissed for a duck!

This exceptional case aside, in first-class matches each innings starts with a new ball which, in virtually every instance, is taken by the fast bowlers. Why should this be?

Placing the field

There are two main reasons: shine – which is one factor in affecting the ball's swing; and hardness – which makes it bounce more. There are, however, occasions when the pitch so much favours spinners that they should take the new ball; and I have found that, if they are really keen to bowl, they have little difficulty in gripping the shiny ball after a single over from a seamer, if not from the start.

Normally, though, the seamers will take the new ball. Sometimes, its lacquer skin makes it swing alarmingly for an over or two only. Even the fastest of bowlers, like Holding, may find it swinging out of control at the very time when they themselves are clammy-handed from nervousness. Once this skin has been knocked off by pitch or bat the ball may swing less, if at all, until the fielding team has polished one side, allowing the other to remain dull.

In England, the shine stays longer, on the whole, than abroad, as both pitch and outfield have customarily been less hard and dry. In Australia, the ball would typically lose both shine and hardness within a dozen or so overs, so that the contrast between all-out attack with a new ball and all-out defence with the old is sharper than in England. Harold Larwood, describing the 'Bodyline' series in 1932–3, recalls how England would start an innings with bowlers maintaining a conventional line of attack, around off-stump, and the usual slip-cordon. 'After a while, though,' he adds, 'the skipper would move the slips one by one over to the leg-side.' Leaving aside the ethics of bodyline, the tactic was to create an alternative mode of attack once the ball stopped swinging.

This contrast has become less clear-cut in recent years, thanks to the increased use of fertilisers and watering. Everywhere outfields are lusher. My own view is that colour television may have increased the appeal, for the groundsman, of creating an aesthetically pleasing effect by means of rich, green swathes across the field – no matter that the outcome is an extremely slow outfield and a ball cushioned against the ravages of hard earth! The ready availability of water tempts many groundsmen to over-water the pitch, too, as an insurance against its breaking or dusting. Even watering the outfield can lead to damp on the pitch, either because of drifting spray or from underground seepage.

These developments have not only given seam bowlers an advantage for much longer in countries where the opportunity to attack sensibly had mainly been restricted to the initial overs with a new ball; they have also further tilted the balance against spinners. Other extrinsic, technical factors have contributed to this one-way trend, such as covers, automated ball-manufacture and even diet and training. Until 1913 no part of the pitch was covered against rain. Therefore, all sides were forced to include at least two spin bowlers, as no one else could keep his feet on soggy footholds. For many years after 1913, only the ends of a pitch were covered; this meant that, on drying tracks, there was a great likelihood that spinners would find conditions more to their liking than quicker bowlers. Machine-made cricket balls have far more prominent seams than those made largely by hand thirty or more years ago: here too the gain is proportionately greater for the seam bowler. In every sport where achievement is measurable, there has been an unremitting improvement in performance thanks to better diet and training. I find it hard to believe that cricketers alone have failed to benefit; but the major gains must be for faster bowlers. Finally, the decline in over-rates means that fast bowlers can bowl a higher proportion of the overs bowled in a day.

To revert to the argument: the new ball should almost always be used by quicker bowlers because it is more likely to swing and will certainly bounce more steeply and lose less pace on contact with the ground. Boycott enjoys saying that the new ball goes through 'like a fire-cracker'; certainly a batsman's reflexes need to be sharper against it.

The shift towards faster bowling has, as we have seen, affected the composition of teams, so that it is now rare for a side to have less than three front-line seam bowlers. One outcome, for the captain, is that he then has to choose two to open. They may not, necessarily, be the two fastest bowlers, as I have discussed in Chapter One. Some fast bowlers prefer the old (but not too old) ball. Jeff Thomson, Wayne Daniel and Colin Croft are just three who find that they can control it better than a slippery new one. Moreover, the captain may wish to allow his two fastest bowlers to have the wind and/or slope behind them, so he will need to operate them in turns. Moreover, speed and bounce are not the only weapons. Some new-ball bowlers, like Alan Davidson, Kapil Dev, or Andy Roberts have been masters of movement, though they may have been marginally slower than some of their partners. Oddly, one of the fastest bowlers in the world, Imran Khan, is far more dangerous in his second spell. He seems to be able both to swing the older ball more sharply and to control its direction better. Presumably, he and Sarfraz Nawaz, for years his opening partner for Pakistan, had to learn to swing the old ball under unhelpful conditions; both are remarkable in their ability to do so without noticeable loss of pace.

Another element in the choice of new-ball bowlers may be compatibility. I never liked the opposition to get off to a flying start; with England, therefore, I would, at times, ask Hendrick rather than Botham to partner Willis. Hendrick was steadier and more consistent than the others, an admirable foil to their adventurous flair. The captain must remember that, if all else is equal, batsmen would choose not to face quite different threats from a pair of bowlers (just as bowlers prefer not to have to bowl at two very different types of batsmen, left- and right-handers, for instance, or front-foot and back-foot, or forceful and defensive). Fast bowlers, it is said, hunt in pairs (or in the case of the West Indies, in packs): and the pairs often complement each other. Fred Trueman was fast, aggressive and bowled predominantly outswingers, while Brian Statham, who was neither so volatile nor so variable, relied more on movement off the pitch.

Placing the field

RIGHT Dennis Lillee bowling with nine slips against New Zealand, Auckland, 1977.
An extreme example of the classic fast bowler's strategy, to aim for off-stump and just
outside, hoping for an outside edge. The actual field-setting may have an element of
arrogance about it: but only a man of Lillee's speed and accuracy could get away with
it. He took eleven wickets in the match for 123 runs.

Lillee at Perth, 1974, where 95 per cent of his deliveries would go over the top of the
stumps. Here he is bowling at the left-handed David Lloyd, so his stock movement
would have been in to the batsman: hence the three short-legs. Australia were on top
in the match; thus they could afford to do without a deep fine-leg. Lillee does not
intend to pitch many balls right up to the batsman; he can therefore afford the open
spaces at mid-off and mid on.

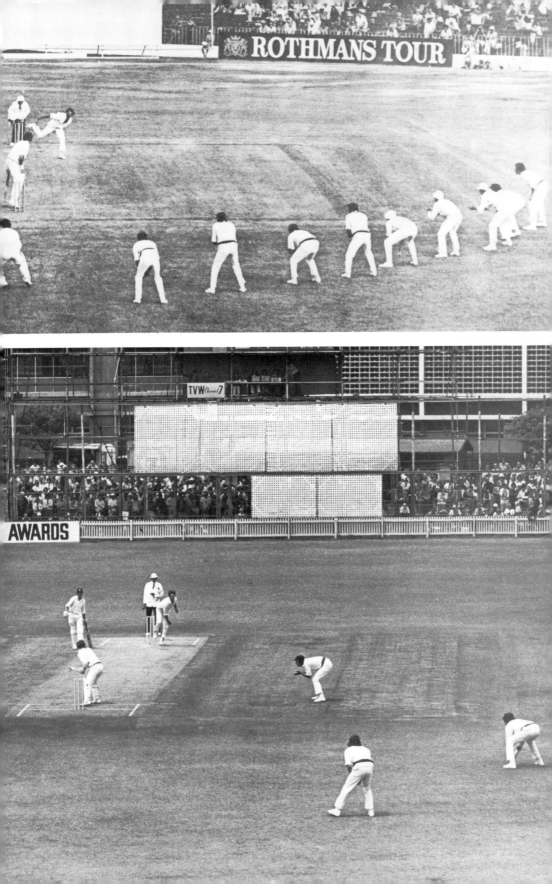

Placing the field

The captain should have some pattern of attack in mind. Suppose he has a normally balanced attack, two quickish bowlers, a medium-pacer, and two spinners. If, as is usual, he opens with his quicker bowlers he will not expect to give both maximum-length spells, since then neither will be capable of bowling for a long time. He is more likely to take off one, B, after four overs or so, and bring him back at the preferred end (A's) after A has done eight overs. Meanwhile he will use the medium-pacer, C, from B's original end. One exception would be if the match is desperately close, and he is willing to risk exhausting his main bowlers, A and B – Hutton's tactics in 1953–4. Another would be if they take early wickets, and he aims for a complete breakthrough.

In 1978, Hogg made it clear to everyone that he was not keen on long spells. ('They use up all the juice I've got,' he said.) But we were amazed when he was rested after only four eight-ball overs at the start of the Perth Test when his analysis was two wickets for no runs. If A and B both rely on speed, while C moves the ball much more, the captain may, on a damp or slow pitch, open with A and C, planning to keep C going while A and B alternate from the other end. If the make-up of the side is one fast and two medium-paced bowlers, the fast bowler must be used shrewdly. He needs, in Hogg's terms, some juice to come back on at new batsmen, especially at those known not to 'fancy' it, or at tail-enders; but he should not be kept out of the attack too long. The captain's arc of attention will constantly oscillate between the short-term and other needs; between changes or schemes that concern the next ball or the next over, plans for the disposition of bowlers in the next hour (who will take over at the top end, say, and when) or for the rest of the session, and indeed some outline of strategy for the whole day. (He may know that the second new ball will become available after tea, so he will calculate on using at least one spinner in the period leading up to this break.)

Let us go back to the beginning. What field should a fast bowler have at the start of an innings? What line and length should he be encouraged to bowl?

As a rule, a batsman has an area of uncertainty just outside the off-stump. He has to move quickly to get eye and feet in line with the ball; he has to judge whether it can be safely left. Most new-ball bowlers aim for this area, hoping to find an outside edge for the 'keeper or slips. The bouncier the pitch the more invariable the rule. Lillee used to reckon that 95 per cent of his deliveries would, at Perth, bounce *over* the level of the bails; only the yorker or full-toss would hit the stumps. So his dismissals there were almost all to catches. On a dead-slow pitch, on the other hand, with little bounce, the edge would often drop short of the slips and the batsman has more time to adjust; but the ball would far less often bounce over the stumps. So Lillee's (and others') *line* of attack would change. He would try harder to hit the stumps or trap the batsman LBW, and would have fewer slips.

In normal conditions, midway between Perth and, say, a slab of lifeless mud at Karachi, any self-respecting new-ball bowler would want at least two and probably three slips in a three-, four- or five-day match. (The longer the match, the more you can afford to attack.)

My first question of a bowler was often 'Do you want a 6–3, or a 5–4 field?' – that is, did he want six on the off and three on the leg, or five and four? Let us suppose we agree on 6–3. The next question is how attacking should we be? The answer will depend on many factors – the nature of the pitch, the bowler's confidence, the type of batsman, the state of the match. There will have to be at least one defensive fielder in front of the batsman on the off-side.

Two general rules: the faster the bowler and the shorter he bowls, the more often the ball will end up behind square. So the issue of whether a mid-off is needed as well as a man in the covers will depend on the bowler's speed and length. The risk of *over*-attacking in field-placing may be that the bowler *under*-attacks in the length he is prepared to bowl; without a mid-off he may fear being driven, and therefore bowl a shorter, more negative length.

On the other hand, a gap on the off-side might induce a fatal drive, too early in a batsman's innings. J.J. Warr, the Middlesex captain and outswing bowler of the '50s, used to leave square-cover open, hoping to tempt a batsman to follow the ball away from his body. I remember Sarfraz dismissing me when Middlesex played Pakistan in 1974; his first two balls were inswingers, just short of a length; the third was temptingly pitched up, almost a half-volley. There was only one man in the covers. Excited, I went for the drive. The ball swung away and found the edge. Brearley c. Asif Iqbal (third slip) b. Sarfraz 0!

Puritanically, I always preferred the opposition to score boundaries from honest drives than from inadvertent or even sneaky nudges or thick edges; so if it came to a choice between having a third-man or a mid-off I would tend to opt for the third-man – though not, of course, on a slow pitch and outfield. In Test matches, we would be more likely to do without either, and pack the slip-area: most Test openers are hoping for a long and initially defensive occupation.

I have often felt that gully is an over-used position. The genuine defensive edge rarely goes as wide as gully, and the mishit drive or square cut would be as likely to end up in the hands of a one-saving fielder much deeper than conventional gully. The latter is needed, though, on a bouncy pitch where the quickie may find the shoulder of the bat or a self-protective glove. On ordinary, slower pitches, Fletcher's plan with Essex has a lot to be said for it. He would often set four slips, a backward-cover, and an extra-cover as his off-side field.

To sum up so far: a conventional attacking off-side field for a quick bowler with the new ball would be four slips, a gully and an extra-cover. A conventional defensive field would consist of two slips, a gully, third-man, cover and mid-off.

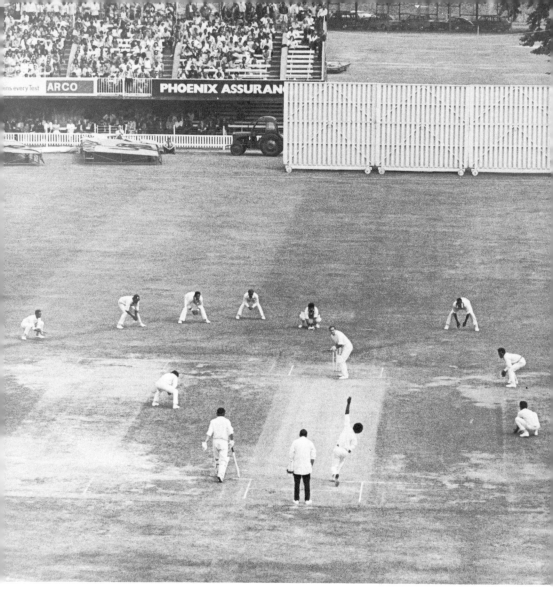

Lillee was capable of bowling to a 7–2 field without either giving away leg-side runs or wasting the ball outside the off-stump. In the Centenary Test in Melbourne, on a helpful pitch, he bowled with six men in the slips and a square-cover. On the leg-side he had only a short-leg and a deep fine-leg. I managed to survive for at least an hour against him in each innings, and I cannot remember being able to let anything go without difficulty; nor did he offer us any runs on the leg-side. (Later in the match, as the ball got softer and the pitch more placid, Lillee tried a few more inswingers – hoping for LBWs – and bowled to a more normal 6–3 or even 5–4 field.)

To return to our captain's ordinarily talented opening bowler. Where will he put the three leg-side fielders? A deep fine-leg is almost always

Bernard Julien bowling to Ray Illingworth, third Test at Lord's, 1973. West Indies had amassed 652 for eight declared; so they could attack all-out. I am puzzled, though, by the short extra-cover and the short mid-wicket, as I cannot readily imagine what sort of shot, from Illingworth, would lead to his dismissal in either position.

called for. Since Hutton and Bailey saved the Headingley Test against Australia in 1953 by packing the leg-side, the laws of cricket have been changed to prohibit more than two fielders being placed behind square on the on-side. As a result, this area, unlike the off-side, cannot in any way be covered by the close-in fieldsmen. And only a medium-pacer like Tom Cartwright or Derek Shackleton could hope to bowl regularly without a deep fine-leg; with their accuracy they were able to operate with only a leg-slip and a backward square-leg.

Of the other two fielders, one is likely to be at mid-on, to prevent firm pushes from being expensive. For many batsmen, this fielder can be quite wide, almost at mid-wicket. The final fielder will be either at short-leg or near the square-leg umpire. Short-legs are essential when

Fred Titmus felled by Jeff Thomson, third Test, Melbourne, 1974–5. Titmus's method against the fierce pace of Thomson or Lillee had been to move way across his stumps to the off-side, evading the short-pitched ball. By this means he had scored a courageous 61 in the preceding Test at Perth. The Australians then moved their line to outside off-stump, and Titmus found himself in trouble. This delivery was not a bouncer; in fact the batsman was struck on the side of the knee. The slight grins on the faces of Greg Chappell and Ashley Mallett are not so much expressions of callousness as of an involuntary amusement at the indignity of the collapse.

the bowler is capable of extracting sharp lift and finding the batsmen's gloves, or when the predominant movement is from the off. Where exactly the short-leg should stand is a nice matter that can become a lottery. Really fast bowlers sometimes do without a mid-on; but then they cannot afford to pitch the ball up too often.

Now for an entirely general point: the captain should notice which side of the ball a batsman tends to get. Against fast bowlers, does he back away? Does he look to play the ball on the off-side? Does he sway back from the bouncer and/or attempt to cut it? In all these cases, any 'floating' fielder should probably be placed on the off-side. (The other alternative is to shift the line of attack towards leg.) On the other hand, the batsman may move way over to the off-side, and play more to leg. He may aim to get inside the bouncer and either hook it or let it pass behind his back. John Dyson, the Australian opener, was a good example of this. For such batsmen, an extra fielder may be put on the leg-side.

Perhaps some examples will make my meaning clearer.

On the bouncy Australian pitches in 1974–5 Mike Denness tried to stay to the leg-side of the short-pitched ball. The only attacking shot he would attempt against it was the cut. Ian Chappell was therefore able to put seven fielders on the off-side, and instruct his bowlers to bowl straight. I am not saying that this technique of batting is inevitably wrong. There are circumstances in which getting precisely into line is both physically risky and tactically unsound. I have seen as correct a player as Boycott look to play very fast bowling in this way; except that he was so quick to spot the length of the ball, and so quick on his feet, that he would be in line for the well-pitched-up delivery.

Clive Radley is another who plays short fast bowling to the off. In 1974, he improvised a marvellous 90 against the bowling of Willis, David Brown and Stephen Rouse on a lively, rain-affected pitch at Edgbaston. But Warwickshire's tactics, with A.C. Smith as captain, were hard to believe; they allowed him to score dozens of runs to third-man before putting a fielder in that area. On this occasion, they would in fact have been better off with a third-man than a fine-leg.

Many other players go the other way. I myself found that much depended on the way a bowler moved the ball. Against an outswing bowler, like Lillee or Richard Hadlee, I would be more likely to stay to the leg-side against a bouncer. Against Croft or Sylvester Clarke, I would move further to the off. I felt less comfortable against Clarke when Surrey placed a man at backward short-leg, taken perhaps from gully or third slip, as I felt that I would not be able to avoid playing certain of his deliveries in the air in that direction. In 1974, Fred Titmus scored a courageous 61 in the second Test at Perth by moving so far across to the off-side that the bouncers kept missing him; until Lillee and Thomson adjusted their line to wide of off-stump.

Even the great players, who are better equipped to play on either side, and are able to commit themselves later than ordinary mortals, show a preference. Viv Richards, for example, plays more from off to leg, while his namesake Barry favoured the off-side; the same ball that, bowled to Viv, might be dispatched to the long-on boundary would be stroked through extra-cover by Barry. At every level of the game the captain can often get a clue about this characteristic by studying the batsman's feet, and their initial movement.

I do not want to give the impression that it is only for fast bowlers that this question is an issue, though batsmen often react against pace in quite special ways, inconsistent with their pattern of play against all other bowling.

Much of what I have so far said about fast bowling relates to line. For, particularly with the new ball, bowling wider often means squandering one's main – or sometimes one's only – chance to attack. Bowling the right length is equally important.

Now, it is true that 'good' length is relative; relative to speed, pitch, the batsmen, the state of the game and so on. But it is also the case that, on a given pitch, what turns out to be the right sort of length will not vary much. However subtle the bowler may be in responding to a particular batsman, his main, and basic task is to see to the mechanics of his own action, and propel the ball in such a way that it lands on what would generally be a goodish length, and travels in what would generally be a goodish direction. It is often sound advice to say to a bowler, 'Just bowl. Don't think about the batsman.' In conditions that help the bowler, this approach is particularly likely to be valid; if you, the bowler, get it right, *any* batsman will be stretched to deal with you. Everything else may be irrelevant. The bowler should feel that *he* will dictate to the batsman, not vice-versa.

The captain must be sensitive to all this. There are, as I have said, many occasions in which the bowler should simply revel in his skill. And there is no point in brilliant tactical ideas if they flummox the bowler more than the batsman. Non-bowling captains in particular are prone to expect too much, too often, from their bowlers. Seeing the game as a batsman, I would often be keen for our quicker bowlers to test the opposition with a bouncer or two. Now, tactically and psychologically, my plan might often have been sound; except that I sometimes failed to take the *bowler's* state of mind into account. As John Lever once said, *he* has to feel right about bowling a bouncer. He may not; he may feel that he is still searching for a rhythm, or that the extra effort of a bouncer would spoil the rhythm that he is building up. Or he may know that, in his present physical state, the bouncer would be all too predictable and all too hittable.

As a rule, the slower the pitch the further up a bowler should bowl. Like the darts player who tries to avoid '1' and scores '5', he may well over-compensate. The thought is: I must not bowl short on this pitch; the result is half-volleys. At Middlesex we used to feel, particularly in 1980, that Daniel over-pitched for a man of his speed. Eventually, we discovered that he had his eye on winning the *Sun*'s so-called 'Demon-Bowler' contest for the bowler who hit the stumps most in a season (in fact he ended that season winning a different *Sun* award – for his 'outstanding contribution to cricket').

On very easy-paced pitches, which give no help to the bowler, it may be worth trying a few short-pitched deliveries, in the hope of inducing an error. Norbert Phillip, the Essex and West Indies fast bowler, used sometimes to bowl ultra-short, 'loopy' bouncers, aimed to reach the batsman at or above head-height. The batsman, he reasoned, may be greedy, and play too soon; it is not easy to control a tennis-smash. In 1979, Phillip dismissed Roland Butcher – an excellent hooker – with just such a delivery – and Lillee got Gatting out similarly in the Test at Manchester in 1981. Sunny Gavaskar bowled a single over consisting of six deliveries so short that they bounced like tennis-balls at the start of England's second innings in the Test match at Bangalore in 1977. (But his main aim was to scuff up the pitch for India's spinners, a ploy which, remarkably, he was allowed to put into action at each end by means of an extravagant follow-through.) More sensibly, I have seen Indian opening bowlers pitch the ball up, looking for swing, for the first few overs, and revert to a much shorter length when the ball stops moving.

Bouncer-frequency should depend not only on the batsman's ability to deal with the short-pitched ball but also on his all-round skill. Dennis Amiss used to object to the amount of short-pitched bowling he received when he played against Middlesex. I would retort that this was his fault, for playing so much better off the front foot than off the back. Amiss was one of those batsmen who like moving *to* the ball rather than letting it come to him. He also took his eye off the bouncer. Illingworth even went so far as to say that, 'if protective helmets had not been introduced, Amiss would now be dead'.

So far, I have mainly been discussing faster bowling. In fact, it is with spin bowling that the art of captaincy has more scope. For spin bowling calls for a resourcefulness and cunning that are less mandatory for the more physical, more violent qualities of fast bowling, and it is up to the captain to encourage and contribute to the spin bowler's ploys.

On pitches that are likely to take spin, it is an advantage, if the balance of the side can afford it, to have three spinners rather than two, despite the old saw that if two spinners can't win the match nor can three. It was Illingworth who taught me that individual spinners have characteristically different lengths: that he, Illingworth, pitched his stock ball a couple of feet further up than, say, Titmus; and probably three feet further up than the taller Emburey. (Though Edmonds, equally tall, bowls a fuller length than any of them.)

Illingworth attributed his own practice to having learned his art on the wetter, slower pitches in the north of England. Spinners also have quite different actions, trajectories and delivery points. Lance Gibbs, for example, had a high action for an off-spinner and delivered from wide on the crease. Moreover, he did not drift the ball out, towards slip. Contrast the three English off-spinners; when Illingworth, Titmus and Emburey let go of the ball, their hand was probably over middle-stump. They could actually pitch on middle-stump and hit off; whereas for Gibbs to hit off-stump the ball would have to pitch several inches outside, even if the ball did not turn. Now, of the many consequences of these differences – for example, that Gibbs was less likely to get LBWs, but with his high arm and greater spin he was harder to play on dry, bouncy pitches – the one that is relevant to my present concern is that different spinners can make use of different bits of the pitch. Having three spinners in a team (or even four, as Illingworth regularly had at Leicester), improves a captain's chance of exploiting worn patches. To give another example: John Steele and Chris Balderstone both bowled slow left-arm for Leicestershire. Steele had a low action, and bowled from the very edge of the crease. He did not spin the ball much, being inclined to make it skid through (though he had an infuriating habit of turning one just when you, as batsman, had decided that he wouldn't). His stock delivery would pitch two feet shorter and one foot wider than the slower Balderstone's, who bowled from nearer the stumps, and with less in-slant. Leicester were fortunate that all their spinners could also bat; I am not advocating the selection of four spin bowlers as a general rule.

But this is not the only reason for preferring three spinners to two. People forget that spin bowlers tire; I have often noticed that they make the ball turn less after eight or ten consecutive overs. So, on pitches where they are likely to bowl a large number of overs, it is an advantage to be able to switch them. The simple fact of variety, too, is often a relief to the captain, and the cause of a batsman's undoing.

Indeed, I maintain that spinners and seamers should work in harness more often than they do. How often, in county and club cricket, does one see all the seam bowlers tiring at about the same time, so that after thirty overs of unmitigated seam one gets twenty of unmitigated spin? I remember making this error at Northampton in 1975, when I over-bowled the three seamers in the morning (hoping for a decisive break-through) and was left with few options in the afternoon, when the home team scored freely, ending up at 338 for five.

Whether or not the spinner is operating with a seamer at the other end, it is his responsibility to work hard at keeping a shine on the ball. Seam bowlers are rightly furious if the spinner disregards this task.

Little is lost by trying a spinner early on. Occasionally, there may be sufficient morning damp to help him as well as the seamer. Batsmen are geared up for facing quicker bowlers. And, if nothing happens, the spinner concerned can be quickly withdrawn from the attack. Sometimes, of course, a spinner comes on *faute de mieux*.

My first questions when discussing a field with a spinner would be the same as with a seam bowler: how many of the fielders do you want on each side of the wicket? and how many close catchers?

Take a slow left-arm bowler, operating, as he usually will, round the wicket. The choice will normally be between 6–3 and 5–4 off-side fields. If we settle on 6–3, we are likely to have one of two aims in mind. Either the ball is turning, and it should be hard for a batsman to hit to leg, against the spin, even when the ball pitches around leg-stump; or we may be trying, on a good pitch, to induce the batsman to make an error outside the off-stump, in which case the 6–3 field may be predominantly defensive. In the first case, the field might look like this: there could be three close catchers on the off-side (slip, gully and silly-point) backed by three fielders saving the single (short third-man, cover-point and mid-off). The slip and gully would be looking for catches off the outside edge, while silly-point and short-leg would expect catches from the inside edge, usually in conjunction with the pad. The leg-side fielders would be mid-on, short-leg (usually square) and a man behind square on the leg-side – deep if the batsman is a powerful sweeper, otherwise placed to save the single or to catch a top-edged sweep.

In the second case, we might have only a slip in close. This leaves five defensive fielders on the off-side. We may well start without anyone back on the boundary. It is important that these fielders are not deployed in a haphazard and untidy ring, as often happens. To my mind, there are two possibilities. One is a W formation, in which alternate fielders are closer and the others deeper than the usual one-saving position. The advantages of this arrangement are, first, that the closer fielders may catch drives that are not quite kept down; second, that the field invites the batsman to hit over the top, while keeping some fielders deepish for the mishit; and, third, it is difficult to judge singles, as the ball has to be hit hard enough to evade the closer fielders and yet not too hard if driven straight at the deeper fielders. The other alternative is a box in which short third-man, square-cover, cover and extra-cover form a line parallel with the pitch. It will be clear that extra-cover is much deeper than square-cover; but each fielder should tend to move to the right, challenging the short single. Captains should insist on practice at both formations, and on the players' taking care about their precise location.

With either defensive off-side field, the leg-side field is likely to be mid-on, mid-wicket and backward square-leg, though for some batsmen short-leg will be needed, and for others deep backward square-leg. Sometimes, a long-off or long-on and/or deep extra-cover will be called for.

Rather more frequently, a 5–4 field will be chosen, whether for defensive or attacking bowling. The ordinary version might have one slip with four men in the covers; a leg-slip, backward square-leg, mid-wicket and mid-on.

Naturally, all sorts of modifications to these basic fields are possible. The more interesting variations concern attack. Some batsmen either block or hit. For them, one may have an in-out field, with two or three deep fielders and three or four close catchers. Others may hit less hard, and be more adept at stroking and placing the ball; for them, a ring of fielders behind the close catchers may be more appropriate. During a phase in the Bombay Test in 1977, Bishen Bedi, then India's captain, placed an in-out field for Greig, and a ring for me – exactly right in the circumstances. His tactics, after I had scored quite fluently early on when the fields were more aggressive, drove me to desperation, and eventually made me make the mistake that got me out: I charged down the pitch too early against Prasanna, who saw me come, bowled the ball wide, and had me stumped.

The captain and bowler also have to sense where the chances are most likely to go close to the bat. Even on a turning pitch, some batsmen are more likely to be caught off the inside edge and pad than off the outside edge. Thrusting their leg at the ball, and allowing for spin, they are most likely to be caught on the leg-side, or at silly-point, than in the gully.

I have already described the alternative of bowling over the wicket. This can be used either to attack, as it was with Underwood at Old Trafford, or as a defensive variation. In either case, the leg-side field will need to be strengthened.

Now let us take the off-spinner. During the tour of the West Indies in 1959–60, under May's captaincy, MCC used their off-spinners in a

Jim Laker dismissing Ken Mackay at Manchester, 1956. A typical off-spinner's field to a left-hander on a sharply turning pitch. The fielders are Cowdrey, Oakman (slips), Lock (point), May (short-cover), Washbrook (extra-cover), Evans ('keeper). One main difference between Laker's fields and those of a contemporary off-spinner occurred when he bowled at right-handers; for without the restriction on fielders behind square on the leg-side, Laker could have two backward short-legs plus a fielder behind them.

purely defensive way, setting 6–3 off-side fields. Nowadays, we would be more likely to defend with a 3–6 field, aiming at leg-stump, and basic fields will be 4–5 or 3–6. Having six men on the leg-side may also be attacking. Now that only two men are permitted behind square, it is rare that more than two short-legs can be afforded, for the off-spinner needs someone deepish behind square; and only a player who is both timid and inept will allow him to bowl with two forward short-legs. So an attacking leg-side field will comprise: two short-legs (one forward and one backward), a deep backward square-leg, a mid-wicket and a mid-on. On a turning pitch, many players will be prepared to hit over the top on the leg-side, calculating that the risk is worthwhile, as they are likely to get out if they play defensively: for them, the sixth fielder will be at wide long-on. He may, for other batsmen, be at short mid-wicket for the drive, especially if the ball tends to 'stop'. On the off-side, there will usually be a choice between having a slip or a silly mid-off. Finally, there will be a mid-off and either an extra-cover or short third-man.

If more emphasis on attack is required, one of the three defensive fielders in front of square on the leg-side can be brought to a close-in position on the off-side.

Having only three fielders on the off-side may, of course, be a defensive move. Bowling at or outside the leg-stump to a packed leg-side field has long been recognised as a run-saving device; Warwick Armstrong apparently used it eighty or so years ago. But it has been refined and developed as a regular feature of cricket by the demands of the one-day competitions. In fact the change in the laws referred to above means that a good deal of skill is required to make it effective: the two fielders behind square will have a busy time if the bowler bowls too many deliveries outside the leg-stump.

The Australians have always tended to bowl on or outside the off-stump. Even their off-spinners often bowl with five on the off-side. The wounds of the Bodyline series are still apparent in their reflex antipathy to leg-side fields. In 1977, during the MCC v Australians match at Lord's, Geoff Miller was bowling to Greg Chappell. The Australians were cruising along, without much difficulty. So, for variety, I suggested to Geoff that he try an over or two with seven on the leg-side. I remember Chappell throwing his bat down in disgust.

More extraordinary was the reaction in Australia eighteen months later, when we won a remarkable Test match at Sydney by bowling the home side out for 111, Miller taking three wickets and Emburey four. The ball was turning sharply, so at one point I set a field with only two fielders on the off-side. The field was: silly-point and mid-off; two short-legs; deep square-leg, mid-wicket, short mid-wicket, mid-on and long-on. At once, Kim Hughes, trying to run the ball through the vacant third-man area, was caught off bat and pad. After the match, many Australians, though not, I think, the players, complained about these tactics; they could hardly call them defensive, as we had bowled Australia out in only 49.2 overs; but they felt in their guts that it was all somehow unfair.

Such a field-setting will always be provisional in that it might make a bowler stray too far to the leg-side. More usual would be a field consisting of four men on the off-side; three saving one, the other either at slip or at silly mid-off. The more bouncy the pitch, the more likely the ball is to go to slip, though the decision will also depend on the technique of each batsman and the line the bowler expects to bowl. The leg-side field would be: one short-leg (probably behind square), a deep backward square-leg, square-leg, mid-wicket and mid-on. Again, the variations on this pattern are endless.

When should off-spinners bowl round the wicket (and left-armers against left-handed batsmen)? The main rationale for doing so is to increase the likelihood of LBWs and, for this, the pitch must be taking spin. In such conditions, it is hard for an off-spinner to get an LBW decision from over the wicket, unless the batsman is back on his stumps, since the ball that strikes him in front of off-stump is likely to miss leg, whereas the angle of delivery from round the wicket means that the ball can, after bouncing and turning, travel along an imaginary line from wicket to wicket. (Inswing bowlers, of whom the most notable example was Mike Procter, also make use of the same device when the ball swings sharply.) Going round the wicket may, in these circumstances, be a method of counteracting both pad play and the sweep-shot. It may also, of course, be used for variety when the ball is not deviating an inch.

All good spinners cause the batsman trouble in the air. I mean by this that it is hard to tell early in the flight of the ball exactly where it will pitch. Bedi was a master of this art. By minute changes in action, he could make two deliveries that, to the bemused batsman, appeared identical, end up in quite different places. For instance, by undercutting the ball slightly, he could make it curve in from outside the off-stump; as he may also have bowled it a little quicker, it arrives sooner than the batsman expects. This delivery, let us say, pitches just outside off-stump, and would hit leg-stump. The next one looks the same; but now Bedi cocks his wrist more, imparting more spin and less swing. Though the arm action looks the same, he allows the ball to come out of his hand more slowly. The batsman may well feel that it is just like the last; but no, this one does not curve in, and, being slower, it lands shorter than he expected; moreover, being spun more, it turns. So this delivery ends up perhaps nine inches outside his off-stump. All great spin bowlers have something of this quality. Now, on helpful pitches, the bowler relies on all this subtlety rather less. Here he knows that, so long as he pitches the ball regularly in the right place, the pitch will do the rest.

It is on unhelpful pitches that defeating the batsman 'in the air' is most valuable. On such pitches, there will not usually be much point in having too many close-in fielders. If the ball will not turn, it will not often find the edge. So here the bowler, with the assistance of the captain, will have to devise means of persuading the batsman to make mistakes. One part of this will always include wearing him down by making run-scoring difficult. Some bowlers, like Underwood, blessed with patience and accuracy, are invaluable to the captain for their ability to keep control in this way. Others are prepared to risk more by way of variation, flight and enticement. The latter invite the batsman to drive, but deceive him in the air. Hugh Tayfield, the South African off-spinner, often bowled with two men 'on the drive' – twelve or fifteen yards from the bat on the leg-side – for just such an end. 'Flight' does not, incidentally, simply mean bowling the ball more slowly, or pushing it higher in the air. It is hard to say what the difference is, except that the man who deceives the batsman in the air *bowls* his slower ball, he doesn't just toss it up.

The captain must know a bowler's range. Curiously for so marvellous a spinner, Underwood has always found that he tends to lose much of his zip when he bowls appreciably slower than usual. His range of pace needs to be small to be most productive. He has, nevertheless, the ability to confuse the batsman in the air without ever bowling really slowly. In Pakistan, in 1967, I encouraged Underwood to flight the ball. The result was that he lost not only this elusive elusiveness but also his accuracy. (Since when I would grin at him down the pitch whenever he bowled me one of his rare slow balls; except once, at Lord's in 1971, when one of them clean-bowled me!)

Even when a bowler has a wide range, the captain should not assume that he can confidently operate at one particular end of it at any time. (The problem of bowling slower than usual is not unlike that facing a quickie who is trying to bowl faster and shorter than his usual pace.) There are, however, conditions which cry out for genuinely slow bowling. In the first Test at Wellington, in 1984, there seemed, from a distance, to be a time in New Zealand's second innings when Nick Cook, the slow left-arm bowler and our only spinner, might have experimented; New Zealand were battling to save the match with their lower-order batsmen. The pitch was docile, and as Jeremy Coney likes to drive at the ball, and against the spin, it appeared that England could have risked a few boundaries in the search for a breakthrough, if Cook had had the confidence to bowl slower. For it often happens that the ball will only turn when it is bowled slowly; the problem is that the margin of error is then reduced.

Edmonds is capable, on occasions, of beautifully controlled, genuinely slow bowling. Not only does he then turn the ball more, but also the extra little loop of the ball, added to his height, makes it bounce higher. He bowled in just this way on the first morning of our match against Kent at Tunbridge Wells in 1982, dismissing Bob Woolmer and Chris Tavaré. Any other style of slow bowling was on that firm but springy pitch relatively innocuous.

The captain *may*, when things go well, be able to instil enough confidence in his slow bowlers for them to feel free to operate over their widest possible range. Often his field-placings will reflect not only their joint aims, but also their hope of persuading a batsman to play the way *they* want him to. They may put men in the deep in order to prevent him from hitting out; conversely – if there are runs to play with – keep an attacking field to encourage him to play shots.

So far, I have been talking about bowlers who spin the ball from the front of the hand; they are sometimes called 'orthodox'. The leg-spinner has always been a dubious character, unorthodox by implication. It has become a cliché to speak of his magic and sleight of hand. I find it hard not to refer to him in orotund Edwardianese as a 'purveyor of leg-spin', or 'back-of-the-hand merchant'. The word 'googly' reminds me of that stretch of the sacred Ganges that emerges into the Bay of Bengal near Calcutta under the egregious name 'Hoogley'. And the leg-break's mirror-image has been stamped with the mark of inscrutability by being christened, if that is the right word, the 'Chinaman', though it is more likely that the name derives from Ellis Edgar Achong, a slow left-arm bowler of Chinese origin who played for West Indies between 1929 and 1935. What the leg-spinner has to offer is not what it seems.

Or seemed. For the species has all but become extinct, at least in England, as anachronistic as the language used to describe it. There are many reasons for the decline, and I will return to them later. Now I will mention just one: the misuse of leg-spinners by captains temperamentally unsympathetic to them.

I can give three examples. Johnny Wardle was a most versatile cricketer. He was a highly competent orthodox spinner, a brilliant bowler of Chinamen and googlies, and even an adequate swing bowler. In many conditions, his orthodox bowling was the best bet; it was more accurate, and he could defend one side of the wicket. On wet pitches in particular he could bowl sides out more cheaply than with the Chinaman. In other circumstances, though – and especially overseas – he could be a genuinely attacking bowler only with the Chinaman. In the other style, he was reduced to defence: he might force good players to make an error, but was unlikely to get them out when they were defending. Now, Len Hutton, as captain of England, had a deep respect for fast bowling, and an equally deep mistrust of leg-spin; the outcome was that he used Wardle as a stock bowler whose job was to allow the fast bowlers to rest. He was allowed to bowl Chinamen and googlies in the last Test of the 1954–5 series, when the Ashes were safe, and took eight wickets in the match. Jim Swanton wrote that he bowled well enough in this game to 'make clear what he might have achieved by this method if it did not go so much against the grain, in Yorkshire and England circles'.

I think Hutton, like many Yorkshiremen, found leg-spin bowling disturbingly enigmatic. Wardle once told me of an occasion when he was bowling orthodox spinners to Hutton in the nets at Headingley. Hutton, he said, kept dancing down the pitch and hitting him everywhere; not least way back over his head. Wardle became fed up with this, and switched to Chinamen. 'I don't want to sound immodest,' he went on, 'but I have never made a great player look so much at sea.'

I will let Hutton have the last word: Middlesex have a tradition of leg-spinners, and they often took wickets against Yorkshire. In 1965, Harry Latchman took six for 52 against them at Lord's. After we came off the field, Len visited us in our dressing-room. John Murray and Fred Titmus teased him. 'How is it,' they said, 'that you Yorkshiremen have no idea against leg-spin?' And they quoted examples – Jim Sims, Ian Peebles, H. G. Owen-Smith, R. W. V. Robins, R. V. C. Robins, Denis Compton, and now Latchman – all Middlesex leg-spinners. Hutton let them finish. Then: 'The further north you go,' he said, pointing to the ceiling, 'the slower they get.' And he tapped the side of his head with his finger.

Leg-spin bowling with its flourish and strut, its long-hops and its patches of brilliance, is anathema to the Yorkshire mentality. It is difficult

John Gleeson, like Jack Iverson, was unorthodox even among the unorthodox. Both bowled with their middle finger bent double behind the ball and both were extraordinarily difficult to 'read'. Such rare skills are less likely to emerge today, with the glut of one-day cricket and the frequency of Test and International series.

to imagine Abdul Qadir being allowed to survive and flower in Yorkshire; and if the next small, flexible-jointed Qadir happens to be born in Bradford, his best chance would be to move south (if not also east) at an early age.

In my other two examples, the captains used their leg-spinners, but more as stock bowlers than as potential match-winners. I refer to Bill Lawry with John Gleeson and Trevor Bailey with Robin Hobbs. Gleeson was not unlike Sonny Ramadhin: both bowled leg-breaks and off-spinners from the front of the hand, with a quick whirly action that made picking one from the other hard. In 1970–1, few if any of the English batsmen could 'read' Gleeson. Yet Lawry rarely used him to attack, rarely crowded the new batsman with close fielders. Like Hutton, he had a vivid respect for fast bowling. When I saw him at the Centenary Test in Melbourne in 1977 a few years after his retirement, I commented on how young he looked. 'I haven't been ducking and weaving these last years, have I?' he replied.

In the case of Bailey and Hobbs, there was far more excuse. Hobbs always claimed that his captain wanted him to bowl like a slow left-armer – pushing it through, capable of bowling defensively and for long spells. The result was that Hobbs lost his ability to spin the ball sharply, and became exactly what his captain wanted; he even drifted the ball in, like the left-armer. But this may, in fact, have been his best chance of building a career, and surviving in a form of county cricket which already included one-day matches. Possibly, too, Essex were never in his formative years powerful enough as a side to be able to afford a potential match-winner who was also quixotic and experimental.

Leg-spinners are, in fact, of most value in a team that can score plenty of runs, and score them quickly. Middlesex's immediate post-war successes were based on a marvellous batting line-up, adventurous captaincy and three leg-spinners. The leg-spinners are most effective on dry pitches and in warm weather; in short, in relatively high-scoring matches. The climate, as well as the character, of Yorkshire has militated against them.

But why have leg-spinners all but disappeared? Part of the answer lies in the factors that have counted against spin bowlers in general, and helped seamers: the use of fertilisers, the watering of outfields and the changes in ball-manufacture. More specifically, though, leg-spinners have suffered from a change in attitude. Cricketers have become less cavalier. It is no longer thinkable that a wicket-keeper should have 64 stumpings in a season, as Les Ames did in 1932. Contrast Ames's career record (415 stumpings, 698 catches) with John Murray's (257 stumpings, 1270 catches) or Jim Parks's (93 stumpings, 1089 catches). Tail-enders no longer slog gaily, thereby becoming quick victims for a slow leg-spinner. Selectors, captains and cricketers in general have become more conscious of containment; and the leg-spinner, especially in recent English conditions, has become a luxury. One-day cricket, which calls for attacking batting but defensive bowling, has hastened his demise, but it, too, is a symptom as well as a cause. His decline is the saddest loss for cricket, and if Abdul Qadir's, and, more recently, the young Indian Sivaramakrishnan's English victims contribute in any way to a revival of the art then their successes should be cheered by Englishmen, however partisan. For of all the skills of the game, theirs are the most subtle, charming and delightful. Leg-spinners are a pleasure to play against, and to have on your side. And they are a rewarding breed to captain.

The changes in attitude that have affected leg-spin bowling have, of course, other aspects; and I will conclude this chapter by discussing how these have influenced field-placing.

Fewer batsmen, nowadays, hit over the top. Bowlers tend, too, to bowl flatter and perhaps shorter; which limits both the opportunity and the temptation. So long-offs, long-ons and deep extra-covers have become rarities in two-innings, first-class cricket. A few batsmen will still go for the lofted shot even when the field is back; Botham is an example, as

Fred Titmus batting in calmer, less torrid times, against Sussex at Lord's. Tony Greig is at silly-point and Alan Mansell behind the stumps. Titmus was inclined to get his legs to the off-side of the ball against the spinners, too; he also played with his bat ahead of rather than behind his pad, so he was unlikely to give a pad-bat chance to the off-side. In fact he rarely got into trouble against off-spinners, despite a lunging style that suggested he might.

was Chris Wilkins, the South African who played for Derbyshire in the '70s. For them, the captain would be foolish not to place one or two fielders on the fence straight away. For many players, however, there is a strong case for keeping the field in at least until they have hit once over the top. As Cartwright used to say, the first time is the hardest; it takes nerve, and a summoning of courage. No batsman can feel really confident about the shot the first time. I used to find, however, that many spin bowlers preferred to pre-empt the shot rather than gamble on a mishit. Titmus, for instance, would want a deep wide long-on for any batsman who he knew had hit him over the top in the past. (Titmus also used to want two short-legs for the price of one, but that is another story!)

The changes over, say, Titmus's career, between 1949 and 1982, have been no less striking with regard to attacking fields. In the '50s an off-spinner would almost never operate without a backward short-leg and a slip. Silly-point, and a very close, short square-leg, were almost unknown. Thirty years later, it is not uncommon to see an off-spinner bowl with fielders in these new positions, but no one at slip or backward short-leg, and similar changes can be seen in the fields used by slow left-armers and leg-spinners. Even for quicker bowlers, the short-leg is more likely to be in front of square; and silly mid-off is not unknown. Why?

I think there are two main explanations. The lesser cause is that pitches have become slower. The edge is less likely to carry to slip or leg-slip; whereas fielders in front of the bat can stand closer in for the ball that pops up off bat and pad (or pad and bat). Far more significant is the change in defensive technique. In Titmus's early days, the forward defensive shot involved pushing the bat way out in front of the pad. Coaching books will still advocate this as the 'correct' way to play. The inside edge would, therefore, miss the pad and go behind square, while the outside edge would travel further towards the slips the harder the bat was pushed out towards the ball.

Increasingly, however, batsmen have tended to play forward with their bat level with, or even behind, the front pad. (I believe that the change dated from the May-Cowdrey stand of 411 against West Indies in 1957, in which the pad was used to counteract Ramadhin.) With this method, the inside edge cannot get to backward short-leg, as the batsman's pad and leg are in the way. If the ball hits bat first, it will then hit the pad, and may well go forward of square. On the other hand, when the ball is played with pad ahead of bat, misjudgement of line such that the pad is too close to the line of the ball will result in the ball brushing the front pad before hitting the bat. Then the pad tees up the ball, which may pop up on the off-side even off the middle of the bat. I have seen one batsman caught at orthodox mid-off from this pad-bat combination; and I myself was so much a sucker for it in my young days that I was caught twice in the match in this way when Cambridge played Middlesex in 1962, once thrusting my front pad at the ball with such vigour as to be caught and bowled by Titmus.

I am glad to say that field-placing and the courage of close fielders, combined with the change in the LBW law that allows a batsman to be given out even if the ball strikes his pad outside the line of the off-stump provided that he does not offer a stroke at the ball, are gradually eliminating the unattractive habit of pad-play that became the vogue after 1957.

CHAPTER NINE

Strategy, tactics and unusual ploys

There was once a lionkeeper at the Dublin Zoo called Mr Flood, who was remarkable in that over the years he had bred many lion cubs, but never lost one. When asked his secret he replied, 'No two lions are alike.' No doubt he had strategies and general lines of policy. But like a good cricket captain, he responded to each situation afresh.

Strategy is as essential for a cricket captain as for a lionkeeper, but for both flexibility is equally important.

Broader policy-lines may be formulated for a whole tour, or series. For example, in 1976 Tony Greig decided that, with the limited fire-power at his disposal, England's best chance against West Indies was to play a defensive game in the field. (He was also in favour of picking Brian Close and me to blunt their pace attack.) He had watched them in Australia the previous winter, and had seen the mercurial quality of their brilliance. They had lost 5–1 against Greg Chappell's team, despite scoring at the prodigious rate of 4.66 runs each eight-ball over throughout the series. Tony's policy made sense; it would be all too easy to set fields that would be appropriate for stolid English players, and find the score mounting uncontrollably.

Next winter, for the tour of India, he also had a clear idea of his plan of campaign. When he had played in India four years earlier he had seen the remarkably high standard of spin bowling throughout the country. He noticed too how competent the top Indian batsmen were against spin. And he concluded that we should rely on faster bowling for our main weapon of attack, as indeed of defence.

Both strategies were sound; but both needed to be applied with flexibility. In the first Test against West Indies, at Trent Bridge, Greig missed, I thought, a fine opportunity for attacking on the first day. The weather was cloudy, the ball moved about; yet we never had more than two slips and a deep gully in close-catching positions. The West Indies were anxious about batting in these conditions, and played cautiously.

Strategy, tactics and unusual ploys

Yet Close spent two days lumbering across from square-leg to square-leg, dismayed at not being allowed to field at short-leg. Typically, Greig afterwards accepted that he had made a mistake; equally typically he reacted by going to an opposite extreme at Lord's, in the second Test. Defending a meagre total of 250 on a slow pitch, he nevertheless posted five slips. The immediate effect was dramatic: West Indies lost three wickets for 40 runs (Larry Gomes, I remember, being brilliantly caught by Bob Woolmer left-handed at fourth slip) and were all out for 182, but I think this success was fortuitous. In general, my main criticism of Greig as a captain is that he swung too violently between the opposite poles of attack and defence.

In India, Greig's policy worked wonderfully. Lever, Willis and Old fired away, while Underwood kept the batsmen quiet – as well as taking wickets – at the other end. On the following tour of India, however, five years later, I felt that Fletcher, who had also been impressed with Greig's campaign in 1976–7, persevered with a seam-dominated attack for too long after the loss of the first Test at Bombay.

So, over a series of games the captain needs to have some overall plan, however tentative. Equally, when taking the field for a particular match he should have some idea of a strategy. He will have assessed the pitch; and should know the main strengths and weaknesses of both teams. Occasionally, he will start with a firm conviction of his intentions. On a grassy pitch, in overcast conditions, he will expect to employ his fast bowlers for most of the time, and his main problem may be how to combine them in order to make best use of their energies. On a dusty turner or on a drying pitch he will expect to have his spinners on almost at once. In each case, the bowlers who are unlikely to be his main wicket-takers will be used to rest the others, or to provide variety against batsmen who have become set.

On most occasions, the outlook will be less clear-cut. The captain will expect to have to use all his main bowlers in the course of the innings. On unknown pitches, whose behaviour may be hard to predict, the captain's approach should be even more experimental; he should try all his bowlers early, to find out whom the conditions assist most.

Whatever the situation, the captain should not work to rule. One county captain used to decide before every Sunday League game started who would be bowling each over. He gave his players slips of paper before they fielded with their positions for each bowler written down. Such a method is a travesty of proper captaincy.

I have argued that strategy depends on the captain's view of the opposition and of the conditions. It also depends, of course, on the resources available to him. In 1982, Willis dropped out from the second Test against Pakistan at Lord's because of injury. His absence left David Gower with an unbalanced attack. He had four seam bowlers, none really quick, in Botham, Robin Jackman, Derek Pringle and Ian Greig; and an off-spinner, Eddie Hemmings. It is perhaps harsh to criticise

Gower for his handling of such an unpromising attack in his first Test as captain, but he did, I think, fail to make the best use of it.

For of all the seamers, the one man capable of bowling above military medium was Botham. The situation demanded that he be persuaded, cajoled or instructed to concentrate on attacking in short bursts, as he did in the first innings of the Adelaide Test in 1979, when he took four for 42. Yet Botham was allowed to bowl immensely long spells at far below his fastest speed. Since Hemmings, the only slow bowler, opted to bowl at almost medium-pace, the potential for variety was squandered, and the entire attack condemned to mediocrity. Pakistan scored 428–8, Botham's three wickets costing 148 runs and involving no less than 44 overs of effort.

I have stressed the need for flexibility. A captain must keep an open mind about how a pitch may play. I remember starting the fourth day's play of an Edgbaston Test by bowling Edmonds, since on the Saturday the pitch had become docile for the fast bowlers but was beginning to offer some purchase for the spinning ball. However, we noticed that each delivery made a greenish mark on the beige surface: instead of gripping and deviating, the ball was merely skidding through. This unexpected trace of moisture must have been caused by the weekend covering. We quickly replaced Edmonds with a seam bowler.

At many grounds, and particularly at Leeds, the captain must be alert to changes in the weather. If it becomes overcast, he should try a seamer, as the ball will often move around in the air and off the pitch.

There are spin bowlers who have much to offer on a green pitch. Emburey, like Titmus before him, is a master of swing and variation, and batsmen often play him for non-existent turn. Len Hutton in a delightful story against himself once told me about being caught at slip off Titmus. 'In the north,' he said wryly, 'when they go like this' – here he indicated an off-spinner's hand-action – 'you expect the ball to turn. But with Fred, it goes that way!' – miming the drift from leg to off. Emburey enjoys bowling in such conditions, 'fiddling' the batsmen out. In 1982, he took four for 32 against Notts at Trent Bridge without making a single ball turn from the off.

Equally, some seam bowlers can adapt to unfavourable conditions. The finest bowling I ever saw was in 1980 on a Melbourne track that was totally unhelpful to fast bowling. Lillee, after an unpromising start to the match when after five unproductive overs he had to leave the field because of a headache, came back into the attack with the score over a hundred without loss. For the remainder of the match he cut down his pace, bowling a mixture of leg-cutters and off-cutters interspersed with swingers and quicker balls to such effect that he ended with eleven wickets for 138 runs. As a batsman, it was easy to see from Lillee's action whether he was attempting the leg-cutter or the off-cutter; but none of us – bowler, batsman or fielders – had any idea whether a particular ball would deviate.

Strategy, tactics and unusual ploys

Before an innings, a captain will formulate some vague plan about the best arrangement of bowlers and ends, taking into consideration factors like wind, slope, irregularities of pitch and length of boundaries. I have discussed some of the problems bowlers find in running up or down slopes; there are also grounds (most notably Lord's) where the slope is from side to side. Lord's offers significant home-team advantage for this very reason; the slope is a trap for the inexperienced and an asset to the knowing. When he bowls from the Pavilion End, the raw bowler may find that the ball keeps drifting down the leg-side. When he tries to adjust this, by getting his left shoulder round more, he runs on to the pitch in his follow-through. Even as great a bowler as John Snow preferred the Nursery End for these reasons. Yet the Pavilion End has traditionally been the first choice for quick bowlers, not least because the main ridge, now much less prominent, was at a fast bowler's length at the Nursery End, and because the prevailing wind comes from behind the pavilion. Moreover, the slope from the off-side sets the batsman additional problems in deciding which ball to let go. I know of no other first-class ground with a comparable geography; perhaps these tactical remarks will be more relevant for village captains than for their seniors!

The captain will have to take account of the preferences and whims of his bowlers, while encouraging them to become confident about coming in at either end. In one-day matches, where a minimum of five bowlers must be used, at least one bowler will have to bowl from each end (unless six bowlers are used).

Short boundaries cause additional anxiety. Everything – slope, bare patches, direction of wind – argues for putting your off-spinner on at the Pavilion End, except that for a particular match the leg-side boundary is a mere fifty yards. Short boundaries are a bane, especially with regard to spin bowling, in that they can at times override so many purely cricketing considerations; bowlers even have to change their length, aiming for the blockhole, simply to avoid being slogged for an easy four or six.

There has been, as I have already hinted, a marked overall change in the approach of captains to field-placing, especially for defence. The new attitude may be summed up as follows: there is no point in having fielders in attacking positions if there is precious little chance of a catch, and if they may be better deployed elsewhere. Now, despite my regrets about the passing of the leg-spin era, I entirely approve of this maxim. Bradman himself admits that, even disregarding the lower over-rate, such a way of thinking would have made him work harder for his runs.

All too often, a ring of slips is, or was, purely ornamental; a gesture to a conventional requirement. It was a mark of Dexter's originality that he saw before others how maladaptive attacking fields often are in one-day cricket; an originality that paid off with Sussex winning the Gillette Cup for the first two years. I was struck by M. J. K. Smith's willingness to follow through this policy to what seems to me to be a perfectly logical conclusion when in 1972 he put the wicket-keeper on the boundary for the last ball of a limited-overs match: we, Middlesex, needed three runs to win, and Smith was taking no chances. Seven years later, in a day/night match in Sydney, I had the opportunity to copy Smith, in exactly similar circumstances. West Indies wanted three to win from the last ball of that match. I posted David Bairstow, our 'keeper, on the boundary at long-stop. The Australian crowds, not over-enthusiastic about the prospect of a 'Pom' win (even against someone else), pelted Bairstow with beer cans, and me with abuse. But Botham bowled Croft, and we won the match by two runs.

I was also impressed by Close's more creative captaincy when he did away with slips in a championship match at Lord's in 1972. The pitch was very slow, and after the ball had lost much of its bounce few edges would have carried anywhere near slip. But Close did not resort to unqualified defence. He experimented shrewdly in field-placings for close catches in front of the bat, from bat and pad, or, a little deeper, from half-hit drives. His bowlers bowled straight, and gave nothing away. It was, in the best sense, a professional display, which showed up what has been a short-coming in the Middlesex side ever since the war – an inability, or unwilling-ness, to settle for rigorous containment when needed.

Greg Chappell, in the Melbourne Test in 1980, employed similar fields to Close's, without needing to go so far as doing without slips altogether. And I was always willing to allow Botham to wander in to an extremely close slip position on slow pitches such as we found in Pakistan.

I find that the phrase 'cost-effectiveness' comes to mind to describe this symptom of a more careful and cautious age. The regrettable aspect of this increased concern for productivity and economy is that in dull hands the game gets duller, and some captains forget that there are times when the most effective method *is* to attack, or to experiment, or to risk early losses in the hope of a longer-term gain. Besides, there is unending scope for creativity and purposiveness, even in defence.

Let me give an example of a day when such probing seemed to pay off. In 1980, Middlesex played their first championship match at Uxbridge, against Derbyshire. We lost the toss, took an early wicket, but soon discovered that it was likely to be hard work bowling the opposition out. The pitch was slow, and there was little movement or turn. Their best player, Peter Kirsten, a neat, quick-footed batsman in the Doug Walters mould, began to play with authority. With the score at 51, he was joined by David Steele. This was not a pitch to suit Steele, who often gives his most valuable performances in more embattled circum-stances. He was somewhat out of touch, too; and we realised that he was having difficulty getting the ball away, provided that we did not bowl short for him to play the hook, his favourite stroke.

After some time, we noticed that Kirsten was becoming restless. I had put some fielders on the boundary, in particular at deep third-man for Edmonds, to stop Kirsten scoring fours from his pet shot, the cut; so he was scoring singles, and Steele was not getting runs at all. More important, Kirsten was becoming edgy at losing the strike and at having his own rate of scoring reduced. We went further, exaggeratedly giving Steele a single at the end of the over, hoping to inflame the resentment between the partners. We looked bored but amused, intending the batsman to feel that, really, on such a friendly pitch and fast outfield they should be scoring faster than two runs an over. The ultra-defensive fields were meant partly to convey, or underline, the idea that there was nothing in the pitch for the bowlers.

After an hour or more of this game, I reverted to a normal field, with two slips; Kirsten drove hugely, and dragged the ball on to his wicket. His 91 took three hours thirty-six minutes; the last 41 taking up ninety-nine minutes of that time.

I remember, as a young batsman, being virtually shamed out by the groans and curses of a Surrey team which, as Worrell's comments confirm, was not known for fresh-faced innocence. Later in my career, I should not have been so easily embarrassed into such spinelessness. I suppose we find ourselves here on slippery ground, from which the slide into sledging begins. But I am sure there is a legitimate space here for 'tactical' grumbling, sarcasm and conning – I am reminded of the story told of R.W.V. Robins, confronted by a newcomer to first-class cricket. After the youngster had taken guard, Robins held the bowler up. 'Wait a minute,' he said, publicly. 'This fellow can't hit the ball there; or there; or there.' And one by one the fielders were brought in to close-catching positions. This strikes me as entirely legitimate and enjoyable. Bowlers' threats can be simply nasty or malicious; but they can also be good-humoured, as when Fred Trueman said to me, 'Good shot, son, but tha' won't do it again.'

Putting pressure on a batsman is mainly a matter of making things as difficult as possible for him tactically, especially when he is himself insecure. 'You're only as good as your last innings,' is used to prick conceit: even more to the point is the remark that you're only as good as your *next* innings. For every batsman feels a measure of uncertainty at the start of every innings, and however obvious it may seem it is vital to remember that this is the very best time to get him out. It is often worth asking oneself, as captain, whom the new batsman would *least* like to face; and where would he least wish him to bowl? For most players, one should begin with attack. I am still annoyed with myself for not setting a short square-leg for Martin Kent's first ball in Test cricket, at Edgbaston in 1981. The bowler, Chris Old, and I discussed this question, but decided that there was not enough bounce in the pitch to justify this close fielder, and were reluctant to let him get off the mark with a 'squirt' on the leg-side. But the outcome of the next ball, which looped up off bat and pad from his nervous stab to just where the short-leg would, and should, have been, proved us wrong.

For a few players, it is as well not to set too attacking fields initially. I

There was never a dull moment when R. W. V. Robins was around as captain, or indeed as batsman, bowler and fielder. A brilliant cover-point, he was an impetuous and dangerous partner; the story is told of when he came in to join Maurice Leyland – who had been in a long time – on a hot day in Australia. Soon Leyland found Robins running alongside him between the wickets, the former on his second run, the latter on his third. England needed about 500 to win with four wickets left. After the muddle had been sorted out, Leyland said, sternly, 'We can't get all these runs toneet.'

Robins was a brilliant captain, but not always kind. Later, as manager and selector, he became cantankerous and inconsiderate. Yet he made cricket worthwhile for many players and spectators. Ian Peebles, who often played under him for Middlesex, described him as 'the most enthusiastic and joyous cricketer I played with'.

"WHERE DID YOU LEARN THAT? WHO ARE YOU?"

And W. G. must have been intimidating, too.

am thinking of excitable batsmen like Viv Richards and Rohan Kanhai, whose excitability sometimes makes them set off at a gallop. Both these great players tended to play more shots in the first twenty minutes than in the following hour; they played themselves into a calmer, more defensive approach. So, in this early patch, one could do with fielders placed back somewhat for a mishit. Kanhai's running and calling could also, at the start of an innings, be erratic and nervy.

Derek Randall has always been a bad starter, and has been out for a remarkably high percentage of ducks for such a good player. He has twice been dismissed for a 'pair' at Trent Bridge by Middlesex. On the second occasion, in 1981, he knew well that I would tell our fast bowler, Simon Hughes, to bowl a bouncer early on. Indeed, Derek and I had had long conversations in Australia about his compulsive hooking before he had played himself in. Sure enough, in the Notts first innings the second ball Randall received was a bouncer; he went for the hook, and was caught by Radley running back from deepish square-leg. Randall had several days to wait before his second innings, including an evening that I spent at his house. I stayed the night, and we drove to the ground together next morning. There was a certain amount of verbal fencing about which ball the bouncer would be later that day. I told him I might well counter-bluff, by getting Hughes to bowl it on Randall's second ball. He did. Randall hooked. Radley caught.

Such schemes are not limited to new batsmen. The captain should continually be trying to work out what the batsman would least like of the available possibilities. I remember Boycott remarking that Bev Congdon, the fine New Zealand batsman, was a firm-footed player, a bit static, who would be likely to deal less well with a swinging ball than with sheer speed. Jeff Thomson once said that Kim Hughes was less of a player if he was forced on to the back foot; it is also true that when he does start coming forward he tends to lunge at the ball, so it is worth while bowling slightly wider of his off-stump than to some players.

Some batsmen hate being kept quiet, while with others their strengths would also be their weakness: Steele used to get out hooking, but he scored a lot of runs that way. David Hookes, the Australian, is a free-flowing off-side player; but he is often caught in the slips. It can be hard to decide whether or not to bowl at such players' strengths. The answer usually depends on other factors, like the state of the pitch or the number of runs with which one has to play.

Hard-hitting tail-enders fall into a category of their own. Way back in 1964 I learned an uncomfortable lesson from a match between Cambridge and Surrey. Their wicket-keeper, a club player called R. G. Humphrey, came in at Number Eight, and started to smash the ball on the off-side. It went everywhere – off the edge, over the slips, through extra-cover. In my inexperience, I was too much struck by the riskiness and vulnerability of his approach, and not sufficiently aware of the number of runs that accrued. I kept the field too close for too long; and

I did not instruct the bowlers to bowl at his leg-stump, to 'tuck him up', rather than give him room to swing his bat in this scythe-like manner to such effect that he ended up with 58 runs, and Surrey ran out winners by 36 runs.

In the Test match at Trent Bridge in 1977, Australia collapsed on a good batting pitch from 121–1 to 155–8. The last two wickets added 88 runs; more, I think, than they would have done if I had placed a more defensive field, with a mid-off and a third-man. Mind, the captain is also in the hands of his bowlers. It is essential to run in and bowl with venom against Numbers Nine, Ten and Eleven, taking nothing for granted. Greig taught me this lesson in India, in 1976–7, when he drummed it into Lever, Old and Willis that Prasanna, Bedi and Chandrasekhar should be made to feel uncomfortable at the crease. This aggressiveness saved us runs.

Another method of dealing with tail-enders is for the slow bowlers to try some especially slow deliveries. Ray East, of Essex, would get Wayne Daniel every time, as the latter could hardly contain his excitement. Just occasionally Daniel would connect and the ball would be retrieved from the Southend municipal duck pond. The possibility of such big hits inhibits some bowlers; Illingworth is alleged to have retorted, when someone encouraged him to toss one up at a wild hitter on the grounds that he would hit one six and then get out, 'I can get him for less than six!' A Yorkshireman's reply: circumstances would normally dictate whether the view was reasonable or not.

There are also some front-line batsmen who hate to have time to think about what shot to play; they may be excellent players of pace, or indeed of the spinners when they push the ball through. David Smith, once of Surrey, now of Worcestershire, used to be such a player.

This is perhaps a suitable place to mention two unusual fielding positions. The first is fly-slip: this is sometimes called for on bouncy pitches against players who like to cut or slash fast bowlers, or indeed for those – like Eddie Barlow, the South African, Gary Cosier of Australia, and Alan Knott – who deliberately slice or uppercut the ball over the top of the slips. Oddly, I regularly though rarely placed a fly-slip but cannot ever remember getting anyone caught there. Indeed, for many years I myself was the only batsman I had actually seen caught at fly-slip, and that was by accident.

Against Essex at Lord's, I cut the first ball of an over from Lever high over where fourth slip would have been; the ball flew exactly to where Graham Gooch was standing, about halfway to the boundary; he had been dawdling, and had not reached his position in time! Since then, I have seen people dismissed in that way; it happened twice, remarkably, in the series against Australia in 1981, both times planned by Hughes and Lillee: the victims were Willey at Headingley, Knott at Old Trafford.

Another unusual position was also devised to try to cope with Knott's impish batting, this time against the spinners. In India, in 1976–7,

Strategy, tactics and unusual ploys

Gavaskar would be in charge of the Indian team when Bedi was off the field; and he often tried to deal with Knott's particular brand of sweeping by placing himself at a deep short-leg, just behind square. Not that he ever caught anything there; but then Knott is a marvel of the sweep: against Middlesex he once swept fifteen consecutive balls from Edmonds and Emburey without missing or mishitting a single one. He has told me that if he sets his mind to it he can sweep virtually any ball, with the possible exception of the low full toss. His secret is to keep his head still and not try to hit the ball too hard.

I should mention three other topics: the question of whether, and when, to take the second new ball; the welcome problem of deciding whether to enforce the follow-on; and the rare chance of claiming the extra half-hour.

I suppose that the intention behind making a second new ball available after a certain number of overs was to help the fielding side; and often they will take the new ball as soon as they can. They will be particularly keen to do so when their main method of attack is with their fast bowlers, who prefer a new ball for its bounce and swing, though spinners too are often grateful for its extra bounce. In such circumstances, the batting side may be in a quandary during the last few overs with the old ball; for while the main strike bowlers are being rested there is a temptation to cash in with some easier runs. At the same time, it is a great bonus to the fielding side if an established batsman throws his wicket away at this stage. His successor will not thank him for doing so, either. In Australia, in 1974–5, Underwood used to claim that Titmus got out – to Ashley Mallett, the off-spinner, or to Doug Walters's gentle swingers – just when Lillee and Thomson were loosening up for the second new ball which he, Underwood, then had to face.

This period of the game calls for a certain cunning in the fielding captain, to take advantage in the inner, mental game that constantly goes on within each player's head and, so to speak, between their heads. Frequently, as I say, the new ball will be taken immediately it is due. However, there is often a case for waiting. If the fast bowlers are exhausted the new ball may simply go faster off the bat. Towards the end of a day, the captain may wait until half an hour before the close, so that his quickies will have two bites at the new cherry – one that evening, and the other in the morning. The captain may also see no point in taking the new ball if wickets are falling fast with the old one; and occasionally he may choose to continue with a soft, ragged ball simply because it is so hard to hit far. We decided on this line in the Melbourne Test in 1978–9, on a dreadfully slow pitch; and took the last four wickets cheaply with the old rag.

Captains rarely, in any cricket, decline to enforce the follow-on. Again, the main reason for hesitation would be the exhaustion of the main bowlers. In hot weather, and on an easy-paced pitch, a captain *may* choose to bat, giving the bowlers a rest, and perhaps hoping that the

Alan Knott turning the pace and bounce of short-pitched fast bowling to his advantage: second Test, Perth, 1974.

pitch will deteriorate. This was Illingworth's justification for not asking Australia to bat a second time in the Adelaide Test of 1971–2. I cannot remember an occasion on which I did not enforce the follow-on when in a position to do so. In Test matches, the traditional timetable by which the third day is followed by a rest day encourages the captain to enforce it, as the day off is likely to follow their first fielding stint; the introduction of Tests without rest days may lead to Illingworth's example being more frequently followed. In England, in particular, there is almost always a risk in not inviting the opposition to bat again that rain will reduce the time available for bowling them out in the second innings.

Middlesex did once lose after enforcing the follow-on – against Kent at Dartford in 1976, when a series of dropped catches by us, combined with some fine batting by Kent, enabled them to set us 194 to win on a turning pitch. However, I have no doubt that my decision was the right one. Captains should, it need hardly be said, be aware of the rules governing follow-ons: that it does need to be said is proved by a mistake made by a pretty wily captain, Norman Gifford, who in 1974 declared Worcestershire's first innings 148 behind Northants's score of 294, hoping, in the rain-affected match, to make a game of it on the last day. Unfortunately, however, he had forgotten that, as the first day's play had been entirely lost, the regulation for two-day matches applied; since their first-innings deficit was more than 100 runs, Worcester were forced to follow on.

In county cricket, there is a playing condition that allows a team to request an extra half-hour's play on the first or second day if there is a possibility of a result in that period. I suppose that the saddest occasion on which it was claimed was when Lancashire beat Somerset in a single day at Bath in 1951. What made it sad was that the match was Bertie Buse's benefit, when he was entitled to all the money collected at the gate.

Normally there is no reason for hesitation if one is in with a chance of a two-day victory. Apart from the fact that the weather might intervene, any sportsman likes to finish a match off, especially if it means an extra night at home. Only once can I recall there being an issue: we were playing Yorkshire at Scarborough in 1980. Thanks to a marvellous 173 by Roland Butcher, and some fine fast bowling, we made them follow on. In their second innings, though, they fought well on a benign pitch. By 6.30, they had lost only five second-innings wickets; and our bowlers were very tired. Nevertheless, I claimed the extra half-hour. My reasoning was, first, that I thought we might need as much time as possible to clinch a win; and the half-hour claimed on an earlier day is not deducted from the hours available on the last day. Secondly, the Yorkshire batsmen had geared themselves to a finish at 6.30; I thought that they might lack concentration in addressing themselves to an extra half-hour's play. I knew that our bowlers were tired; but I felt that one more wicket would justify the extra effort, and that the scoring-rate would not be high since the opposition would be concentrating on defence. In the event, we did get one wicket, Graham Stevenson's, and managed to win the match; though not until after tea on the last day.

Some administrators feel that it is anomalous that the extra half-hour is repeatable. I welcome the anomaly. Any match in which a side that has been so close to defeat on the second day is still in the game near the end of the third deserves to be allowed another extra half-hour in which a result can be tried for. There is a danger, in these days of necessarily stringent regulations, of over-systematisation; of knocking down the game's higgledy-piggledy outbuildings and replacing them with streamlined glass structures of less charm. For example, a few years ago the playing conditions for county cricket were changed so that pitches are now covered against rain at all times. Though I could understand the reasons for this switch, I regretted it, since it removed from the cricketer's repertoire a wide range of skills, notably, that of batting against a spin bowler on a drying pitch. It was a drastic departure, as for a hundred years and more rain had played its nourishing part in the vagaries of cricket.

Similarly, I was sorry when the twenty-four-yard delivery was banned. Peter Walker, of Glamorgan, used to enliven a quiet afternoon with the occasional ball bowled from at least two yards behind the stumps. Once he timed it to coincide perfectly with the moment when Eric Russell, the Middlesex opening batsman, was looking at the ground in his little ritual of preparation; fortunately for Russell, the ball, which he never saw at all, narrowly missed his off-stump. There was a move recently to outlaw the reverse sweep, initiated by the Pakistani batsmen Mushtaq Mohammad and Javed Miandad, and also used by Ian Botham. And in the attempt to prevent a repetition of Greg Chappell's instruction to roll the last ball of a limited-overs match against New Zealand along the ground, there were those who wished to rule *all* underarm bowling illegal.

In all these cases, I am against the restrictions (though I agree that some more limited legislation was called for to prevent Chappell's ruse). As one of the few bowlers to have bowled underarm in modern first-class cricket (not, I should like to stress, as a protest, but as a practised last resort), I believe that it is not impossible that this art should be, to some small extent, revived. Let us not, at any rate, rule permanently out of court the possibility of a Simpson-Hayward gracing the 1990s with prodigious underarm leg-breaks. As a boy, I can remember only one thing about C. H. Palmer, the Leicestershire captain; and that was his lobs. I was fascinated that such outrageous things might occur deliber-ately in *proper* cricket. In 1980, for Middlesex, I bowled a few overs of lobs myself, when we were stuck, or trying to winkle someone out. On the whole, they were not approved of, by our team let alone the opposition (I was terrified that Brian Davison was going to split my skull open with his bat after the first lob I bowled to him!). Nor were they successful. My season's bowling figures were 15.4 overs, 65 runs, o wickets.

Strategy, tactics and unusual ploys

G. H. Simpson-Hayward, of Worcester and England. 'The last of the lobsters', he was the most successful bowler in the one series in which he played, against South Africa in 1909, taking twenty-three wickets in five Tests. A decade before, lob-bowling was already rare; but Ranjitsinhji was all for encouraging 'the boy who has most cheek and is least sensitive to chaff' to practise it and to persevere. He was also in favour of an occasional high full-pitch 'which falls on the very top of the stumps'. 'When runs are of no consequence,' he said, 'and getting wickets all-important, a lob-bowler is a treasure.'

Ranji also wrote that 'the kind of underarm balls known as "daisy-cutters" or "sneaks" are only found in village matches'. I imagine he would have found Trevor Chappell's underarm grubber, bowled to Brian McKechnie of New Zealand as the last ball of a limited-overs match in 1981, beyond the pale.

I have mixed views about lobs myself, now. But I am convinced that cricket, and particularly first-class cricket, must avoid too much solemnity or pedantry. Captains have a responsibility to keep the game fun, however serious. In fact, county cricket often is humorous, playful and relaxed, and some of its more memorable moments include the outrageous as well as the absurd.

I enjoyed hearing about Snow's bouncer bowled with a soap cricket ball, on a wet Thursday at Leicester (and the Sussex scorer's asterisk against the dot in the analysis, referring to his explanatory note: 'ball exploded'). I admired the cool way Snow bowled four Middlesex batsmen including me with slow full-tosses on a bright August evening at Lord's; he discovered, quite by chance, that we 'lost' the ball in the glare of reflected sunshine if he bowled it slow and full enough. I was delighted by the unusual dismissal of Alan Rees at Lord's in 1965; Titmus and Murray had for years tried to trap the unwary batsman who moved down the pitch too soon by a ball wide down the leg-side, designed to get him stumped. At last, against Rees, the plan seemed to have worked. But with a desperate instinct for survival, the batsman, losing his balance as he tried to kick the ball away, palmed it down with his hand. He was out, 'handled the ball'; but Titmus and Murray were robbed of the credit for this dismissal!

Finally, I enjoyed a little game within a game that Edmonds and I indulged in, against Yorkshire, who were batting without much sense of adventure. We decided to do away with the short square-leg; and rather than place the helmet in the normal position behind the 'keeper, we had the idea of putting it on the square, at short mid-wicket; the idea was that the lure of a five-run bonus for the ball hitting the helmet might tempt Jim Love or Richard Lumb to play against the spin and give a catch from the leading edge. Childish? Probably, but if it were not for the child in us we would never play games at all. (The outcome, incidentally, was a new regulation: unworn helmets can only be placed immediately behind the wicket-keeper.)

I will end these chapters on captaincy in the field with two general points. First, the team – and the captain in particular – must never give up. Occasionally things get so bad that you have to laugh. But cricket is full of surprises. A wicket falls, and three more go, for no good reason. And, secondly, do not mistrust your intuition. Mike Gatting commented, when asked about taking over at Middlesex, that this was the main lesson that he had learned from me; what in fact he would certainly have noticed was my irritation when hunches that I did not follow turned out to have been right.

CHAPTER TEN

Kicking over the traces:
the place of aggression in cricket

It is a commonplace that modern sport, like society in general, exhibits more violence, aggression and dissent than it once did, and that cricket is no exception. I think there is truth in this view, and in this chapter I shall explore some of the ways in which these changes affect the captain, particularly at the level of first-class cricket.

What, then, are the changes? Until 1963, limited-overs matches played no part in the structure of top-class cricket. Its arrival and popularity have been both symptom and cause of the demand for excitement and the stress on winning and losing. Over the last two decades crowds have become increasingly partisan, noisy and critical. The media intrude more. The game itself has become harder, physically – at least for batsmen. Helmets are routinely worn, and fast, short-pitched bowling aimed at the player is far more common than it was twenty years ago.

Kerry Packer's World Series Cricket (1977–9) epitomised many of the less attractive aspects of these developments. I have always believed that Packer offered some bold new ideas to the cricket scene, both in content and in packaging. And he was successful in bringing a wider audience to the game. But in the process World Series Cricket set out to fuel the more elemental passions of the crowds. The television coverage, generally excellent as it was, still tended to linger lovingly over moments of violence or injury; for the entertainment of the viewer, the cameras were allowed into the sanctity of the dressing-room during play, and microphones were planted near the stumps to pick up grunts and expletives.

I shall look at these elements in turn: one-day cricket, crowds, media and bouncers.

Games, like art, achieve their impact in the way they reflect and symbolise life outside the frame, the stage, the arena. Of all games, cricket embodies life's passions most richly. It can, too, be unspeakably boring, as drab and futile as a pointless journey. And it is both curious and lifelike that cricket allows for the 'draw', so that two sides can play for a week without deciding a winner. The timeless Test at Durban in 1939 was entering its most fascinating phase on the tenth day, when the match had to be abandoned to allow the England team to start their two-day train journey in time to catch the boat home. The draw is a 'result' which has little in common with the tie or the dead-heat, for there are many draws in which neither side is within a mile of winning, and others in which one side has utterly outplayed the other but still requires a single wicket or a handful of runs. What is called a draw in football has the very different implication that another minute's play could suffice to turn the draw into a victory or a defeat for either side.

It is hard to imagine anyone inventing a game today with the inbuilt possibility of a cricket-style draw. With hindsight, it seems inevitable that it was baseball rather than cricket that caught on in the USA at the turn of the century. And society's demand for excitement led directly to the invention and spread of limited-overs cricket, designed explicitly to achieve outright results within a day.

More broadly, club cricket in the south of England as well as the north is now much more likely to take place on the basis of leagues rather than as a series of 'friendly' matches; and the rules for these leagues are often more or less complicated versions of limited-overs cricket. There is, too,

Big Brothers. World Series, 1978.

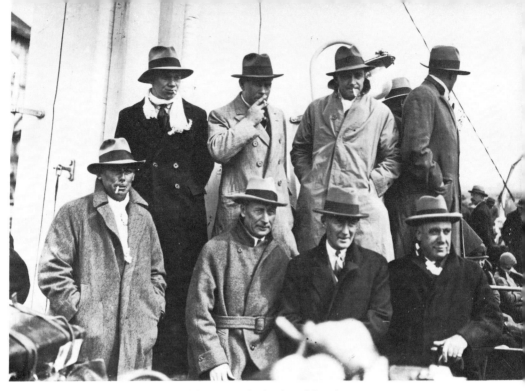

More leisurely days. Some of the MCC team on the last leg of their home journey after defeating Australia 4–1 in 1928–9. Back row: George Duckworth, Patsy Hendren, Wally Hammond, George Geary. Front row: Maurice Tate, Phil Mead, 'Farmer' White and Frederick Toone (manager).

a national indoor cricket competition in England, in which each match is even briefer than the forty overs each side which seems so hectic in the Sunday league.

Detractors of these modern innovations have sometimes said that limited-overs cricket isn't really cricket; a paradox which forces one to pay attention to the radical nature of the new form of life. In a game that does not allow for a draw, taking wickets is often irrelevant, even for the team fielding last (which can win without getting anyone out at all).

Tactically, there are, as we have seen, many varied demands on a captain. I want to stress here the extra psychological demands. One-day cricket aims precisely at tension, excitement and results. For a county team, a month of the season will now include anything from four to nine one-day matches. At least half these matches will be close, so that at certain stages each captaincy decision will be, or at least feel, crucial to the outcome. In the 1950s, before all this started, perhaps one or two of the twenty-four days' cricket would contain this sort of tension; now there will be several times as much. The whole attitude in one-day matches is less leisurely, more urgent than in traditional three-day games; and in addition, some of this sense of urgency spills over into the latter.

More generally, the British have become less inhibited in the last generation, less afraid of intimacy, but also more volatile. In cricket, as

One of county cricket's safest pairs of hands: Alan Ealham of Kent catches Andy Kennedy of Lancashire in the Gillette Cup final of 1974. Crowd and player reaction – with the Law remaining suitably neutral – is evident.

elsewhere, there are good and bad consequences of this. Shared, overt pleasure in a team-mate's success has always seemed acceptable and enjoyable to me. Cricketers have not yet gone in for widespread kissing, but hugging is not unusual and I have seen cheeks chucked. David Shepherd, then the rotund Gloucestershire cricketer and now a trimmed-down first-class umpire, was once fielding at third-man when an important catch was held at wide long-on. He set off at his usual single-gear chug, reached the cluster of congratulatory fielders and arrived back at his corner of the ground after his 300-yard trip just in time for the next ball.

Such expression of shared emotion seems harmless to me, though the other side of the coin appears when disappointment becomes a sulk or dejection dissent. I think it a sign of maturity to own the desire to do well collectively and individually, but of childishness to let it run away with one.

Many older cricket-lovers, by contrast – and not all of them colonels in Surrey – take exception to the hugging. I had a friendly letter from a

sixty-six-year-old man from Tynemouth, in which he wrote, 'When you skippered England, why, oh why, didn't you discourage all this ridiculous back-slapping and cuddling? ... To an old square like me it was reprehensible and inexplicable.'

The contrast between the attitudes of two generations of players was nicely displayed during the Headingley Test in 1977. During a stoppage for rain, we watched, in the dressing-room, a film on television of Jim Laker's match at Old Trafford in 1956. After a few dismissals, Derek Underwood, incredulous, said, 'But they don't seem pleased about taking wickets!' The players' reactions looked, to our eyes, low-key. The bowler might allow himself a modest hitch of his trousers as he sauntered down to a group of fielders whose 'creams' were unlikely to be sullied by any mark of mud or grass. It was, for them, all in a day's work.

One result of the new attitudes is that captains are under more pressure. They have to make decisions quickly, in response to rapidly changing situations. They have to deal with players, including themselves, who are at a generally higher pitch of excitement, anxiety, elation or

West Indian batsmen Viv Richards and Gordon Greenidge mobbed by spectators at Edgbaston during the World Cup match between West Indies and India, 1979. Greenidge had just reached his century. Crowd invasions of the peaceful type have become hard to control. They are annoying for players, umpires, administrators, and most spectators, and they can end in police brutality and riots (Pakistan) or in player retaliation (Australia) which in turn led to Terry Alderman's dislocated shoulder.

dejection. It is not surprising if traditional courtesies are eroded in such an atmosphere, or if the captain's own temper is liable to become flustered. Indeed, a certain amount of heat is required of a captain; aloofness at any rate is not a quality that goes down well with the average cricket team. In 1977, Greg Chappell started the tour capable of shouting at his players; he ended it yawning more frequently, more phlegmatic but also more resigned.

I once commented to a county opponent about his captain, whose calmness and politeness towards his players I admired. The man replied, 'Yes, but we never know what he's thinking. We know *you* better, from playing against you once a year.' I am afraid I was not able to live up to Ian Chappell's aim, which was never to shout at players. I used to hope that my

impatience was a shortcoming that would be forgiven because it came from minding; it showed that my energy was flowing into the job. Moreover, I do not believe that all these changes in behaviour have been for the worse. It would be ridiculous to expect the same decorum on a battlefield as would be appropriate at the vicar's tea-party.

We will return to standards later in the chapter. I now want to discuss another aspect of the stresses under which – poor fellow! – the modern captain lives. Cricket crowds are getting more unpleasant. Policemen have been beaten up at drowsy Taunton; a pint of beer was thrown from the balcony of the pavilion at Old Trafford, narrowly missing Mike Smith and myself as we walked off for bad light during a Gillette Cup match; police dogs were brought into the ground at Headingley after fighting broke out between England and Pakistan supporters during the World Cup match in 1979.

Vocal violence is also worse. Jeering, exultation and abuse have all increased, while humour has decreased. Mindless chanting is commonplace. Crowds are less generous, both more and less easily pleased. They demand instant satisfaction; their criticisms are crudely sexual. A cricket match is often, now, an outlet for a vicious streak. Perhaps dogs, wives and children are getting fewer kicks at home.

County cricket used to be more sedate. There was the slow rhythm of three-day matches, with close finishes rare. Play would be held up while aeroplanes went overhead, or until barracking died down. Occasionally I have been reminded of these leisurely days, as when Middlesex played Glamorgan at Lord's in August 1979. The crowd, aware of the passing of summer, basked soporifically in the quiet sunshine. The cricket, between sides both low in the table, was unspectacular, until Phil Edmonds rescued us with a powerful 141 not out. Glamorgan's bowlers posed no physical threat. The day seemed an echo of the past, a balmy, peaceful idyll.

Such reminders are rare, and of course the contrast is even more striking in Australia. John Arlott reckons that something snapped, some sacred barrier of behaviour was crossed, when John Snow was grabbed by hostile spectators in front of the hill at Sydney in 1971. During the 1974–5 tour, part of the crowds' armoury consisted of banging empty cans on the terraces. Colin Cowdrey describes one such situation in his autobiography, *M.C.C.*

> It was not a pretty sound, but it raised a chorus of caustic criticism and bitter condemnation in the England dressing-room. Sitting silently beside me was the Australian golfer, Peter Thomson. He had listened with interest to our team's reaction and later said, 'I believe your players should be clear-minded about it, because although the crowd's demonstration was ill-mannered, this kind of alien reaction is something that we, as performers, must now accept.' He then quoted an instance of how his own nerve had been similarly tested in an important play-off in an American tournament. (Thomson's iron shot to the 17th green was caught in the wind, and just dropped into a sand-bunker.) 'What hurt,' said Thomson, 'was a sound I had never heard before on a golf course. A huge roar of delight went up as my ball went down in the sand. Hundreds actually stood there clapping . . .' What I had to realise was that crowd values have changed. They are not always going to lean over backwards to show generosity to the visitor. We've got to learn to live with it.

It was in Australia, too, that our fielders quite reasonably refused to stand right on the boundary for fear of bombardment by means of refilled beer cans. I revised my earlier tendency to criticise Boycott for paying too much attention to the crowd by signing autographs during play.

Kingston, Jamaica, 1968. Captains Gary Sobers and Colin Cowdrey appeal for calm from a crowd whose fury had erupted with flying bottles. Tear-gas followed, some of which blew back into the dressing-rooms. The players were keen to forget cricket for the day, but the Jamaican Cricket Association officials, deeply apologetic to their guests, intimated that calling the game off would lead to immense difficulties. This was an occasion on which purely cricketing considerations take second place; I am sure Cowdrey and the MCC management were right to go back on to the field. In the event, the riot caused them to lose momentum, and a match which they seemed on the verge of winning ended with England desperately trying to save the match on 68 for eight wickets. The extra time on the sixth morning that had been added on as a gesture of generosity to England ended as a source of torment.

Ray Illingworth leads his team off the field, Sydney, 1971. The series of events was as follows. John Snow had struck Terry Jenner on the head with a bouncer. When umpire Rowan warned him for intimidation, Illingworth intervened, pointing out that this was an isolated bouncer, and asking under what playing condition the warning was being given. The crowd reacted strongly to all this and when Snow went back to his fielding position on the boundary he was grabbed by an angry and inebriated spectator. Beer cans rained on to the field; and the England team first sat down, then walked off. They returned when the umpires warned that they could forfeit the match if they did not return. I can sympathise with Illingworth in most of what he did, though he was perhaps challenging the umpires' authority in taking his players off. This was the match in which Illingworth's shrewdness and canny bowling played a crucial part in England's win – by 62 runs – which clinched the series at 2–0.

The situation was quite different from a riot I experienced in Pakistan in 1977. On that occasion I had told the team to keep their eyes on me if there were any crowd disturbances and I would indicate what we should do. But when five or ten thousand angry spectators plunged over the fence towards us orderliness gave way, I fear, to a dash for the pavilion.

The least acceptable walk-off occurred at Melbourne in 1978 when the Indian captain, Sunil Gavaskar, having been given out LBW, tried in a flurry of temper to take his partner, Chetan Chauhan, off with him. The team manager had to meet the pair at the gate and order Chauhan to get on with the game.

Geoff Boycott keeping some Melbourne youngsters happy, 1980.

When I realised just how nasty they could be, I saw that appeasement was undoubtedly not a bad bet. After some unsavoury episodes in 1979–80, the authorities decided to restrict the number of beer cans that each spectator could bring in to the ground, but the limit was twenty-four, a more than generous allowance, one felt, of liquor as well as of potential missiles.

Crowd incursions are stupid and annoying, but not, on the whole, vicious or unpleasant. In 1982, however, one had a serious sequel. Terry Alderman, in trying to tackle one of the oncomers, dislocated his shoulder and was unfit to bowl for several months. It was foolish of him to take the law into his own hands, however understandable his irritation at these mindless incursions.

It would be a mistake to imply that Australia has a monopoly of bad crowd behaviour. It was, after all, at Lord's that two MCC members manhandled umpires Dickie Bird and David Constant after a pitch inspection during the Centenary Test in 1980. Moreover, humour is not entirely dead, or inaudible, in Australia. In the fourth Test in 1978–9, I opened the batting after the speculation about whether I would leave myself out of the team, as Denness had done four years before. Anyway, I played, and in the first few overs survived two loud appeals for LBW; after the second, a wag shouted, 'Breely, you make Denness look like Bradman!'

The crowd's sarcasm is not reserved for opponents. In the Test at Trent Bridge, in 1978, when I was still wearing my skull-cap head-protector, it and my cap kept falling off as I ran between the wickets. At length, someone shouted, 'Why don't you stick it on with a six-inch nail, Brearley?' And Tony Lewis records dropping an awkward swirling catch at Neath, his home town. Instead of sympathy, he heard the comment, 'It should have knocked your bloody teeth out.'

I like the story Keith Tomlins, then a young Middlesex player, told of a cagey Yorkshire supporter at Scarborough; this young lad was collecting autographs, and had provided himself with book, pen, pencil and rubber. When Tomlins emerged from the pavilion after play, he was asked, suspiciously, who he was, before being offered only the pencil. After signing his name, Tomlins saw the boy study the signature quizzically, then carefully rub it out.

Such little blows to the ego are an accepted part of life in the public eye. I was often asked how crowd reactions made me feel. I think that it all depended on how I was already feeling about myself. If I was all too aware of my inadequacies, the crowd's jeering tended to add to my insecurity. If I was convinced that my methods were right, or that I was handling a situation reasonably well, such hostility would make me all the more determined. Once, at the Oval in 1980, I was being barracked by a cluster of regulars on the East terraces. As it happened, the pitch had been recently relaid, and the bounce was frighteningly uneven, especially from the dangerous Sylvester Clarke, and I was pleased with the way I was battling it out, despite occasional ungainly reflex responses. After I had managed to fend down one delivery from somewhere near my Adam's apple, this little band of East-terrace heroes piped up again. At this point, in mainly mock-anger, I marched towards them, offering them the bat.

But I was not, on the whole, good at defusing such situations, or winning a crowd round to me. Ken Barrington would have enlisted them by an apt piece of comic mime. Tony Greig would have matched the grossness of the crowd with a gross and good-humoured communication of his own. Greig understood pageantry. The vast crowds in India in 1976–7 responded adoringly to his simple idea of having the team, resplendent in orange-and-yellow-trimmed blazers, salute all sections of the stadium shortly before each Test began. We even did a lap of honour after the Calcutta Test, a popular gesture despite the home team's defeat by ten wickets. But then Calcutta crowds take to England teams, and their South African entertainers; Matthew Engel, writing in the *Guardian* on the 1985 Test there, described the last day as the 'Allan Lamb show'. Lamb, he said, has the knack of being 'just a little human and irreverent from time to time' in ways which 'amuse and sometimes defuse an Indian crowd'.

During the tour of Australia in 1979–80, I was seen by the man in the Sydney street as the embodiment of all that's bad in the British. I talked too much, too glibly, and with the wrong accent. And when they had a go at me on the field I ignored them, like the stuck-up Pom that

Ayatollah Brearley.
Australia, 1979–80.
Cartoon by Bill Beacham.

they knew I was. That beard, too, which led to the nickname 'Ayatollah', and that I had grown to express my capacity to be rough and abrasive, struck them as archaic and foreign. I also took the brunt of the hostility directed, in the aftermath of World Series Cricket, against English cricket for the refusal to go along with some aspects of the new playing conditions. Whatever the reasons, whenever I walked on to the field, especially at Sydney or Melbourne, I was greeted by a tremendous roar of boos. Near the end of the trip, Bob Hawke, then Leader of the Opposition and a long-term trade-unionist, told me that he thought I could have mollified that hostility if only I had communicated in some direct way with the crowd. He did not want me to leave the country with an entirely unfavourable view of his compatriots. Many of the fans must have been his supporters, too, and they were not bad fellows. I think he was right in saying that what annoyed them most was my apparent indifference: my ignoring them rather than responding, as Greig, for example, would have done, by some recognisable gesture. If I were to start that trip again with the help of this advice, I might make more of an attempt to share a joke with the crowd, but I could not regularly interact on a flag-waving scale. I am not Tony Greig.

On the whole, then, crowds have become more unkind, opinionated and noisy. They have made the captain's job just a little more fraught. The same can be said of the media, at least as they affect the Test captain. The sheer expansion in their numbers increases the demands on him. They phone up on off-days, or on the evening of a match; little deputations may turn up at one's hotel room after an incident. They have come to expect captains to answer questions at press conferences at least three times per Test, and players to be quoted after notable performances.

Kicking over the traces

Before the war, press coverage of Test series was minimal. On D.R. Jardine's tour of Australia in 1932–3, only two correspondents accompanied the team. One was a lawn-tennis writer, the other the 'ghost' for Jack Hobbs's daily reports. There was no TV, and scarcely any radio. Jardine could achieve a reticence, not to say secrecy, that would be unthinkable today. Far from announcing the team to the world on the day before a Test, he would not inform even his own players about the side until twenty minutes before the match, when, according to Harold Larwood, Jardine would hang up the list on a hook in the dressing-room, and everyone would cluster round to see who had been selected. (Larwood also said that no one from the press would have dared ask Jardine if he was considering leaving himself out of the team, for fear of a punch in the face.)

The attention paid to the modern captain's every word does have its advantages. In the first place, many correspondents are players manqués. Tom Clarke, himself the sports editor of a national daily paper, once described sports writers as 'the eunuchs at the harem'. Court writers, he added, do not typically identify with the rapists or frauds; whereas sports writers usually love the game they cover and, on the whole, wish the players well. (English cricket writers also wish England well, and tend to become jittery when we bat!) Secondly, the publicity is no doubt of benefit to cricket as a whole. At a press conference, the captain may be able to get across his no doubt excellent reasons for a particular course of action. It is an opportunity to educate the public via the media. Moreover it is hard to know what actually happens on a cricket field. It is amazing how often expert witnesses, close to the scene of the crime (the fielders), disagree about, say, which side of the bat a ball passed, or whether a batsman edged a ball. How much harder for a writer, a hundred yards away, perhaps over extra-cover, to have much clue about the finer points? He needs help, and the captain can offer some.

I admit that I enjoyed press conferences, even when we had lost (though, watching Graham Yallop wriggle on the hook in 1978–9, I would have anticipated hating them as much as he did). I found it interesting to try to put my finger on the differences between the two sides, or on moments when a match was lost and won. I was glad, too, to be asked each question once, rather than time and again, as happens when there is no formal conference. My policy was never to say anything I thought to be false, and to tell as much of the truth (as I saw it) as possible. You don't *know*, most of the time, what's going to happen, so why pretend? Yet if some awkward cat is out of the bag, don't deny it. I tried not to put down our players, or criticise the opposition in anything but a restrained and courteous way. It is best, morally and prudentially, to be generous to them whoever is on top. And I, like most England captains before and after, made it a rule never to criticise the umpires. These meetings with the press were, in fact, games in which one tried to keep one's balance like a cat on a wall without falling off either on the side of indiscretion or on that of vapidity.

For my own peace of mind, I had to impose clear limitations on the times at which I was available. At Tests, I would see journalists once on the day before, once on the rest day, and once at the end. We usually arranged for either the manager or the chairman of selectors to visit the press-box around tea-time each day, in case there were any matters of information that we could pass on.

Since Jardine's day, press coverage has become not only more wide-spread but also more intrusive. Television has intensified this pattern. The style of its coverage has also changed, in the direction of more explicit presentation of the personality of a sportsman. There is greater use of close-ups of a player's face, both under the stress of the game, and while being interviewed. The viewer has an illusion of intimacy with him: the public figure becomes a member of the family, a regular visitor in the living-room. Alan Knott noticed this change in the mid-'70s. Suddenly, like other cricketers, he was recognised far more frequently in streets or restaurants, and his quirks had become public property.

Players are in a position to turn the media's interest to their own advantage, whether through columns of their own or through the opportunities in advertising that familiarity offers. Sponsorship and promotion have expanded enormously, and much of the reason has been the style and matter of the television coverage.

Another aspect of World Series Cricket was that players, umpires and commentators were all employed, *qua* performers, by the same company that ran the game – Packer's Channel 9. Here, the game's administration was too much at the mercy of the commercial interest that supported it, and the players paid for their wages with lack of independence.

The media have, then, contributed to cricket's survival and to players' incomes. Nevertheless, exposure does involve risk, especially to captains, whose responsibility it is to act as spokesmen for the team and themselves. The danger lies as much in their own misjudgements as in misrepresentation or unfair comment. One *faux pas* may haunt a captain who, as cricketer, did not embark upon his profession with public speaking in mind, nor did he have any training in the process.

Some become excessively cautious. Illingworth in his book on captaincy tells of a game at Bournemouth when he bowled a tight spell without luck. Afterwards, the correspondent of the *Yorkshire Evening Post* asked him whether the ball was turning. Illingworth writes: "'A little,' I answered, only to be contradicted by Len (Hutton), who later told me, "Never say it is turning when you have not taken any wickets."' Illingworth rightly says that Hutton's denial of a plain fact was 'petty and needless'.

But Hutton also had a masterly way with the press. Cowdrey describes the initial press conference in Perth in 1954, when Hutton 'dazzled the toughest and most cynical journalists with a performance that would have outshone Bob Hope . . . The Australian press, I suspect, were expecting a lot of bravado, even bombast. They received the opposite . . . It was all underplayed. "Noo, we 'aven't got mooch boolin'. Got a chap called Tyson, but you won't 'ave 'eard of 'im because 'e's 'ardly ever played . . .'"

A single remark can be costly: it can be used as ammunition against yourself. It was premature of Botham to announce, early in the Trinidad Test in 1980, that 'you couldn't get a result in ten days on this pitch, let alone five' and on the rest day that 'heads would roll' if his side were defeated. West Indies won by an innings and 79 runs despite a whole day being lost because of rain. Greig's choice of words in promising in 1976 that England would 'make the West Indies grovel' would have been tactless from any source; but in the mouth of a blond South African it carried an especially tasteless and derogatory overtone. I imagine that it was this remark that Hutton had in mind when, a few months after this series, he gave Greig a piece of advice on the eve of the tour to India. He kept us waiting a few seconds for the words of wisdom, before saying, laconically, 'Don't *say* too much.'

Crowds and media *are* at times hostile. Peter May's retirement from Test cricket was said, by Illingworth, to have been hastened by press comments on his ability. However, cricketers, including captains, may perceive them as more unfriendly than they in fact are, and react with anxiety or rage. Unfair or malicious responses *do* hurt. But a measure of insensitivity in this direction can help: I once had a letter complaining of my 'having a skin like a rhinoceros's', which I took to be, in this context, a tribute.

One of Botham's main shortcomings as captain of England in 1980–1 was, as I have mentioned, his touchiness about criticism, and his tendency not to be able to differentiate between its types. Thus Viv Richards has described how in the Caribbean Botham would, in the later overs of a one-day match when he might be fielding near the boundary, edge around the fence trying to pick out anyone who was harassing him. On the journey home, Botham threatened Henry Blofeld of the *Guardian* and the BBC who, he thought, had been malicious. But he also saw malice where there was none: what was meant as helpful comment from members of the team could strike him as threatening and disloyal if it happened not to coincide with his own views; so he came to cut himself off from the most powerful and helpful source of advice and constructive criticism available to a captain.

The fact is that there is an essential divergence of point of view between spectator/critic and performer, and a real conflict of interest between any journalism (but especially the trashy kind) and the players. Some friction is inevitable, in sport as in other fields. Sometimes the friction has a vicious edge. Kim Hughes, the Australian captain, in a speech shortly before the final Test in 1981, agreed that his team deserved criticism. But, he went on, some of the things said about them were such that, 'If you were walking along a street and a fellow said that to you, if you had any "go" about you at all, you'd deck him!' Three years later poor Hughes finished his Test captaincy in tears, unable to read through his prepared statement of resignation.

Spectators look for spectacle, drama and excitement; players for security. Onlookers want heroes and villains; performers want to be understood and loved, whatever their failings. Writers are subject to their own pressures (of deadline, competition and bloodthirsty editors); players feel that writing about a game is easier than playing it. Journalists seek quotes; most players will at best speak off the record. (And some in each category manage to muddle the situation, as when, in Australia, Tony Francis, of ITV, quoted some remarks made by Geoff Boycott that were disparaging to me; the former was convinced that they had agreed that the conversation was *on* the record, while Boycott's version was that it was informal and private.)

But the press need not be, and often are not, uncreative and obsessively down-putting. As literary critic and novelist Walter Allen said about the world of books, 'The main function of a critic is to encourage people to read. I've been pretty excited by many books. All I want to do is communicate this excitement to others.' The same can be said of most cricket commentators.

I cannot remember a player who was indifferent to what was shouted, printed or broadcast about him, or who was not more sharply struck by a sentence of blame than a page of praise. As Maurice Leyland said about facing fast bowling: 'None of us likes it, but some of us shows it more than others.' It is up to the captain to make the best use he can of the media, and to establish as much trust as possible.

So: changes in the game's structure reflect and encourage aggression and the will to win, and these attitudes are expressed by crowds and by the media. On the field, too, there has been a move towards overt aggressiveness – most obviously in the prevalence of bouncers.

A little more than twenty years ago, a predecessor of mine at Middlesex, Bob Gale, told me that in his experience as opening batsman he would receive no more than half a dozen bouncers in an entire season. He modified his remark only by adding that fast bowlers would of course bowl bouncers at batsmen who could not deal with short-pitched bowling, and at batsmen who 'took them on' by hooking. Gale himself was a big man, who preferred playing off the back foot and who did not attempt to hook. But even if he was exceptional in these ways the fact remains that if his career had been delayed by fifteen or twenty years he would certainly not have been able to make the same claim.

What has brought about this change? Partly the number of genuinely fast bowlers now playing in English cricket. Nowadays, almost every team has at least one. But more important is the change in attitude. Bouncers are no longer displays; they are bowled in earnest, and aimed to skim through at chest or throat level. In some matches, Gale's seasonal ration gets used up in three or four overs. The TCCB were so concerned about the trend that in 1979 they introduced an experimental playing condition limiting bouncers to one per over, any subsequent ones being deemed no-balls. They tried to persuade other cricket boards of control to adopt this rule for Test matches; but the response depended purely on self-interest, so that countries with limited pace attacks opted for the experimental rule, while others preferred to continue without it. The outcome was that English players had the worst of all worlds: no let-up against West Indies; less chance to bombard India; and, in particular, a different set of playing conditions in county cricket from those in force in many Tests. As a result, the experiment was discontinued in 1984.

People often overstate their case, on intimidation as elsewhere. When Lillee writes (in *Back to the Mark*), 'I bowl bouncers for one reason, and that is to hit the batsman and thus intimidate him,' he tells a fraction of the truth. For he clearly has other reasons for bowling bouncers, as well as the one he owns to. He often hopes, in the first place, to get the batsman out with a bouncer, whether mishooking or defending. And, secondly, he intends to force the batsman to change his technique; to be wary of pushing forward to him, for example. Good bouncers are unsettling technically as well as psychologically.

On the other hand, Jim Swanton (*The Cricketer*, March 1984) wishes, if I understand him, to outlaw the bouncer altogether, by having lines drawn across the pitch so that any ball bowled short of the relevant line would be a no-ball. I find the article uncharacteristically unclear. Swanton says that the umpires would have to instruct the groundsman where to draw these lines ('according to the pace of the pitch'). Much would therefore depend on where the lines were drawn, and with what precise intention. I assume that he means that the line should be drawn in such a way that the best fast bowlers cannot get the ball up above a certain height (rib? throat? head?) by bowling legitimately; so that the 'something that is repugnant to the traditions of the game . . . the evil' is, in Swanton's eyes, *the* bouncer, *any* bouncer. I think this must be his aim; for if the line allows only the good bouncers, it outlaws only harmless ones pitched too short to be dangerous, and this does little to eliminate persistent bouncers. In my view the only evil is the *persistent* bouncer.

I cannot believe that Swanton's scheme would work. Should the line be drawn with the new ball (which bounces more steeply) in mind or the old? With a fresh first-day pitch in mind, or a slow fifth-day one? With Garner in mind, or Gatting? And since when have umpires been selected for their ability to 'read' a pitch before a match starts?

More important, I should think even less of it as a plan if it *did* work. I enjoy seeing bouncers (provided there are not too many of them). I never objected to receiving them as a batsman, and I often encouraged bowlers to bowl them. The occasional bouncer is an adornment to, an enrichment of, the game.

Moreover, I agree with Lillee in so far as he is saying *one* reason for bowling them is to intimidate – that is, to make the batsman apprehensive and less confident about playing forward to the next ball. Physical courage, allied to skill, plays a part in many games and sports; I see no reason why it should cease to be one of the qualities called for in batsmen. Intimidation may be against the laws of cricket; but it would be naive to think that it has not always played a part in the armoury of fast bowlers.

Swanton, like Lillee, exaggerates his point. Both leave out of account the thrill of watching the perfect bouncer and the batsman's attempts to deal with it, as well as the skill and variety involved in each player's role. The bouncer should, like a slower ball, or a googly, or an inswinger from an outswing bowler, be a surprise delivery. It should involve bluff and gamble. The good bouncer may need to be on the line of the off-stump to one player; outside leg-stump to another. To one it may be above head-height; to another rib-height. Bouncers sometimes swing disconcertingly. Some bowlers, like Andy Roberts, bowl two bouncers in succession, the second much faster than the first.

The complete batsman will have many resources for dealing with all this, some of them thrilling. He may hook, or give himself room to cut. He may duck (a method which takes skill) or weave – which involves a different skill. He may prefer to stand high and play the ball down defensively. He should never take his eye off the ball.

The bouncer can be utterly inappropriate and wasteful, just what the batsman ordered. Tony Greig used to rile Lillee deliberately, who then bowled worse. Imran Khan became a much better bowler when he stopped trying to hit batsmen. In my view, bowlers should be allowed to fall into the error of giving batsmen runs by bowling short on slow pitches. Think of Fred Trueman to Peter Burge at Headingley, 1964, when the latter's 160 rescued Australia from 178–7 to a first-innings score of 389 (a lead of 121) and, ultimately, to a seven-wicket win.

To return to Swanton: that which 'is repugnant to the traditions of the game' is, to my mind, the *persistent* bouncer, combined, as it often is, with slow over-rates.

I suggest that we do not give up attempts to restrict the bowling of bouncers to one an over, and that we also explore 'Bomber' Wells's suggestion to limit to three the number of bowlers in a side who can run in more than a stipulated number of yards. But cricket without bouncers, and without a streak of intimidation, would be an impoverished game.

The captain's job is complicated, I think, by the heightened atmosphere of aggression. He has to mobilise the team's aggression, without letting it run wild, and without losing touch with his own. In the face of overt aggression from a side that may be more powerful than his own, he has to counteract the tendency to become timid. At Perth, in 1979, I think that some of our batsmen were secretly unnerved by an image of Australian toughness. We lost contact with our own combative powers, and surrendered to the legend of Lillee and the Perth pitch. (I remember

Patsy Hendren returns from Australia, 1929, carrying a pith helmet. In 1931, he was to be hit on the head by a short-pitched ball while batting in the West Indies; and in 1933, when West Indies played Middlesex at Lord's, Hendren appeared wearing a special cap made by his wife. 'It had,' Geoffrey Moorhouse writes in his book *Lord's*, 'three peaks, two of them covering his ears and temples, lined with foam rubber; in appearance not at all unlike the thing Mike Brearley was to adopt forty-four years later.' Hendren may well have been the first first-class cricketer to wear a protective helmet; though we know that the fine Notts batsman Richard Daft batted with a towel round his head on a dangerous Lord's pitch in the 1870s.

that Botham was so angry about this tentativeness that he batted with a kind of reckless fury himself – yet another inappropriate reaction.) Mastery in cricket can be achieved by all manner of means, and a side's need to muster all its grit, cunning, patience and team spirit is even more crucial when it lacks the edge in sheer power.

The most visible sign of the new exercise of power is the helmet. Yet the helmet is not, in my view, a merely negative or defensive asset. While helmets have brought aggressive comments from the pundits and the general public, I am convinced that they improve the game, for spectators and bowlers as well as for batsmen. Critics have argued that helmets would make batsmen reckless rather as opponents to seatbelts claim that car drivers would be less cautious. Viv Richards declines to wear a helmet for that reason. He wants to keep alive the element of risk, without which he might be tempted to rashness. I maintain that for most batsmen it's a good thing to be less cautious, but that the helmet does not make them rash.

Critics have also claimed that a helmet provokes a fast bowler into more hostility by announcing the batsman's awareness of risk. I have not found this. Indeed, when Michael McEvoy, then of Essex, opened the innings *without* a helmet in a match against Sussex, Imran took umbrage and bowled like a wild man, as if trying to hit the batsman with almost every ball. The helmet makes a bouncer more what it should be, a means of getting someone out (whether mishooking, or fending the ball off, or playing differently to the next ball) rather than a way of *knocking* him out.

Lastly, critics have said that the helmet is a sign of cowardice. Denis Compton wrote recently that if helmets had been in vogue when he went back in to bat against Lindwall and Miller in 1948 with five stitches in his eyebrow, he could not have worn one. It would have been, he said, 'an insult to my manhood'.

The most obvious response is, what's so special about helmets? Is it unmanly to wear pads or gloves? And what about the box? A fearless man might be more sensitive about protection nearer to home. Or is it, perhaps, a matter of visibility? Would a multi-coloured codpiece be unmanly, an invisible helmet not?

These days, the word 'manly' jars. Women cricketers need courage too. So the question should be reformulated: is wearing a helmet cowardly? Is it cowardly to protect oneself against a danger? The answer depends, partly, on the extent of the risk. Some danger there certainly is, as the parents of the two children killed by being hit on the head by cricket balls on a single Saturday in Melbourne in 1980 would tragically confirm.

And wearing a helmet has not turned out to be a line of action taken by cowards. No one would call Botham a cowardly batsman, or Boycott, Gower, Gooch, Greenidge, Haynes, Kallicharran or Clive Lloyd. All these at times wear a helmet and all had previously faced without flinching the fastest bowling in the world. When the risk does become minimal – the bowlers slow or medium, or the pitch docile – a helmet may appear unnecessary or ridiculous. But some batsmen prefer to continue with it so that their balance is not changed; they may even feel uncomfortable without it.

In the company of starving people, it is indecent to complain that one's steak is underdone. If the Greeks had had to play cricket under the walls of Troy, Agamemnon might well have unbuttoned his breastplate and doffed his helmet, however rough the pitch. There is here an analogy with the immediate post-war years. A man who had for months piloted low-flying fighters in raids from which, at times, only two out of three returned safely, may think that it is indecent to guard against the pathetic risks involved in batting. Such a man was Bill Edrich. He, and others like him, may well have felt in 1947 that they were living on borrowed time; that having cheated death they had no right to be alive. This attitude might induce a recklessness, and even an indifference, that would court danger rather than rush to avoid it.

For us pampered post-war (or mainly post-war) children, however, unused to extremes of danger, a sickening blow to the head is not an accident to be relished. Middlesex's Ian Gould's batting career was set back when he was concussed by a bouncer from Colin Croft. Mine was rejuvenated by the assurance a helmet brings. I felt more confident about hooking quickish bowling. The excitement of facing, say, Sylvester Clarke on that uneven pitch at the Oval was still there, but the streak of fear was not.

'Ah,' you say, 'the streak of fear!' There were indeed moments of fear. But near-misses, and the occasional blow, did not so much produce fear as a lack of eagerness for further bombardment. My reaction was the cricketing equivalent of the stiff upper lip. I stood up behind the ball, and took whatever punishment was going. The attitude was: whatever happens, don't let fear show. I did not flinch, though I may occasionally have frozen. It is not an attitude to be despised. But I discovered that wearing the helmet enabled me to be less rigid in response, more varied, more playful, more creative. I was able to use a range of responses to the short-pitched ball, rather than only one. Richards may need to rein in his own adventurousness: ordinary mortals need every encouragement to be spontaneous.

A day's batting against the West Indian attack will still, as Geoff Boycott has written, be comparable to standing in the fast lane of the M1 and dodging the traffic. But batsmen are likely to remain lively (and perhaps alive) for longer with their comfortably solid headgear. Wearing helmets, they will be more likely to summon up their zest for the contest, more likely to counter aggression with their own aggression.

There are of course excesses which a captain must act to prevent or curb. But a more central part of his job is to enable players to be less inhibited in their aggression. Often their uneasiness in this area is not acknowledged. At the individual level, there are many examples of people who are afraid of prominent success. At school, few children are desperate to be top of the class, though most are keen not to be bottom, and many like to come in the first few. Simon Hughes, the talented young fast bowler, fell into this category early in his career at Middlesex. He was over-anxious not to be chosen for representative cricket too soon. Moreover, he would often bowl a bad ball early or late in an over. After four perfect deliveries, he would bowl two leg-stump half-volleys. When once I berated him with this, he looked at the ground and, with a mixture of embarrassment and self-satisfaction said, 'I'm not good enough to bowl *six* good balls in an over.' I found his lack of ruthlessness infuriating. I was sure that if he could bowl four good balls an over, then he could bowl five, or even six.

Ewen Chatfield, New Zealand's Number Eleven, deflected a bouncer from England's Peter Lever onto his temple. His heart stopped beating for several seconds; he was unconscious for some hours; and he sustained a hairline fracture of the skull. Heart massage and mouth-to-mouth resuscitation from Bernard Thomas probably saved him from death. Lever left the field behind the stretcher weeping, and could not be consoled.

If one sets one's standards high, one has a lot to live up to. And the top dog does expose himself to envy and resentment. This shortcoming may arise from a fear of one's own destructiveness. Some individuals (and teams) let their opponents off the hook when they have them at their mercy. They fail to ram home an advantage. Some find it hard to play all out to win; if they did so, they might be revealed as nasty and unlikeable. We dislike our own barely suppressed tendency to gloat. A tennis player often drops his own service the game after breaking his opponent's, perhaps feeling guilty at having presumed so far; while the opponent, *his* guilt now assuaged, is stung into uninhibited aggression. The sportsman, like the doctor, should not get emotionally involved with his 'patient'. Neither should he let pity get in his way. Hutton's advice to me on the eve of the England team's departure for India in 1976 was,

'Don't take pity on the Indian bowlers.' Respecting an opponent includes being prepared to finish him off.

Roland Butcher and I had some fruitful conversations in this area during the summer of 1980. He had noticed that every successful player in the Middlesex side had a full measure of his own style of – usually controlled – aggression. He admired the way Edmonds, for example, would often be stung into bowling at his best by the arrival of the opposition's best player, while Emburey would never allow his grip on a side to relax and would often pick up the last few wickets. Occasionally, too, Edmonds would snap his fingers at a lazy piece of fielding, and Emburey flush at the effort to contain himself after a confident appeal had been turned down. He liked the way Clive Radley and I showed in the slips a passionate desire to get rid of each batsman.

Butcher felt that only now was he allowing himself to accept and even to nurture his own aggression. He had been afraid, before, that any even inadvertently aggressive remark would be held against him. Now he realised that the consequences of speaking his mind, of the telling riposte, of a more robust interaction, were not after all catastrophic. At the same time, he became more aggressively determined in his batting, particularly in defence, a possibility not so paradoxical as it sounds and epitomised by Boycott's ruthlessly dead bat. Butcher's emergence, both personally and in his play, helped him to his most successful season both as a batsman and as a fielder. He ended the summer with an average of 41.

Some players need to be stirred into a positive response. We could often get Botham to run in harder by a well-timed insult, as when I named him 'the Sidestep Queen' in 1981. Willis and Peter Willey would instil a new bounce into Botham's stride with sardonic remarks from mid-off or mid-on. Late in the Old Trafford Test in 1981, I shouted at Ian from slip: 'Run in and *bowl*: don't just *put* it there.' He retorted by asking from halfway down the pitch if I found it tiring at my age to stand at slip all day, and muttered something about this being his thirtieth over of the innings. But the next ball was much quicker!

On the other hand, some players need more carrot than whip. Willis himself is more easily deflated than I for one appreciated. I was slow to realise that the ribbing he received in 1979–80, especially from Botham, who called him 'The Wounded Camel', was getting him down, and even hindering his performance.

The captain, then, has to deal with aggression from many sources. There is the opposition's, in the first place. Then he must cope with that of the crowd, and the media. He is responsible for the appropriateness of his team's degree of ruthlessness, including his own. I have been claiming that the inappropriateness lies often on the side of an insufficiently developed will to succeed, rather than the opposite. Nevertheless, most of the contentious behaviour on a cricket field stems from a misplaced or exaggerated desire to do well. Winning is *not* the be-all and end-all of sport. In cricket the captain has the prime responsibility for the standard of behaviour of the team. This standard is expressed both in the attitude the side takes to the game as a whole and in its (and the captain's) position on particular issues: in its general approach and in its tolerance or otherwise of disgraceful outbursts. The captain must take a stand and set an example in both areas. It is hard to speak in general terms on such an issue; the best guideline that I can think of is, again, respect – for the game, for the opposition, crowd, umpires and one's own colleagues.

Such a statement needs to be fleshed out with examples. I have already, at various places, tried to explain my attitude to bouncers and intimidation, and I do not need to expand on it here. To sum up, I think that umpires have the main responsibility for taking a firm line to prevent too much short-pitched bowling, and I favour the rule that restricts a bowler to one each over. Captains, too, should not allow their fast bowlers to resort to viciousness. In my opinion, they should instruct them not to bowl out-and-out bouncers at those who are unable to defend themselves. However, bouncers are a physical threat to *any* batsman, and I see no reason why a tail-ender should specifically be protected from them. I welcome the availability of helmets, which make bouncers into tactical rather than physical weapons. I have, as I have said, no regrets about allowing Willis to bowl bouncers at Iqbal Qasim, especially as he had come in as night-watchman.

England's 'Bodyline' bowling in 1932–3 was another matter. Not only was the batsman's body systematically used as a target; but also the placing of six or seven fielders on the leg-side, several of them behind square, *on top of* bowling short outside the leg-stump strikes me as going way beyond what is acceptable. Leonard Crawley, a batsman who had been asked about his availability for this tour, made the point succinctly in a letter to *The Times* on 27 January 1933: 'The real objection of the Australians . . . is to the array of leg-fielders. I submit that it is to this, in conjunction with bodyline bowling, that the Australians, very rightly, in my view, take exception.'

Some maintain that protective clothing enables fielders to stand unduly, even unfairly, close. I do not agree. As a captain, I felt much easier after the advent of helmets about putting fielders (including myself) in dangerous positions. I have explained in Chapter Eight the changes of technique which had already, before helmets, dictated the move towards the current practice of having short square-legs and silly-points. Whatever the fielders wear, the batsman has the remedy in his own hands.

I have also described in Chapter Nine the Australian reaction to my placing ten fielders on the boundary for the last ball of a match. The strength of feeling was later shown by this being compared with Greg Chappell's instruction to his brother Trevor to roll the last ball of a one-day match against New Zealand along the ground, to ensure that they did not score the six runs they needed. I think the two pieces of captaincy were entirely dissimilar, one totally justified, the other not.

Kicking over the traces

Douglas Jardine. A friend, hearing that Jardine had been made captain of England for the Australian tour of 1932–3, is alleged to have remarked, 'He may win us a series and lose us an Empire.' He had the sort of icy passion that enabled him to conceive of Bodyline as an answer to Bradman, inaugurate it, and what is more carry it through to the bitter end. But Bodyline was a blot on the history of cricket, and Jardine will be remembered for this above all else. He seems to have been one of those whose senses of proportion and feeling became as nothing against a chilling logic. It is typical of the man that when West Indies used the same tactic at Manchester in 1933 with E. A. Martindale and Learie Constantine (though on a slow pitch), Jardine batted without flinching for five hours, scoring 127.

The key difference lies, I think, in the fact that Chappell's move eliminates the need for skill. His aunt could, no doubt, have done the job as well as his brother. The essence of sport is a contest of skills. Rolling the ball instead of bowling it undercuts in an unethical way this aspect of the spirit of the game, while putting all the fielders on the boundary is a minor extension of existing practice and an ethical way of developing your tactical skills to make the opponents' exercise of theirs more difficult.

Cricket is not a game based on physical contact. There are, however, occasions when fielders and batsmen may collide or get in each other's way. The laws prohibit the batsman from obstructing the bowler: I do not think they explicitly preclude the reverse. It can be a moot point, in a scramble for a short single, to decide who obstructed whom. An unspoken rule is that the batsman is entitled to run straight; he does not have to swerve to allow a fielder to pick up the ball. (At the same time he would be foolish to risk a collision that might both injure him and leave him stranded.) Rarely do players resort to barging or other unfair tactics. I suppose the most notorious case was when John Snow, in frustration, shoulder-charged Sunil Gavaskar at Lord's in 1971 when the latter was running on a perfectly legitimate course. Snow's act was, I thought, wrong and petty; the reaction of the media exaggerated and unnecessary.

It is also generally accepted that a batsman is entitled to run between the man throwing the ball and the stumps aimed at; he may not, of course, deliberately get in the way of the ball, but he may deviate in his running and keep his head down. I once saw Colin Bland, the marvellous South African fielder, run Jim Parks out in a Test at Lord's in 1965 despite Parks's adoption of this method; Bland managed to hit the stumps by throwing the ball between Parks's legs.

One point at which interference with the batsman may occur is when the striker approaches the end of his first run. He may well be looking at the ball to decide whether he can manage a second. At this moment, he is vulnerable to the possibility of a particularly nasty form of obstruction or blocking by the bowler after his follow-through. A few bowlers make a point of queering the batsman's pitch here; though again there are often cases of accidental mutual inconveniencing. As captain, I did once, many years ago, at a stage in a match when feelings were running high, turn a blind eye to a deliberate piece of obstruction by one of our bowlers in this situation; but such behaviour is totally unacceptable and I ought to have made this clear to the offender.

I remember, too, in my early days as a captain, allowing myself to overlook a ruse adopted by one of our fielders in a match at Folkestone between Cambridge and Kent. The fielder was edging round behind square-leg as the bowler ran in to bowl. Colin Cowdrey, who was batting, quite rightly protested when he realised what was happening, and I never

John Snow barges Sunil Gavaskar at Lord's, 1971.

allowed this to occur again. Very rarely, this trick has been used against England by Australian teams; once at Perth, in 1977, when we played Western Australia, and once at the Oval Test later that year. On the first occasion, Dennis Amiss had the presence of mind as non-striker to stop Lillee as he was about to deliver the ball. (This took courage too, as Lillee was not amused.) The second incident happened when Geoff Boycott was facing Mick Malone. As the ball was about to be bowled, mid-wicket dropped back about thirty yards, and fine-leg moved perhaps twenty yards squarer. Malone bowled a bouncer, Boycott went for the hook. He hit the ball in the air, thinking he had only to clear orthodox mid-wicket, and was appalled to see that the two fielders were both in the vicinity of the ball. Fortunately, neither could quite reach it. Boycott was right to criticise the non-striker, Derek Randall, for not preventing these unfair tactics. The umpires, too, ought to intervene in such cases.

There can be a comical side to the lengths to which some players will go. I liked W.G.'s nerve in shouting 'I declare' as a fielder was about to catch him, and in reminding a timid umpire that the crowd had come to watch him bat, not the umpire umpire – though these stories, like many about W.G., may well be apocryphal. I have heard batsmen shouting loudly to distract fielders when they are waiting under a skied ball; and have heard a batsman calling 'mine' after hitting the ball up between two fielders. I have even suspected the reverse, fielders shouting 'Yes!' to confuse the batsmen. All this is not to be encouraged.

International cricket is, rightly, a serious matter, but it does not need to become malicious. Injuries are not wished on an opponent; and players sympathise with each other when they occur. Fast bowlers are actually more soft-hearted than they sometimes make out. Jeff Thomson was appalled when he hit fellow-Australian Graeme Wood in the cheek during Middlesex's match with the tourists in 1982 (and not simply because he was a compatriot). It is not callousness that makes Bob Willis walk away after hitting a batsman; it is rather the fear that he will become over-tender, and lose his aggression. But I did suggest to him that his apparent lack of concern looked boorish.

On the other hand, I see no reason why players should have to pretend to an attitude of camaraderie on the field that they may not in any way feel. I was on Rod Marsh's side in an interchange with Randall during a Test in 1977.

RANDALL (having just taken guard): 'How are you going, Marshy?'
Silence.
After the next ball: 'What's the matter, Marshy, not talking today?'
MARSH: 'What do you think this is, a garden party?'

Australians find Randall, with his perky, nervy humour hard to under-stand; I think his quirkiness is in fact used to boost his own confidence and, unconsciously, to make his opponents ill at ease. Whenever Middle-sex played Notts, I would be aware of Derek's mannerisms and chattering as a sort of benign gamesmanship; and once I reversed the situation by mimicking him while he was batting. It was then his turn to feel uncomfortable.

Pretending that a hard contest is a garden party may smack of hypocrisy. As I have said, I admire the Australians' straightforwardness with regard to 'walking' – that is, not waiting for an umpire's decision if you know that you are out. After the Second World War, 'walking' gradually grew in English county cricket. By the early '60s anyone who did *not* walk was considered a cheat. Unfortunately, this admirable approach lends itself to abuse. Many batsmen will walk when their score is, say, 53, or 77, or 143, but not on 0 or 99. Some walk for the obvious 'nicks' but not for the faint ones. There is a temptation to walk when the match is not too important, and your place in the team is safe; but not at a crucial stage of a game, or if your last five innings have yielded 10 runs and your entire career is in the balance. Moreover, fielders are sometimes wrong about whether a batsman touched the ball, and certainly about whether he knew he did.

They may even mishear. In a county championship match at Old Trafford in 1965, Middlesex had to score only 44 to win on the last day. As it happened, I already knew that I had been dropped for the next match – quite justifiably, as I had scored 29 runs in my last seven innings. Soon after I came in, I played at a ball from Ken Higgs and missed. The Lancashire players appealed, and I was given not out. At the end of the over, I talked to my partner, Eric Russell, in the middle of the pitch. 'They thought I touched it,' I said, 'but I didn't feel a thing.' One of the fielders overheard, but thought I said that *I* thought I touched it. Bad feeling resulted, and I felt resentment at being falsely accused.

Again, the batsman may misunderstand the umpire. A peculiar series of events led to Peter Parfitt's dismissal in a match between Middlesex and Surrey at Lord's. Parfitt swept at a ball from Pat Pocock, which was taken by the 'keeper. On appeal, the umpire, Arthur Jepson, quickly said 'That's not out, over.' His hand-gesture for the end of the over looked, to the striker, like the signal for being given out, and he failed to hear the 'not'. So he walked quickly off, without showing any sign of disagreement. Parfitt was known as a walker, so all those close to the action assumed that he had taken a moment or two to register what had happened, and had then given himself out. As a result, he was not recalled either by me (as non-striker) or by the umpire or the fielding captain.

Once, I got into a tangle with bat and pad; the ball went up off my pad to slip, and I walked; only to think after a few paces that I had not hit the ball. By then, though, it was too late to go back. Since those early days I have more than once remonstrated with young players who can be too placatory or over-keen to avoid criticism.

I mention these episodes as instances of the problems and misunder-standings this high-minded habit can produce. On the whole, I prefer the pre-war attitude, shared, as far as I can gather, between amateurs

Kicking over the traces

The Australians' joy is soon shattered: Gordon Greenidge given not out against Jeff Thomson, second Test, Barbados, 1978. Only the old-timer Bob Simpson, called back as captain after the Packer 'defections', has stood his ground.

and professionals alike; namely that the occasions on which a batsman is wrongly adjudged not out are balanced more or less equally by those on which he is mistakenly given out; and that the umpire is there to decide.

The most unsatisfactory phase is the in-between one, where players have no common ground and there is inconsistency both in behaviour and in attitude. As captain, I regard it as a matter for the individual to decide. But I admit that, particularly in Test cricket, I did sometimes point out that our opponents were unlikely ever to walk.

And I always insisted that the most crucial aspect of the whole matter was that we should accept the umpire's decisions. I would sometimes have to shout at bowlers and fieldsmen to get on with the game rather than stand incredulously when an appeal had been turned down.

I will return to the question of dissent shortly. Meanwhile, I should like to discuss appealing. Modern cricketers are often accused of appealing too much. In my experience, there have been several players who have erred in the opposite direction. I found it annoying to be told by the umpire that a key batsman had been LBW in the previous over, but that no one had appealed. In my view, bowler and/or 'keeper should appeal if they think a batsman *might* be out, and not only if they are sure that he is. I do not mean that players should act as if they are convinced the man was out if they are not; appeals can be unanimous, confident and even belligerent, but they may also, with justification, be made inquiringly, quizzically or tentatively.

Claiming a catch when you know that the ball has bounced strikes me as plain cheating, as there are solid grounds for distinguishing between this practice and staying in, as a batsman, when you know that you were out. The main difference lies in the passivity of the latter. You are, by virtue of the appeal, placed in the dock; you stand accused; it seems reasonable to wait for judgement, and not to give yourself up. It is not the case that the only alternative to a plea of guilty is one of not guilty. By contrast, the quasi-catcher has to *initiate* the process of indictment by an appeal (or at least by making out that he has made a clean catch). He bears false witness for the prosecution. His act resembles perjury, while the batsman merely declines to admit guilt.

The fielder may, of course, be uncertain whether the ball did touch the ground. In most such cases, he should disclaim the catch. He may, however, look to those standing nearby to confirm his impression that the catch was, after all, valid. On occasion, there will be vehement disagreement between the 'catcher', batsman, umpire and other fielders about whether a ball carried. I remember once being absolutely convinced that I had caught Peter Marner, at Leicester, when I had dived forward at extra-cover to pick the ball up. But Mike Smith, fielding ten yards away, was equally sure that the ball had bounced.

Such cases are rare; almost always the fielder knows best, and it is up to him or the captain to call a batsman back if he unwittingly walks off

Gundappa Viswanath's courtesy at Bombay, 1980. He had persuaded the umpire to change his mind and allow Bob Taylor to continue batting. It is hard to imagine any other Test side making such a gesture, or carrying it through with such relaxed acceptance. Ian Botham and Kapil Dev compare notes on bats and grips.

without confirmation, or if the umpire gives him out on appeal from enthusiastic team-mates. The most notable example of such an act was in the Centenary Test in Melbourne in 1977, when Marsh indicated that a ball which Randall edged had not carried to him. The 'keeper had dived for the ball and rolled over; by the time he was aware of what had happened and was back on his feet, Randall was already on his way to the pavilion. In the context of the match – we were at that time well-placed for a remarkable win, and the Australians must have been tired and dispirited – Marsh's was a generous act.

I do not find it easy, however, to say in what circumstances the captain ought to recall a batsman or ask the umpire to reverse a decision. I remember an incident in a qualifying match in the Benson and Hedges Cup in 1972. One of the Essex batsmen went for a short single; being well out of his ground when John Murray received the ball and broke the wicket, he was given out. Murray had, however, dropped the ball.

Kicking over the traces

The Essex captain, Brian Taylor, was incensed by the decision, and appeared from the balcony to be demanding that I withdraw our appeal and allow the batsman to return. I did not do so; and I am sure that I would do the same now. In the first place, from my position near the umpire, I could not be certain that he was wrong. The ball had been dropped; but it may have travelled from Murray's gloves and knocked off the bails before falling – in which case, the decision was correct. But even if I *knew* that the umpire was in error I would hesitate to open the matter with him. For that means publicly questioning his judgement.

Gundappa Viswanath, then Indian captain, took the opposite line at a key moment in the Jubilee Test in Bombay in 1980. We had bowled India out for 242, but had collapsed to 58–5 when Bob Taylor, batting high in the order at Number Seven, joined Ian Botham. The two had added 85 when umpire Hanumantha Rao upheld an appeal for caught behind against Taylor. When Taylor hesitated, incredulous, before leaving the crease, Viswanath walked from first slip to the umpire, and then called the batsman back. Apparently he had persuaded Rao to rescind his decision. This most sporting behaviour by Viswanath probably led directly to our victory, as the sixth wicket pair added a further 86 runs and turned the match. I can wholeheartedly admire his generosity while suggesting that it is not a good precedent, and makes an umpire look foolish. It is of course quite different from calling a batsman back when you know the ball has bounced, as in the Marsh–Randall incident.

The captain should recall a batsman only when the manner of the dismissal is unsavoury, not whenever he believes the umpire to have made an error. A flagrant example occurred during the first Test of the MCC tour of West Indies in 1974. According to *Wisden*:

> Off the last ball of the day there occurred an extraordinary incident which led to angry crowd scenes and a long meeting in the pavilion of cricket officials from both camps. Julien played the ball to Greig at silly point, and turned for the pavilion. So did some of the England fielders, while Knott pulled out the stumps. With Kallicharran walking down the pitch, Greig threw the ball at the stumps at the bowler's end, and Kallicharran was given out. After a two-hour meeting, with the England team besieged in their dressing-room, the West Indies Board issued a statement saying that 'in the interests of cricket in general and of this tour in particular' the appeal had been withdrawn . . . It was emphasised that the umpire, Sang Hue, had been correct in his decision.

Nothing in the report suggested that the decision to allow Kallicharran to continue in the morning had anything to do with the England captain, Mike Denness. In my view, however unfortunate it may be that the reversal was occasioned by crowd pressure and by political expedient, Denness should have tried to effect this outcome. For although the batsman ought to take care not to wander from his ground until 'Over' or 'Time' has been called, it is important for the spirit of the game that such working to rule should not *become* the rule. Otherwise, there would be constant delay when batsmen need to pat down the pitch; and the level of suspiciousness and sharp practice would rise alarmingly. Greig's impulsiveness struck most observers as unfortunate; after all, Knott had already pulled out the stumps at his end. It is hard for the captain, who may himself already have turned away towards the pavilion, to know exactly what had occurred; but as soon as he did, he was, I think, duty-bound to try to withdraw the appeal and have the decision reversed.

Sang Hue was, clearly, technically correct, and an intervention was needed to enable him to change the decision. In 1982, during a county championship match at Southend, Paul Downton was batting with a runner. After playing the ball into the covers, he forgot that he had a runner, and went through for a single. The ball was thrown in to the 'keeper, who broke the wicket and appealed. The umpire gave Downton out; rightly, as the law states that a batsman who has a runner must not be out of his original ground when the wicket is broken. I do not know how I would have acted had I been the Essex captain, but I hope that I would not have allowed the appeal to take effect. Many batsmen forget about their runner in the heat of the moment, and I should not wish to take advantage of such an oversight. Moreover, in such cases asking the umpire if the appeal can be withdrawn is not to suggest that he has made a mistake.

I started the chapter by conceding to the critics of the modern game that cricket is more aggressive than it was. Some aspects of this shift in behaviour are, I have argued, desirable or acceptable, but others to be regretted and deplored. The worst aspects concern the undue pressurising of umpires, mainly by dishonest appealing and dissent.

In 1972–3, Tony Lewis, captaining MCC in India, was so alarmed after two Tests at the nature of the appealing by both sides that he arranged a meeting with his opposite number, Ajit Wadekar. Both captains then agreed that they should instruct their players to moderate a level of appealing that had degenerated into cheating. This series contained a large amount of spin bowling on helpful pitches. As a result, there were often several close fielders, and frequent occasions when the ball popped up off the pad with the bat somewhere near. These bat-pad, pad-bat decisions are probably the hardest of all for the umpire; and his job is made still harder if fielders claim catches with absolute conviction when they know that the batsman has not hit the ball. Moreover, bitterness and retaliation quickly creep in, in such circumstances, especially when the umpires are inexperienced or incompetent. It is not an excuse for dissent and bad behaviour to assert that most of it occurs when the umpires are actually bad; and it is a fact that only in England do ex-players regularly become umpires, and only in England are they recognised as fully professional.

Notorious examples of dissent include Lillee's refusal to exchange his aluminium bat for a wooden one when instructed to do so by the umpires (after holding the game up for several minutes, he at last petulantly hurled the bat away). In 1980 Michael Holding, usually a quiet and courteous cricketer, kicked the stumps down during the first Test against New Zealand in reaction to an umpiring decision.

What sort of response is called for by the authorities to such displays of bad temper? The captains should make it plain that they disapprove. At Perth, Greg Chappell did indeed convey this message, himself walking out with a selection of alternative bats for his fast bowler. The Australian Board of Control, however, took no disciplinary action. In New Zealand, Clive Lloyd consistently failed to support the umpires publicly during a series in which his team members were guilty of some appalling misbehaviour. Colin Croft, for example, shouldered umpire Fred Goodall during his run-up after being no-balled, and the whole team refused to take the field after tea during the second Test at Christchurch, saying they would not continue unless Goodall was removed. Lloyd's lack of firmness was compounded by the stance of his manager, Willie Rodriguez, who actually insinuated that there had been collaboration between the New Zealand administration and its umpires to ensure a home victory.

In both cases, the Boards of Control and/or their representatives failed to fulfil their obligations to cricket by being so loth to punish the players concerned, whether by reprimand, fine or suspension. I do not believe that cricketers' committees set up to judge their team-mates (as happens in Australia now) are an adequate solution. For one reason, such 'courts' may be biased for or against individuals. More importantly, it is the administrators who are in the end responsible for the welfare of cricket in a country – they make the rules, appoint the umpires, select the teams, raise and disburse the money and so on. Obtaining the active support of the cricketers in looking into allegations of misbehaviour is one thing; allowing them to have the final say in the matter is quite another.

The uncouth side of Dennis Lillee, tossing away his aluminium bat at Perth, 1979. He got his publicity. Geoff Boycott reckoned I made a mistake in challenging Lillee's use of the wretched bat; he thought it fired the great fast bowler up to an extra effort with the ball.

Only two things can be said on Michael Holding's behalf about this outburst at
Dunedin, New Zealand, in 1980: one is that he has rarely shown dissent in a fine
career, and the second is that no other cricketer could manage to make a deplorable
action look so graceful. West Indian behaviour reached a nadir in this match, which
they eventually lost by one wicket. The batsman is John Parker, the fielder Derek
Parry, and the 'keeper Deryck Murray.

I will end this chapter by reiterating my view that on the whole top-class cricket is played in an admirable spirit, in which umpires and opposition are given due respect, and by discussing one view as to the cause of such decline as there is.

'Some of the old chivalry and morality, which put cricket apart from other games, has ebbed away in the tide of awards and prizes, sponsorship in its many forms, and larger appearance money.' So wrote the experienced cricket journalist Alex Bannister, in *Wisden*, 1980. The first part of his statement has some truth. The English first-class umpires let it be known in 1982 that in their opinion dissent has increased, especially the sort of dumb show in which, for example, a batsman does not look at the umpire after an appeal. (The umpire must then either give him out again, or stand there feeling foolish with his finger statuesquely up.) Alternatively, or in addition, the batsman looks or glares for all too long. Overt disgruntlement is not confined to batsmen; fielders and bowlers also display dissent. The umpires felt less strongly about chorused appeals, but noted their growth as another factor adding an unpleasantness to their job.

The English players also acknowledged their anxiety. After their meeting in April 1982, the Cricketers' Association resolved that 'it is totally against any action or gesture which puts unnecessary pressure on umpires. All players will make every effort to maintain the traditional standards and status of the game.' Some players, moreover, called for stiffer penalties for misbehaviour on the field.

I would support the now unfashionable view that one of cricket's lessons for life is to teach its players to take the rough with the smooth, and, in particular, to accept the umpire's decisions, however erroneous. I agree that the time has come for players to remind themselves of the validity of this ideal, and for the moral to be reinforced by the authorities.

But is money part of the explanation for the falling-off noted by the umpires and implicitly accepted by the players? Is Bannister right in the second half of his opinion that the cause lies in the financial rewards for winning? Do such incentives encourage a damaging ruthlessness?

First, we must consider the extent of these rewards. In county cricket, a regular member of a highly successful team in the mid '80s stands to make perhaps two or two and a half thousand pounds in prize money on top of his salary. Such a sum, when compared with what is available in, say, football and tennis, is almost derisory. It may, however, represent a healthy proportional bonus on top of basic pay. Since Packer, the pay for Test cricketers has been greatly increased, though the sums are, again, small compared with the financial rewards available for the top performers in other sports. And prize money constitutes a much lower percentage on the basic pay than in county cricket. Certainly Test players are no longer paid less than the man who pushes the sight-screen (as Marsh is alleged to have claimed, with good cause, during the Centenary Test in 1977). And county cricketers stand to earn more in real terms now than they did in, say, 1972 or 1977. However, I cannot believe that it is the financial potential that leads to pettiness or shabbiness on the field, nor would it if that potential were to be further increased.

In the first place, money is the last thing cricketers have in mind while involved in an important match. A bad decision hurts not because of its financial implications, but because of the injustice and its bearing on the outcome of a match that we care about winning.

As I have said, I believe that wanting to win – and minding about losing – are felt more intensely now than before, though many cricketers from earlier generations might find this inconceivable. Wanting to win badly is amongst the emotions that fifty years ago it would have been unacceptable to express, something that adults were supposed to have grown out of.

But does money affect the desire to win? Hardly, I think. It may be a *dis*incentive. Players gradually become disaffected if they feel under-valued, and one of the many ways in which this may occur is financial. Money *may*, in the short term, motivate, but only if nothing else does; for example, if a millionaire were to arrange a match which had no other point than, say, one hundred thousand pounds in prize money, I suspect that both teams would be keen to win. Money also makes a difference to whether or not a young man takes up the game: one of the unquestionable advantages of all the current talk about prize money and pay is that it helps to create an image of a rewarding career for the young. Pay affects *what* set-up a player allies himself with; as in any job, his dissatisfaction with one employer may be based in part on rates of pay, and both Packer and the South African Breweries were able to lure players away from conventional cricket by the guarantee of large sums of money. Many people would be willing to be traffic wardens for twenty thousand pounds a year; one well-known actor said that he would be prepared to show his bottom on television – for an astronomical sum.

What cricketers do, and *whether* they do it has a great deal to do with the money at stake; it is far less clear that the money affects *how* they do it. The same actor as mentioned above has performed Shakespeare for a director he admires for fifty pounds a week, and he puts much more effort into that than he would do into pulling down his trousers or into his far more remunerative run-of-the-mill work.

He is likely, in fact, to be anxious about failure at the Shakespeare, and concerned to do well to satisfy himself, the director, his colleagues and the public – probably in that order of importance. The situation is similar for the cricketer. He, too, performs, and is anxious, on account of his self-regard and that of his team-mates and opponents. The spectators matter less. Remarkably, most players will give of their best on a damp Thursday in Ashby-de-la-Zouche as much as on a bright Saturday at Lord's. I have always doubted the argument that financial incentives will improve performance. I preferred to think of the extra money earned as reward. I have known time-servers and old lags in cricket, the type of player who always knows when a patron or a selector is in the crowd, and who adjusts his level of effort accordingly; who cares little about his own contribution to the team or about the team's performance. But such players are rare. For the majority, the passions of the game correspond to those that excited them when playing as boys on the beach or in the park. Professional cricketers, like actors and musicians, are fortunate in that they are paid to do that which they would otherwise have done as a hobby. Their motivation is more inner, and less dependent on extraneous factors like money. Most players love the game. It is for this reason that their aggression can readily be harnessed by a good captain, and that motivation is easier for him than for managers in many other walks of life.

CHAPTER ELEVEN

Many hands make light work – sometimes

For a team game, a striking feature of cricket is that it is made up of intensely individual duels. Despite the spiritual support of his team-mates in the dressing-room, and the company of a partner a pitch-length away, the batsman who takes guard for the first ball of a Test match, against Michael Holding or Dennis Lillee, is entirely alone. One error, and he is *hors de combat*, possibly for a whole day or more. A string of low scores, and his average, published for all to see, has plummeted. Success and failure can be all too measurable, and the players themselves take a ghoulish interest in the averages. One member of the Middlesex Committee used to bring an exhaustive set of Middlesex players' averages into the dressing-room every two or three weeks; I remember, not to my credit, how much more amenable towards him I felt when my own was high. Our jobs are laid bare by the statisticians. One consolation is that it makes it hard, in the long run, for a cricketer to kid himself.

Even so, figures can mislead. Jack Hobbs had this to say about batting at the Oval in the '20s:

> Well, Andy [Sandham] and I would go in, and, if we were going well, say we had 70 or 80 on the board a bit before one o'clock – and the best of the bowling was not so sharp; well, Surrey had a lot of batting in those days . . . so, you'd have a bit of a hit, against one of your old pals, you know, the chaps who did the real work . . . Sometimes it went wrong and you didn't get out, and before you knew where you were, you'd got a hundred. But more often you'd be out for 60 or so . . . There were other times, though. Say Sandy went early, and we were on a difficult pitch, or someone like Maurice Tate, or Ted McDonald, or Harold Larwood was bowling really well; that was the time you had to really earn your living. After all, Surrey paid me to make runs, not just runs when we didn't need them but runs when we did.

Some runs count more than others, for the side. Averages do not tell the whole story.

Few players have had the generosity, or the wherewithal, of The Master. Private interest may conflict with that of the group. One may feel exhausted and yet have to bowl, or be required to sacrifice one's wicket going for quick runs. One may be tempted into the luxury of a glory-shot rather than be prepared to soldier stolidly on. This tension is inherent in the game, and gives rise to the occupational vice of cricket – selfishness.

But can a cricketer be *too* unselfish? The answer is, yes. He can fail to value himself enough, and this can lead to a diffidence which harms the team. He might, for example, underrate the importance to his confidence and thus to the team's long-term interest of his occupying the crease for hours, however boringly, in a search for form. And I have seen a whole side in flight from selfishness, with batsmen competing to find more ridiculous ways of getting themselves out, in order to prove that they *weren't* selfish (though I suppose the insidious self reveals itself here, in the compulsive need to win the group's admiration).

Team success is, indeed, the product of personal successes. And it would only be possible to have the conflict between self-interest and that of the group in a team game. Each ball is a mini-drama between two protagonists – a bowler and a batsman; but the protagonists' actions take their meaning from, and are strongly influenced by, the group context.

It is not accidental that sporting teams range from around seven or eight to fifteen a side. For a true group cannot exist with much less than seven members; and with more than twenty it tends to become a crowd. Two is not a group; they may combine well together, but too much hangs on the individuals and how they happen to get on. Threes tend to divide into a two and a one; fours into two–two. Five or six people can make a group, but the absence of one or two individuals makes its identity precarious.

Sports teams are, then, big enough for the group to have a character of its own, and for there to be significant division of roles. They are small enough for communication to be simple, for individuality to be maintained, and for each player to know the others extremely well, at least in the setting of the sport. Such groups are the descendants of primitive hunting bands. The well-being of large companies also depends on the functioning of these small teams within them, from the girls behind the counter to the Board of Directors.

Like the individuals who constitute them, groups take on characteristics of their own. They may, for instance, be arrogant, insecure or self-confident. They may be quarrelsome, apathetic or lively; rigid, fragile or resilient. These qualities derive, in complicated ways, from the characters and interactions of the members. But the group, too, may be said to influence the individual, for better or for worse.

For instance, some years ago, we had a player at Middlesex – whom

I shall call 'Brown' – who came to us from another county with the reputation of being temperamental. There he had been a thorn in his captain's flesh. On one occasion, Brown felt that he and not the captain should have been bowling; so, while fielding in the outfield, he allowed the ball to pass gently by him and hit the boundary-board before he lobbed it back. He was a figure of fun to the rest of the team, who revelled in his outrageousness, but were also at times annoyed by it.

We took him on because of his undoubted talent. Besides, I rather liked him. In our pre-season practice matches, he tended to fall over when he bowled (and this produced stifled laughter) and he presented himself as an appalling fielder, spindly and uncoordinated (this produced unstifled laughter, though I knew that we would all be irritated if he fielded like this in competitive matches). He also made rather provocative and odd remarks.

We, the players, decided that we should encourage him not to play the fool, that we should take him seriously from the start, regarding his current standard of fielding as a base-line from which all improvements were to be acknowledged. As captain, I consulted him about his bowling and about tactics generally. A productive rivalry sprang up between him and another bowler in the side. We reminded him of his strengths when he so easily slid into hopelessness. We laughed at him less, and he felt less need to gain attention in this way. Gradually, he spent more time on his feet than on his knees, and his fielding improved remarkably. For a year or two, all went well – until other difficulties intervened.

There is no doubt that Brown invited a certain reaction from the rest of us. Professional cricketers are usually sharply perceptive, and quick to spot a candidate for the role of Court Jester. At his previous county, Brown had achieved acceptance of a sort by means of this. It offered him attention and thus a degree of security, however precarious. It also fed a partly malicious humour in the rest of the team, who could get on with their own jobs while enjoying vicariously some of the Jester's altercations with authority. The group pushed him further into the part.

I do not claim that none of this happened at Middlesex – of course it did. But I do think that our responses as a group were more helpful both to him and to the team.

Brown's problem, and the team's, lay in his social role. I have described in earlier chapters how the suitability of a role in a more narrowly cricketing sense enables a player to make his best possible contribution to the team. Here, I want to stress the need for a person's efforts to be valued by the rest. Without the English team's support, it would have been harder for Tavaré, in 1981, to remain so determined in the face of the crowd's barracking and the press's carping at his slow scoring. He needed reassurance that his role as sheet-anchor was what the side required. Knott, his Kent team-mate, was particularly clear about this need. And Botham, typically, would make a point of acknowledging the value of Tavaré's work.

Leader not essential, Dr Owen says

By Fred Emery
Political Editor

A Prime Minister would not be essential to running a Social Democratic government, which could be led collectively, with senior ministers taking turns to chair Cabinet meetings, Dr David Owen suggested yester-

programme would be put to all the members.

Meanwhile in a flood of speeches Labour and Conservative MPs revealed that they both have a lot to say in denigration of a party they profess to believe has no chance. The insults were studied but added to the publicity.

Whatever the reality might be in the SDP, it wouldn't work on the cricket field.

Roles may also restrict, and the same role may, at different times, work well or badly. A few months after that series against Australia, Tavaré found that, during the tour of India, his steadiness had tightened into rigidity. Now he needed to loosen up, to let his arms flow, to be less cautious, both in the team's interests and in his own. After some net practice in this vein, he proceeded to score a century in the third Test, at Delhi, from only 211 balls – a good rate of scoring in Test cricket.

The attitude of the group affects individuals in many other ways. At this point I will mention only one. Morale can plunge into pessimism. On the arduous tour of Australia in 1974–5, the England players came to refer to a seat which was reserved for the next batsman as 'the condemned cell'. This was not part of a healthy black humour; the side had, I think, virtually given up. Thought of failure may infect a team as it does an individual, and I have seen sides in which the close fielders no longer expect their bowlers to induce an edged shot from the batsman, and the bowlers no longer expect the fielders to catch it.

But there is another element in these complicated inter-reactions. For one member of the team is also peculiarly set apart from it; he is influenced by its character, but also responsible – to a degree – for moulding its character; *of* it, but separate from it; required to act, like the others, but also overseeing their actions. I refer of course to the captain. And in the rest of this chapter, I shall try to draw together some of the ideas scattered in earlier pages about methods of leadership.

Without doubt styles have changed. Today, the Victorian model of leadership could be applied no more to a cricket team than to a cotton-mill or a coal-mine. We who as young players hardly dared to utter a squeak (as perhaps it now seems) have been succeeded by the twenty-year-old pipsqueaks. The Titmus, F.J., of 1950 became Middlesex's first professional captain in 1965. He was the best Middlesex captain under whom I played; but he did not do much to overcome the hierarchical set-up. Indeed, I remember his first formal contact with the playing staff in April of that year. Flanked by senior pros Murray and Parfitt, Fred told us that if we had the idea that having a professional captain would mean some sort of democracy, we'd better think again, 'as some of us have had more experience than some of you, ain't we, J.T.?' Pecking orders were more clearly defined then than fifteen years later, when I exploded at the side in the dressing-room at Cheltenham. Fred was still playing. I harangued them for about ten minutes, along the lines that we seemed to be assuming that we only had to turn up on the ground to win; and I focused on the recently developed vogue of playing, endlessly, mindless card-games. These games went on while the side was batting; players would play with their pads on, and curse when a wicket fell in the middle of a hand. The new batsman would tell the others not to disturb the cards, as he would be back soon. It was a joke, all right; but I began to feel that it was all too much to the point. The climax of my speech was that there were to be no more card-games during hours of play for the next few days. When I stopped, there was absolute silence for about ten seconds. Suddenly the tension broke as a voice from the back was heard to say: 'Who's got the cards, then?' Such a remark would have been unthinkable in Titmus's own early days, or indeed during his captaincy. As Murray once said to me, 'We knew our places then, and learned the hard way.' In recent times, there has been, in some quarters, a yearning for the clarity of the old ways. I have heard umpires, ex-players and older players complaining that the modern generation of cricketers lack discipline. Personally I doubt it. Discipline counts most in respect of performance on the field, and there have always been those who have it and those who do not.

Now, as at any time, there are of course situations in which the autocratic model is appropriate. John Emburey tells of his first-ever game as captain. It happened to be an Under-25 match against Surrey. Middlesex were fielding second, and the game was close. At one point during the last few overs, *seven* of the side converged on Emburey in the middle of the pitch, each urgently pressing his own views. This was not the appropriate occasion for the full and prolonged exercise of democracy! Richie Benaud called Bob Willis's method in Australia in 1982–3 'captaincy by committee' and I agree with him that I too would have found that intolerable. There can only be one captain. At times a decision must be made, and followed, regardless of whether it is absolutely the best course of action (though one hopes it is not one of the worst). The message from the captain, at such a moment, may simply be, 'Do it because I say so.' In a crisis, there may be no time for debate.

Moreover, decisions have to be made in the overall interest of the side, and conveyed clearly to the people involved. At Old Trafford, in 1984, England were fighting to save the follow-on against West Indies.

W. L. Murdoch, C. B. Fry and W. G. Grace photographed in 1902 at Crystal Palace
when the three players were playing for the newly formed 'London County'.
Murdoch captained Australia in no less than seven series against England between
1881 and 1890. A. G. Steel, his opposite number in two series, said of him that he
had a 'thoroughly sound knowledge of the game; but his better judgement was too
frequently hampered by the ceaseless chattering and advice of one or two men who
never could grasp the fact that in the cricket field there can be only one captain'.
Cf. Richie Benaud, on Bob Willis, 1982–3: 'Captaining by committee never works.'
I doubt if Fry or Grace went in for such methods. The photo is by cricket's foremost
photographer of the day, George Beldam.

Many hands make light work – sometimes

Dignity.

LITTLE PERKINS: " Now, you fellows, get a move on "

The captain must exercise his authority.

They needed, for this, 301 runs. With the score 280–7, and Allan Lamb approaching his third century of the series, their chances of reaching this target looked good. At this score, however, two wickets fell, the second from the last ball of a Garner over. As poor Paul Terry had broken his arm while batting two days before, the players began to leave the field. But Terry emerged, his left arm straitjacketed to his body inside his pullover. Now, I could see two possible justifications for allowing him to walk out to the crease. One was to give Lamb six balls to score the two runs needed for a well-deserved century; the other was to instruct Lamb to make an all-out effort to score the 21 runs needed without giving Terry the strike. Either way, the declaration should have been made as soon as the latter was about to face the bowling (unless it was for one ball, say, with only a handful of runs needed). Instead, Lamb took two runs, and started to march off, but was waved back by the captain, Gower. And Terry was allowed to face Garner. This was a case of captaincy that was neither clear nor compassionate.

Illingworth describes a one-day match between Yorkshire and Somerset. Before the match, they discussed their tactics against Richards, and decided to bowl outside his off-stump, at least at the start. When Richards came in, Illingworth reminded his young medium-fast bowler of their plan, set an appropriate field, and watched Richards, from his first four balls, score three fours through square-leg, all off balls pitching around leg-stump. Naturally, he was irritated at the time; later he asked the bowler what had gone through his mind as he came in to bowl. The reply was: 'As I got halfway, I suddenly became convinced that I had to bowl at his leg-stump.'

Such thinking is a sign of lack of discipline; acting on it is worse! There are occasions when a player simply has to do what he is told to do. At some point, consultation, delicacy of feeling, weighing-up of pros and cons need to give way to orders, bluntness, decisiveness. A certain set of qualities hang together here: discipline, will power, effort, arousal and guts, for example. When these alone are the hallmarks of a leader too much is lacking; they represent a narrow view of human nature and of the possibilities of motivation; but, without them, leadership is toothless.

Rodney Marsh tells a story against himself, of a one-innings match between Western Australia and Queensland, at that time the two most powerful state sides in the country. Western Australia had been bowled out for 78. Marsh, as captain, gave a team talk to his disconsolate players. 'Let's at least put up a show for our home crowd,' he said, 'and get two or three of them out.' At this point, Dennis Lillee burst in angrily. 'Put up a show! We're going to win!' He then bowled Viv Richards for 0, took four for 19 and Queensland were all out for 61.

When, during the Peloponnesian War, the Spartans were about to make a landing from Sphacteria, the Athenian general addressed his troops as follows: 'Soldiers, all of us are together in this. I don't want any of you in our present awkward position to try to show off his intelligence by making a precise calculation of the dangers which surround us. Instead we must make straight for the enemy, and not pause to discuss the matter, confident in our hearts that these dangers too can be surmounted.' One way of dealing with a situation like this is to assume that nice calculations are beside the point.

Motivation such as Lillee's, by attitude and example, can lift a side. But it cannot take the side the whole way, especially in a game that lasts so long and requires more than the firing of instinctual skill. In 1979, we laughed at the Australians for bringing in a local football coach as a 'motivator' before the fifth Test at Adelaide. In fact, they did perform with a renewed aggression on the first day, so perhaps his recruitment was not so foolish.

Certainly some players may react best to robust leadership. Stuart Surridge was highly regarded as captain of the talented Surrey team in the early '50s. His method of motivating Tony Lock was, I am told, to castigate, criticise and belittle him.

I think Willis's strengths as vice-captain (and as captain) lay mainly in his possession of these attributes of will power and courage. While no one was in doubt, off the field, about who was in charge, there were times when he appeared to 'switch off' on the field, standing statuesque and expressionless at mid-off. Then, it was reported, the England fielders would receive conflicting instructions, and direction wavered.

Needless to say, there is no such thing as an ideal captain. My point is that the good, or even the good-enough captain must not deny that part of his make-up which is epitomised by the image of a traditional sergeant-major; but nor must he rely on it alone.

Consultation, on any model of leadership, is required. It may take different forms and be used for different ends. It may merely be the means by which the leader gains technical or practical information on which to base his decisions. But it may also be the occasion for a decision. Or it may be seen, and used, more as an end in itself, a process of sharing and sorting out feelings, antagonistic or otherwise, within the group.

Traditionally, cricketers have been sceptical about the value of team meetings. As Hutton said, 'You can have all sorts of fancy ideas, and then in the game you might as well throw them out of the window.' There is, too, often a certain shyness about the expression of feeling within a semi-formal discussion. Cricketers are right to be pragmatic. However, people *do* have ideas of their own; and having fairly regular forums in which they can be expressed has benefits for everyone. The captain has the benefit of ideas from all sources. If they differ from his, he discovers where the opposition lies, and what form it takes. Players learn the habit of thinking for themselves, and not only about their own specialism. Often, in the course of a discussion, new ideas are formulated. It was Oscar Wilde I think who said, 'How can I know what I think until I hear what I say?' The self-respect of all the players is enhanced when their right to be heard is fully accepted.

I remember many years ago being asked a difficult question at a job interview. While I was floundering and tentative, the questioner interrupted and began to correct me. At this point another interviewer said, sharply, 'Let him finish.' Given this encouragement and space, I was enabled to formulate a much better answer. My two winters between 1974 and 1976 working in a therapeutic community for disturbed adolescents helped me to understand all this better. At this clinic, I was excited by the fact that everyone had a say in discussions and in many of the decisions. As junior members of the staff, we could – and did –

challenge the views of our seniors. We clearly influenced the way the clinic was run. I also noticed that confusion about the process could be irritating, as when, for example, a discussion that appeared to be practical turned out to be merely abstract since the decision had already been taken.

Mind, I did not try to introduce meetings of cricketers with anything like the frequency or the therapeutic aims that characterised those in the clinic. At certain times, we would expect to have meetings: before the season started, for instance, to make decisions, to give an airing to complaints or uncertainties, to look at our prospects, and so on. Before Tests or other big games, we would have team dinners, with a discussion afterwards. Otherwise, I would tend to instigate meetings either to talk about a specific topic or because things were not going well.

On the tour of Australia in 1978–9, for example, we had lost the third Test after winning the first two. In the fourth, we were poorly placed with Australia 146–1 in reply to our 152 all out. The whole expedition seemed about to fall apart. At Mike Hendrick's instigation, we started to have intense, brief meetings before each session of play. These talks helped revitalise a unit that had become sloppy and even dispirited. It is, on the face of it, curious that Test players should need such pep-talks. In fact, at any level, they cut through the air of relaxation brought about by lunch or tea; they remind everyone of targets or of basic cricketing truths; and, above all, they can, if realistic and practical, help morale. The philosopher R. C. Collingwood has written that 'a tribe which dances a war-dance before going out to fight its neighbours is working up its war-like emotions'. We do not go as far as the New Zealand rugby teams with their Maori dances, but pre-session talks, like pre-Test dinners, have in part a similar purpose.

Again, in 1981 Middlesex had won only one championship match by mid-June. The poor weather in May had hit us worse than others. But whatever the reasons, we knew we would have to start winning soon if we were not to disappoint ourselves and our supporters. At about this time Butcher asked me what my motivation was that season. I replied lightly, 'To score so many runs that they're forced to pick me against Australia as a batsman alone!' That was all right, he said, but what about my ambitions for the rest of the team? I felt there was some truth in his implied criticism. At the beginning of the season, I had felt unexpectedly sluggish. For the first time, I myself had arrived back for pre-season practice a few days late, and others, notably Daniel and Thomson (who had only recently signed), had returned later still. Moreover, the four who had been on the West Indies tour came home only on 17 April. So there was a ragged start to the season. Butcher's question made me think, and I decided to call a team meeting. There he repeated his remarks, and Barlow supported them, adding that I had not been so firm or determined as the previous year. Downton broadened the discussion, saying that he had noticed a reluctance to help each other out at practice

Roland Butcher batting in a county match against Sussex, Hove, 1982. Ian Gould behind the stumps. Butcher is a thoughtful cricketer and we helped each other on many matters. He believed that conversations with me enabled him to channel his aggression. He also made valuable contributions to the morale of the team, on topics such as my own depth of commitment to the team's success, and the impact of being dropped on a player's state of mind.

in the mornings; often, he added, he could not find anyone to hit him his regular early-morning diet of catches (a habit he had learned from Knott). Out of that meeting came a renewed commitment to each other and the side.

Butcher had also been responsible, a year before, for making us rethink our attitude to players who had been left out. This shift, too, arose from a team meeting. I called this one because of a feeling I had, shared with several others, that the grumpy reaction of some dropped players was damaging team spirit. Mike Smith, who had himself been omitted for much of the season, opened the discussion along these lines. This was helpful, as remarks from someone with his recent experience were bound to carry more weight than the same words from anyone else, especially the captain. Others spoke in the same vein. Then Butcher made his point. Speaking as one who had over five years been in and out of the side, he said, 'Yes. But the rest of us should recognise how we make a person feel an outsider when he's dropped. One day he is part of it all, next day no one talks to him in the same way.' We were surprised; but Butcher was right. For whatever complicated reasons, including, I suspect, embarrassment, our attitudes did subtly change depending on whether a man was currently in the side or not.

Consultation need not occur only in group settings. I have mentioned the practice of calling each player in to discuss a tour or season from his point of view. In 1980, it was again Butcher who put his finger on a sudden decline after the start of the season in which we had won ten consecutive one-day matches and had over the same period been undefeated in the championship. He reckoned that we were all too intent on the *outcome* of a match rather than being prepared to take each one as it came: we were even counting trophies on the mantelpiece, rather than approaching each session as a unique challenge. I was able to convey Butcher's insight back to the whole group after the individual sessions.

Nor is consultation confined to set-piece occasions. Ideally it goes on continuously. It may be informal and indirect, as when the captain talks shop with the players. I remember a lunch in a Bombay hotel with Underwood near the start of the Indian tour in 1976. We talked about left-arm spin bowling in general, and his art in particular. The conversation might just as well have occurred if I had not been vice-captain on the tour, but I found it useful later as I came to know better Underwood's foibles and aims, his preferences and his dislikes. At the end, he told me that he and Mike Denness, his captain at Kent and for England over several years, had never had such a talk. Yet getting the best out of someone calls for a close knowledge of him as a man and as a player.

It is sometimes important to know when *not* to ask for an opinion. I found that, for most of the time, Boycott was a helpful and constructive senior player. His advice would usually be sound, if cautious. But I realised that in certain moods he would be less helpful. And on some topics – as, for example, the possibility of his standing down for one of the pre-Test tour matches in order to give a chance to someone else – it became clear that his view would be inflexible and narrow. As captain, one needs several steadily reliable players who are willing to give advice without sulking if one does not follow it. One also gets to know people's strengths, and to learn which sorts of questions to ask of which players. At Middlesex, Smith was astute about long-term matters, and was perceptive about the characters of other players. Perhaps because he found himself fielding away from the bat, however, his views on short-term questions could be vague. On the field, sheer proximity is often an important factor in whom to consult on a ball-by-ball basis, and I invariably found Clive Radley helpful on these issues.

The view that everyone has the right to a say in how his group is run is matched by the idea that each has a responsibility to see that it is well run. Mutual motivation is essential for success. I nicknamed Gooch 'Zapata' in his early days for England, not only because of his moustache and sombrero-like floppy hat, but also because of the impression he gave in the field of being ready for his siesta. We used to get at him for this soporific air. Now Zap looks lively, and encourages the bowlers more than most. By the same token, one sullen or indolent player can stand out like a sore thumb, and tends to infect the rest. I regard it as part of the captain's task to widen the area of responsibility for each player; to increase his range of thought, whether about his own resources as a bowler or batsman or about the whole side. When Mahatma Gandhi was asked to comment on a proposed constitution for a princely state in India whose ruler wished to make its government more democratic, he suggested only one change: instead of 'rights' of man, he proposed 'duties'.

The word 'duty' need not, however, imply any lack of fun. Cricket is a game, and should be enjoyed. It can be serious without being stern or solemn. As Boycott used to say when the going was hard, 'It's better than being down t' pit.' Mornay du Plessis, the ex-Springbok rugby captain, described in an unpublished talk the spirit of the British Lions in 1974, and contrasted it with the anxiety of the South Africans. The British had won the first Test 9–6, and du Plessis said that the home team arrived at the ground for the next Test in a state of tension. They felt they *had* to win, that nothing less was expected of them. They were overwhelmed by injunctions. At this moment, the Lions bus drew up, and from it issued – singing. Britain won the next two Tests by increasing margins, before drawing the last and winning the series 3–0.

It is the captain's job to find a balance between discipline and creativity. Humour eases tension and softens rivalry. Botham's boisterousness, Willis's zany humour, Hendrick's mordant wit all helped, for example, to enable Boycott to unbend in the England dressing-room and take himself less seriously. Harmony in a team that is full of strong characters is not likely to be bland; it consists of lively and sometimes discordant interplay. The atmosphere in the Middlesex dressing-room always used to be robust and humorous. Occasionally, and especially if things went badly, the jokes could become too biting. At such times, I might try to persuade people to lay into each other less, and I relied even more than usual on the benign influence of those who were steadier, perhaps, and less acid. One season, we were lucky enough to have van der Bijl in our side; his contribution was immense, not only on the field but off it: for he tended to blame himself rather than others, and saw the best in the rest of us rather than homing in so sharply on faults. After a poor performance in the field against Kent in a Sunday League match, for instance, it was refreshing to hear Vintcent say, 'Sorry, men, it was all my fault, bowling those two half-volleys early on.'

If rivalry runs riot, or if envy and malice become too strong, a team falls apart. A player once 'excused' himself to me for dropping a catch – he had his hands in his pockets when the ball was bowled – with the remark that he had had a lot of catches dropped off *his* bowling. Such an attitude can indeed be catching.

On the other hand, rivalry is bound to produce some envy, and it is

Geoff Howarth placing the field, third Test, England v. New Zealand, Lord's, 1983. Howarth has been one of New Zealand's best captains, though he never seemed to take to county cricket. In this picture everyone looks bored. New Zealand had had a first innings deficit of 135, and Gower had scored a century. At such times it is not easy to raise a team. The match was won by England by 127 runs.
Left to right: Jeremy Coney, umpire Dickie Bird, Gower, Ian Smith ('keeper), Richard Hadlee and Howarth.

no bad thing if it can be acknowledged. I warm to the Essex opener, Dickie Dodds, when I hear the story of a county match at Romford in the '50s. He was out for nothing early on. The pitch was flat, the bowling friendly, and his captain, Doug Insole, together with Brian Taylor, scored freely. At lunch Dodds asked Insole, 'Skipper, did you feel any bad vibrations while you were batting?' 'Can't say I did,' said Doug: 'not too sensitive to such things and anyway I was too busy enjoying myself making hay. Why?' 'Well, skipper,' replied the repentant Dodds, 'I'm afraid I was so miserable about missing out that I spent all morning wishing you'd join me.'

Many hands make light work – sometimes

Cowdrey too is honest enough to own to similar feelings in the West Indies in 1959. On the passage out he had been persuaded, much against his inclination, to open the innings. 'Had I been really professional in my outlook, I would have resisted all the appeals,' he writes. 'I could have argued that not only would Wally Hammond have scornfully rejected any such suggestion thirty years earlier, but that he would not have been asked in the first place. Equally I might have suggested that either Ken Barrington or Ted Dexter did the job . . . I cannot pretend that it was not hard to live with when I was soon watching Barrington and Dexter making brilliant hundreds on the placid afternoon wickets which had been so brutish in the early morning.'

Cowdrey's 'finding it hard to live with' strikes me as simply human, and not necessarily harmful to his own performance or the team's. (Indeed, he used the experience to remodel his whole approach to batting, having the courage to pad himself from neck to waist in Dunlopillo.) But such emotions can lead to splits and unhappiness.

I have seen teams divided between stars and the rest. It is true that those who score most runs and take most wickets need to have their successes and hard work valued by the rest. But equally the fringe players and the reserves want desperately to be accepted as integral members of the party. Teams can also become split between party-goers and stay-inners. The party-goers may form an in-group, with in-jokes, from which the rest feel excluded. The stay-inners may become wet blankets exuding disapproval. The former are critical because they are always the ones to volunteer to represent the side at optional functions. The latter suspect that the former put a frivolous social life ahead of the business in hand. It was one of Tony Greig's strengths as captain that he managed to identify with both groups. As poacher turned gamekeeper, he was in a strong position to mix firmness with freedom. I found that it helped to insist on one small detail; that *everyone* be invited to the parties that were going, including those who regularly preferred to decline.

Once again, we return to the importance for a group of individual differences being accepted; in short, of respect. Some thrive on socialising; others are happier with a quieter, more private life. It is absurd for one lot to despise the other, unless either goes too far. A good captain facilitates this generosity of spirit.

The 'military model' would stress uniformity and fairness. The leadership model that I am advocating does not deny the importance of justice, but it suggests that justice does not reduce so simply to the same treatment for each individual, since different individuals have such different needs.

In some matters, the military model is appropriate. On tour, for instance, punctuality is essential. When twenty or so people have to meet regularly and have travel deadlines, it is annoying for nineteen to have to wait for one. What is more, laxity at the start leads to chaos later, as everyone soon assumes that the bus will not leave until fifteen, twenty,

Tony Greig and John Snow, early '70s. Snow was one of the hardest men to captain in county cricket, though Tests were a different matter. For Sussex he could be very awkward, putting in an effort only when it suited him. For all that he was a marvellous bowler – fast but capable of bowling medium-fast when conditions were right.

thirty minutes after the advertised time. As I have said, I think it reasonable to insist on everyone participating equally in training and nets early in the season.

On tour, it is probably advisable to have a uniform; England teams do represent England, and it is best to be on the safe side to prevent extremes of shoddiness. However, I have never believed in the theory that smartness off the field is related to smartness on it. Indeed, Middlesex's first success since 1949 occurred at a time (in 1976) when the players turned up for matches in all sorts of outfits, from neat blazers with badges to T-shirts with dubious messages printed on the front. I am not saying that scruffiness is a virtue; only that any equation of neatness with a productive discipline is facile. Perhaps the same point can be made in another way: it is relatively easy to insist on a superficial uniformity and discipline of dress; it is hard to achieve personal self-discipline on the field. Van der Bijl was one of the tidiest and most self-disciplined of cricketers; yet his corner of the dressing-room was invariably a mess.

Many hands make light work – sometimes

It was Fletcher who told me that in his view the most crucial aspect of captaincy is treating individuals differently. Tony Lewis, who captained England in India in 1972–3, wrote in his diary of the tour that he would ask himself each day what the members of the party wanted from him. It is a good question even if the most common answer was often, nothing – or rather, nothing special – and even if what they think they want may be other than what they really want.

Most people like to be praised if they do well. Some mentors and leaders offer praise too freely or too unctuously, so that it becomes devalued. Harry Sharp, the Middlesex scorer, would explicitly commend players rarely: he said once that everyone knows when he's done well. But Harry conveyed his pleasure, and his judgement was, and is, highly regarded. Gubby Allen tells how he and a friend went to see their housemaster at Eton in 1920 after they had beaten Harrow by 198 runs. No doubt they expected lavish congratulations; instead, the housemaster, C. M. Wells, who had captained England at rugby, said curtly, 'Disappointing match. Could have won by 200 runs if that stupid member hadn't stopped the ball with his paper in front of the pavilion rails' – the umpire had signalled six instead of four – 'You can go.' Nevertheless, whatever the captain's style, he must let the team know he is pleased with them when they do well, and feels for them when not. His concern may surprise. I was quite touched when, a week after the event, Greig told me that he could have cried when I ran myself out early in the Delhi Test.

On the social front, the captain needs to keep himself in touch with what goes on. Room-sharing is important. On tour, we usually changed the pairings every few weeks. At the start, we would often put a newcomer with an old hand. Later, we might put together those who were unlikely to be playing in a Test, so that a late night would not disturb someone who was. The physical layout of rooms may affect the 'feel' of a stay. In Sydney one year, the hotel consisted of twin towers. The anonymity of the floors and rooms was unattractive; but what was even more unsatisfactory was that the tour manager and I were allocated rooms at the top of one tower, the rest of the team at the top of the other. By contrast, Brisbane's hotel had us all on two adjacent floors, each square in shape. We could, and did, drift in and out of each other's rooms. It was like living in a neighbourly terrace where back doors were often open, rather than in tower blocks with inefficient lifts.

Occasionally a captain will take someone under his wing. Cowdrey describes how Hutton did this for him on his first tour of Australia, especially after the news came through that Cowdrey's father had died. I know that Fletcher has made a point of having dinner with one of his players who tends to feel depressed and lonely. F. G. Mann ate in the hotel dining-room on every night of the tour of South Africa that he captained in 1948–9, so that any of the team could join him if they wished.

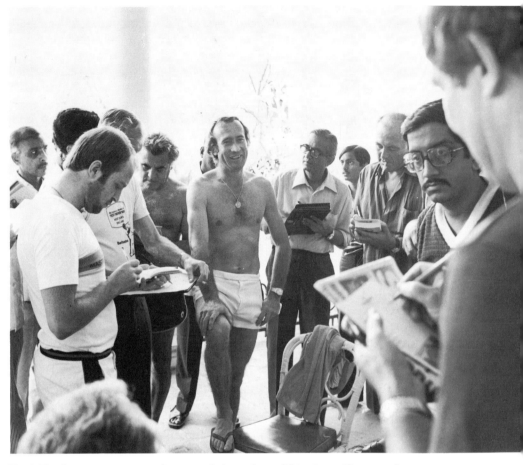

Keith Fletcher gives a press conference in India, 1981–2. This picture illustrates the informality of the '80s, amongst press as well as players. Fletcher was, I feel, hard done by England. He was shrewd, tough, and respected by the team; he knew his players instinctively, and he was considerate of them. His failings were mere peccadilloes.

Douglas Jardine was the type to pay attention to such detail. In 1932 he insisted on all the tourists having dental check-ups before leaving England. He is even said, by Alan Gibson, to have nursed Harold Larwood through, during the lunch interval, with sips of champagne, while outside police were guarding against a riot and Australia was contemplating breaking away from the Empire.

I myself found that I needed to get away from the whole cricket environment at times, and would sometimes go out privately or enjoy a solitary meal in my room. In Sydney, I did once involve David Gower with a group of my friends who had nothing to do with cricket; David was going through a period of feeling low on the tour, when even successful innings seemed flat and worthless afterwards. I wondered if some stimulating company might help him to put things in perspective. He scored 98 in the second innings of the Test, but I think this was a coincidence! But it was a shortcoming of mine, especially on that last tour, in 1979–80, when I was exposed to a lot of hostility, that I did not have enough energy for social cricketing contacts after play. I may have been too little available for the players at that time.

In India and Pakistan, hotels in the smaller centres would be isolated and old-fashioned. As there was no TV or outside entertainments, we depended, like a Victorian family, on each other for company and amusement. There we enjoyed Willis's aptitude for charades, Miller's impersonations of a Derbyshire coal-miner, and Randall's carol (and other) singing. In Australia, where the hotels are usually stereotyped but well-appointed, two opposing tendencies can count against a team's internal friendliness and sociability: one is to stay in the room and watch TV; the other is to leave the hotel every evening for personal arrangements in town.

On the purely cricketing front, different players need different treatment. On tour Illingworth allowed Snow to prepare himself however he chose, provided that he was fully fit for Tests and pulled his weight in the field in minor matches. Botham needed, I think, a framework against which to bounce; he had to be told, for example, that he could not always be bowling. At Headingley in 1981 I took him off after only three overs in his second spell. 'How can I bowl if you give me three-over spells?' he demanded. 'And how can I keep you on if you bowl medium-pace half-volleys?' I retorted. Boycott needed flattery, or, at any rate, since so often the praise was earned, recognition and reassurance.

I am sometimes asked how difficult it was to captain great players; would I have liked, for example, to have had Lillee and Thomson in my team? As Greg Chappell has said, captaining Lillee and Thomson was the least of his problems. Lillee was a genius, who would always try his hardest. His aberrations arose from the same elements in his make-up that made him so good – confidence, fire and guts. At times, Chappell would walk all the way from first slip to the end of Lillee's run, to remonstrate with him. It was, as he says, a long walk back, but Lillee was the kind of man who would in the end take things from a captain he respected. With Thommo there were never problems on the field. A natural athlete, he would always try his best, and his occasional outbursts were directed at himself. He was also the first to help out at practice, fetching balls for other players and giving hints to young bowlers. An easy-going man, he had a good-humoured and genial influence on a team off the field. In fact the only problem was persuading him to work hard enough before a season, or, in Australia, between matches, so as to be fully fit to bowl with control. He preferred fishing to training.

There is no special problem with star players. As we have seen, a captain may find others far more infuriating, whether they are constant jokers, or old lags, or players who are afraid of success, or sulky, or devious, or whatever. And it is relatively easy for everyone to feel well-disposed to the man who has just scored a century or taken six wickets; a much harder task for a captain may be to help the fellow who is in a bad patch to recover his form and his self-confidence.

John Arlott wrote about me, 'He has, though, always been anxious – almost certainly over-anxious – to prove himself as a batsman at Test level.' He went on to comment that I was not able to live up to my full ability in Tests. 'A case, we may assume, of "Physician heal thyself".'

Arlott was right. I had to struggle in Test cricket with an inner voice which told me I had no right to be there. I would then become more tense, try harder than ever, and play further below par. This inner saboteur undermined even success. If I scored 50, I would find it pointing out to me that one of their best bowlers was missing, or that they were tired, or that conditions favoured the batsman. In this mood, I would undervalue the strokes I played well and overvalue those that I rarely played. I would remember the streaky shots.

I was not, of course, the only captain to have found, from time to time, additional problems with my own game. Botham's performances declined during his spell as captain; Kim Hughes did not play at his best as captain. Gower, at the time of writing, has gone through a torrid first season and first tour. Indeed, England captains in Australia have nearly always performed below par. Consider the following list of captain-batsmen, and their remarkably modest records in Tests: Chapman 1928–9, 165 runs at 23.57, Jardine 1932–3, 199 at 22.11, Hammond 1946–7, 168 at 21, Hutton 1954–5, 220 at 24.44, Smith 1965–6, 107 at 17.83. The only captains since MacLaren in 1901–2 to average over 40 in a series in Australia have been May in 1958–9 with 405 runs at 40.50, and Dexter four years later, with 481 runs at 48.10.

There were stages in my career when I despaired of motivating myself, let alone others: when all I wanted to do was crawl into anonymity, rather than bounce back. Once, in 1978, I sought professional help in the form of a few visits to a psychotherapist, with whom I was able to unwind and relax. I also toyed with hypnotherapy in Sydney, as Richards, Willis and others did more extensively. Sometimes, the counselling that a player needs goes beyond what can be offered in the hurly-burly of the cricket setting. Twice players asked me to refer them to this psychotherapist after we had talked about their difficulties: in one case, the effect was dramatically beneficial, in the other, insignificant but harmless.

Other possible conflicts occur because of the captain's dual role within the team: he is both the superior and the partner. I have already mentioned moving from slip in case the sight of me and my supposed disapproval was upsetting a bowler. Someone in authority may *be* authoritarian, but he may also have authoritarianism falsely attributed to him by those who are insecure about themselves. Often there is a mixture of the two.

Wilf Slack, the Middlesex batsman, managed to tell me, after some games as an opener, that he felt inhibited when at the crease with me. I think that his bringing this into the open enabled both of us to be more aware of our damaging tendencies, and him to be freer as a batsman. Of course, such patterns of uneasiness may occur between any pair, because of their characters; when one is the captain, though, additional elements are involved. There are, similarly, bound to be extra complications for the nephew of an industrialist working in the latter's company, or for a schoolboy who finds himself in a class taught by his parent. The captain, like the teacher, needs to oscillate in his responses; reacting naturally like others in the team, but also checking that his response is not dictated by his own needs. To give a different kind of example: the captain who is an opening batsman should not allow his apprehensiveness about batting on a greenish pitch to affect his decision on whether to bat or field; but nor should he go to the other extreme to prove that he is *not* afraid. As a player, the captain has to be an example of responsibility without constricting himself into rigidity.

There are no hiding-places for a captain. In Brecht's play *Galileo* there is a scene in which the Pope changes into his magnificent robes. The Pope needs to be wearing the full panoply of his regalia in order to pass judgment on Galileo, which, at the end of the scene, and fully robed, he does. Like the captain of a cricket team, he is arrayed all in white. Unlike the Pope, however, the captain in a sweaty dressing-room cannot conceal his shortcomings. There is no protective barrier between him and those with whom he has to deal. In this respect, the job is closer to the foreman's than the managing director's; but the captain does not have a heavy hierarchy weighing him down.

The captain, then, has to exercise authority without the aid of distance or subterfuge. He cannot be other than himself. Ultimately it is by example that he earns, or fails to earn, the respect of the team.

No one will follow a prig or a prude; but a captain cannot afford to be dissolute in his personal life. The unreformed law-breaker finds laying down the law for others a problem, and his pronouncements lack credibility even when they imply that someone else is going too far in the opposite direction. When captain of England in West Indies in 1980, Botham, who has never been too keen on training himself, found himself ridiculed by the team when he suggested to Gooch that he was overdoing his early-morning runs.

The proximity of leader and led makes cunning a dangerous tool in man-management. I have always doubted the value of manipulation – that is, the attempt to influence by subtle control in which the controller keeps the strings in his hands – as a method of leadership. Sooner or later people resent being played upon like flutes or tricked into dancing to a certain tune. In sport, there is even less room for such dissimulation. A cricket captain is engaged in a co-operative physical endeavour with the rest of the players, and he is likely to get the best out of them by being to a considerable degree spontaneous and direct himself.

He cannot avoid discomfort. He is required to hold in balance conflicting aims and values. Unless he is in reasonable balance himself, he will not be able to do so. But being balanced does not mean being flat or innocuous or bland. He will lose his forthrightness, energy and contact if he tries too hard to suppress in himself the feelings that he would rather not have. At times of anxiety and stress, the same qualities that have been helpful and vital are inevitably exaggerated or distorted. Just as one of the main requirements for a leader is to be able to tolerate conflict within and criticism from the group, so he needs a capacity to accept them within and from himself.

For example, a captain will sometimes feel lonely and out on a limb. When I first led Middlesex, one or two of the senior players voiced criticisms about my putting fielders in unorthodox positions. But they went on without irony, 'The odd thing is, the ball keeps going to them.' The captain should not ignore advice or convention; but he should not be trammelled with them either. He needs the courage of his convictions. At dinner, Dr Johnson once put into his mouth a whole potato which turned out to be too hot. Hastily he spat it out on to the table. The company held their breath, wondering how the great man would deal with this potentially embarrassing episode. Unabashed, the doctor declared, 'A fool would have swallowed that!'

Again, a good captain will set high standards for everyone. At times, he may become over-critical, either of all others, or of some others, or of himself. In the first case, he blames his team for what goes wrong when they may have tried hard and performed at or near their best. In the next, he finds scapegoats (who often, incidentally, readily fit the role, by being tactless, naive and without malice). In the third case, the captain himself becomes unconfident and depressed. On the other side, a captain may settle for too little from everyone. Far from being perfectionists, they all subside into mediocrity.

No one can steer a course between such rocks and whirlpools without some tendency to veer to one side or the other – or, more likely, to be liable to all mistakes at different times.

Again, in the words of an old north-country proverb, 'If you win a medal wear it.' A leader is there to lead. But this does not mean being a martinet. Equally important, as we have seen, is the role of facilitator for the individual and the group. The good captain enables talents to flower. Like a gardener, he must not prune too hard; but nor can he leave all to nature. We should not forget, too, that there are many pleasing styles of garden, from the formal symmetry of Fontainebleau to the happy wilderness that was, once, Highgate Cemetery.

No leader can escape a sense of responsibility for the performance of his team. Yet this very awareness which prompts him to question and value his own contribution may deviate in two opposite directions. He may feel too identified with short-term outcomes, so that if the team has a good day he is elated; if not, depressed. (As Albert Einstein is said to have commented, before the first attempt to explode a nuclear bomb: 'Whatever happens, it was a damn good theory.') Or he may shrug his shoulders, and say *too soon* that it is impossible to make a silk purse out of a sow's ear. Perhaps an original and useful purse may be constructed from a sow's ear, and maybe a closer or more patient look will reveal richer assets than the porcine appendage.

Bob Paisley has said of managing Liverpool FC, 'A manager has to cut his coat according to the cloth – he has to mould his team's style to the players available. The same applies to the individual player. None of them is perfect, so you have to develop their strengths and cover or reduce their weaknesses. It is up to the manager to study players, to recognise certain factors in their playing ability as well as their characters and make-up.' The illusion of omnipotence is a particular trap for the captain with a well-developed sense of responsibility. And the public and the media lay a seductive carpet over the trap's twigs – twigs that consist of over-conscientiousness and a fragile self.

In these and many other areas there are opposite pitfalls. Top-class captaincy, like top-class sport, calls for combinations of qualities that do not always lie easily together. Yet each in his own way, men like Bradman and Benaud, Illingworth and Close, the Chappells, Fletcher and Greig, have known intuitively when to intervene and when to leave alone; when to insist on well-tried methods being relentlessly repeated and when to experiment. They are tough *and* considerate; they can run a strict ship *and* allow leeway.

On one point they would all agree. A captain must instil the will to win; which means both ramming home an advantage and clinging on desperately when up against it. Greg Chappell told me how the Test at the Oval in 1972 was a turning-point for Australia after a terrible run. They entered the last innings needing 242 to win, a similar target to that which they had failed to reach at Sydney six months before. He believes that the different outcome at the Oval was partly attributable to his brother's bluntness and realism as captain. Ian put it to the side before the Oval Test that they should face the fact that another defeat would mean the ignominy of a third consecutive series lost, by a wide margin; whereas a win would restore pride at 2–2. This match was, incidentally, the first instance of centuries by brothers in a Test, with Greg (113) and Ian (118) adding 201 for the third wicket in the first innings. The result – an Australian win by five wickets – ushered in a new era, Greg claims, of Australian toughness and supremacy, while the alternative might well have led to widespread changes in the team and the need for another start. Test cricket, particularly, calls for a well-developed cohesive will to win, which does not allow a team to relax or give up. Good teams have very few sessions in which everything falls apart; and they are resolute in putting the situation back together at the next opportunity.

The manner of victory is not unimportant: there can be good winners as well as good losers. My experience of the Australian Test teams that

I played against was that they were invariably both, and that those with the reputations for a bristling aggression were most capable of treating the 'twin imposters' alike.

Looking back on my times as a captain, and on what I have written in this book, I sometimes wonder, as I did when contemplating (and declining) a cricket career way back in 1965, about the value of the whole thing, and I find that I am surprised at how much I wanted to win. Now that I am a spectator, I am aware of a certain dreamy distance between the events on the field and me. 'Ah, that fellow's out, is he? More strawberries, please. Hooking a bit early in the innings, wouldn't you say?' In this mood, I can, for a moment, sympathise with what I read in the *Times Literary Supplement* of 26 June 1981: 'The ability to tap the boyhood sources of energy and illusion is essential in most highly competitive activities, and one would hesitate to back a fully adult person (should one exist) in any serious contest. There is nothing like a sudden upsurge of maturity to impair the will to win.'

Nothing, that is, except an upsurge of the various kinds of immaturity. The writer's hesitation is perhaps applied to the wrong part of the process. It may be 'fully adult' to want to win once you have thrown your cap into the ring; the question-mark applies more aptly to the choice of the ring. But I am now less inclined than I was twenty years ago to take a high moral-aesthetic line. Cricket embodies enough aspects of life, and captaincy many more. One who finds a career that fits in with some of his earliest dreams, and finds that career intensely fulfilling, is indeed fortunate.

Bibliography

I have been stimulated by and have enjoyed what these books have to say on the subject of captaincy. The list is not meant to be comprehensive.

Cricket: A. G. Steel and Hon R. H. Lyttelton, Longmans Green and Co, 1888

The Jubilee Book of Cricket: K. S. Ranjitsinhji, Blackwood, 1897

The Game of Cricket: Lonsdale Library, The Earl of Lonsdale and Eric Parker, Seeley Service and Co, 1930

The Art of Cricket: Sir Donald Bradman, Hodder and Stoughton, 1958

Beyond a Boundary: C. L. R. James, Hutchinson, 1963

M.C.C.: Colin Cowdrey, Hodder and Stoughton, 1976

The Cricket Captains of England: Alan Gibson, Cassell, 1979

Captaincy: Ray Illingworth, Pelham, 1980

On Reflection: Richie Benaud, Collins, 1984

REFERENCE:

The Wisden Cricketers' Almanack

Barclays World of Cricket: E. W. Swanton and John Woodcock, Collins, 1980

Acknowledgments

I should like to thank Margaret Fraser for her design work on the book; David Frith both for his specialist photo research and his help on historical matters; Jim Coldham for answering a number of tricky questions on the history of cricket; and Professor G. Derek West for compiling the index. Once again, I am grateful to Philippa Kaye and M. N. Patel for typing from none too legible manuscripts, and to Richard Cohen, my editor, for his support and help.

Illustration Credits

COLOUR PHOTOGRAPHS
Press Association: pages 1 (top), 2 (bottom). Syndication International, page 1 (bottom). Allsport Photographic, page 2 (top); Adrian Murrel/Allsport, pages 3 (bottom), 7 (both), 8 (both); Don Morley/Allsport, page 6 (top). Sport and General, page 3 (top). Patrick Eagar, page 4 (both), 5, 6 (bottom).

BLACK AND WHITE PHOTOGRAPHS
Roger Mann: pages 11 and 261. Patrick Eagar: pages 12, 23, 44 (both), 48–9, 51, 52, 58, 68, 75, 98, 109, 113, 119, 121, 140–1, 160, 162–3 (top and bottom), 178–9, 182–3, 184, 197, 209, 218, 219, 220–1, 244–5, 247, 269, 271, 273; Jan Traylan for Patrick Eagar, page 266. The Illustrated London News Picture Library: page 15. Adrian Murrell, Allsport Photographic: pages 18, 19, 20 (both), 28, 29, 31, 124 (bottom), 132, 133, 155, 216, 225. David Frith: pages 24, 37 (both), 38, 81 (all), 87, 97, 118 (top), 148, 179 (top), 205 (both), 212, 213, 224, 237, 240, 262. The *Guardian*, John Minnion cartoon: page 34. Popperfoto: page 40. The Photo Source: pages 43, 104, 118 (bottom), 167, 195. Express Newspapers: page 154 (both). Sport and General Press Agency Ltd: pages 162 (top left), 190, 241. Associated Press Photo: page 223. *New Society*, Bill Beacham cartoon: page 227. Western Australian Newspapers Ltd: pages 250, 251. *Southland Times*, G. Wright: page 252. Times Newspapers: page 259.

Index

Numbers in italics refer to illustrations; *128A–128H* refer to colour photographs.

Index

Index

Index